THE ANATOMY OF SUICIDE

LECTOR HOUSE PUBLIC DOMAIN WORKS

THE ANATOMY OF SUICIDE

FORBES WINSLOW

ISBN: 978-93-90015-48-1

Published: 1840

LECTOR HOUSE LLP
E-MAIL: lectorpublishing@gmail.com

Vide p. 209.

THE ANATOMY OF SUICIDE:

BY

FORBES WINSLOW,

MEMBER OF THE ROYAL COLLEGE OF SURGEONS, LONDON;
AUTHOR OF "PHYSIC AND PHYSICIANS."

"But is there yet no other way, besides
These painful passages; how we may come
To death, and mix with our connatural dust?
Nor love thy life, nor hate: but what thou liv'st
Live well; how long or short permit to Heaven."

Milton.

1840.

TO
JAMES JOHNSON, ESQ., M.D.

PHYSICIAN EXTRAORDINARY TO THE LATE KING,
ETC. ETC.

This Work is dedicated,

AS A TESTIMONY OF RESPECT FOR HIS HIGH PROFESSIONAL ATTAIN-
MENTS,
AND AS AN ACKNOWLEDGMENT OF THE
ADVANTAGES DERIVED FROM A PERUSAL OF THE MANY ABLE WORKS
WITH WHICH HE HAS ENRICHED
THE MEDICAL LITERATURE OF HIS COUNTRY.

London,—May, 1840.

PREFACE.

This treatise had its origin in the following circumstance:—A few months ago, the author had the honour of reading before the *Westminster Medical Society*, a paper on "Suicide Medically considered," which giving rise to an animated discussion, and evolving an expression of the opinions of several eminent professional men, excited at the time much interest.

It was the author's object in his paper to establish a fact, he believes, of primary importance,—that the disposition to commit self-destruction is, to a great extent, amenable to those principles which regulate our treatment of ordinary disease; and that, to a degree more than is generally supposed, it originates in derangement of the brain and abdominal viscera.

Notwithstanding, however, these points were not considered with the minuteness commensurate with their value, the discussion which followed the author's communication afforded him great satisfaction. It tended to strengthen in his mind an opinion previously formed, that the members of the medical profession were inferior to no other class in a knowledge of those higher branches of philosophy that give dignity and elevation to human character.

To explain more fully the author's views on the subject of Suicide is the object of the present work, which is, strange to say, the first in England that has been exclusively devoted to this important and interesting branch of inquiry.

Hitherto suicide has been the theme of the novel and the drama, and has never, with the exception of an incidental notice in works on medical jurisprudence, been considered in this country in reference to its pathological and physiological character.

That an intimate acquaintance with this branch of knowledge is highly important to the medical philosopher, few will deny; that it is a subject of general and painful interest, all must admit. The apparent coolness with which suicide is often committed has induced many to suppose that the unfortunate perpetrator was at the time in possession of a sound mind; and it is this idea which has induced the profession to conceive the subject as one foreign to their pursuits, and belonging rather to the province of the moral philosopher. How far the author has succeeded in disproving this opinion, it is for others to decide.

He takes this opportunity of acknowledging the assistance he has received from the writings of Pinel, Esquirol, Falret, Fodére, Arnold, Crichton, Willis, Black, Haslam, Burrows, Conolly, Pritchard, Mayo, Ellis, Paris, Smith, Beck, Taylor, and Ray. To the pages of Dr. Johnson's Medico-chirurgical Review, the Medical Gazette, the Lancet, and British and Foreign Medical Review, he is also largely indebted.

In conclusion, the author, conscious of its imperfections, claims for his work no other praise than that it is the first attempt in this country to reflect light on a branch of medical and moral philosophy, the importance of which is only equalled by the difficulties impeding its investigation. He will feel himself amply repaid, should his introductory essay (for such only can it be considered) stimulate others more competent than himself to prosecute the inquiry which he has commenced. Their success will afford him much satisfaction and pleasure; for in the attainment of their endeavours will his hopes be fulfilled, and his ambition gratified.

LONDON,—MAY, 1840.

CONTENTS

CHAPTER IV.

ON THE INFLUENCE OF CERTAIN MENTAL STATES IN INDUCING THE DISPOSITION TO SUICIDE.

CHAPTER V.

IMITATIVE, OR EPIDEMIC SUICIDE.

CHAPTER VI.

SUICIDE FROM FASCINATION.

CHAPTER VII.

OF THE ENTHUSIASM AND MENTAL IRRITABILITY WHICH, IF ENCOURAGED, WOULD LEAD TO SUICIDE.

CHAPTER VIII.

PHYSICAL CAUSES OF SUICIDE.

CHAPTER IX.

MORAL TREATMENT OF SUICIDAL MANIA.

CHAPTER X.

PHYSICAL TREATMENT OF THE SUICIDAL DISPOSITION.

CHAPTER XI.

IS THE ACT OF SUICIDE THE RESULT OF INSANITY?

CHAPTER XII.

SUICIDE IN CONNEXION WITH MEDICAL JURISPRUDENCE.

CHAPTER XIII.

STATISTICS OF SUICIDE.

CHAPTER XIV.

APPEARANCES PRESENTED AFTER DEATH IN THOSE WHO HAVE COMMITTED SUICIDE.

CHAPTER XV.

CHAPTER XVI.

CAN SUICIDE BE PREVENTED BY LEGISLATIVE ENACTMENTS?—INFLUENCE OF MORAL INSTRUCTION.—CONCLUSION.

ANATOMY OF SUICIDE.

CHAPTER I.

SUICIDES OF THE ANCIENTS.—ANCIENT LAWS AND OPINIONS ON THE SUBJECT OF SUICIDE.

Examples of antiquity no defence of suicide—Causes of ancient suicides—The suicides of Asdrubal, Nicocles, Isocrates, Demosthenes, Hannibal, Mithridates, the inhabitants of the city of Xanthus,
Cato, Charondas, Lycurgus, Codrus, Themistocles, Emperor Otho,
Brutus and Cassius, Mark Antony and Cleopatra, Petronius, Lucan, Lucius Vetus, Sardanapalus, M. Curtius, Empedocles, Theoxena—Noble resistance of Josephus—Scripture suicides: Samson,
Saul, Ahitophel, Judas Iscariot, Eleazar, Razis—Doctrines of the
stoics, Seneca, Epictetus, Zeno—Opinions of Cicero, Pliny, on suicide—Ancient laws on suicide.

Human actions are more under the influence of example than precept; consequently, suicide has often been justified by an appeal to the laws and customs
of past ages. An undue reverence for the authority of antiquity induces us to rely
more upon what has been said or done in former times, than upon the dictates of
our own feelings and judgement. Many have formed the most extravagant notions
of honour, liberty, and courage, and, under the impression that they were imitating the noble example of some ancient hero, have sacrificed their lives. They urge
in their defence that suicide has been enjoined by positive laws, and allowed by
ancient custom; that the greatest and bravest nation in the world practised it; and
that the most wise and virtuous sect of philosophers taught that it was an evidence
of courage, magnanimity, and virtue. There is no mode of reasoning so fallacious as
that which is constantly appealing to examples. A man who has made up his mind
to the adoption of a particular course can easily discover reasons to justify himself
in carrying out his preconceived opinions. If a contemplated action, abstractedly
considered, be good, cases may be of service in illustrating it. There must be some
test by which to form a correct estimate of the justness or lawfulness of human
actions; and until we are agreed as to what ought to constitute that standard, examples are perfectly useless. No inferences deduced from the consideration of the
suicides of antiquity can be logically applied to modern instances. We live under
a Christian dispensation. Our notions of death, of honour, and of courage, are,

in many respects, so dissimilar from those which the ancients entertained, that the subject of suicide is placed entirely on a different basis. In the early periods of history, self-destruction was considered as an evidence of courage; death was preferred to dishonour. These principles were inculcated by celebrated philosophers, who exercised a great influence over the minds of the people; and, in many instances, the act of self-immolation constituted a part of their religion. Is it, then, to be wondered at, that so many men, eminent for their genius, and renowned for their valour, should, under such circumstances, have sacrificed themselves?

The famous suicides of antiquity generally resulted from one of three causes:—First, it was practised by those who wished to avoid pain and personal suffering of body and mind; secondly, when a person considered the act as a necessary vindication of his honour; and thirdly, when life was sacrificed as an example to others.

The first class is the most excusable of the three. Pain, physical or mental, puts a man's courage severely to the test. He may have to choose between the alternative of years of unmitigated anguish, or an immediate release from torture. Need we feel surprise at many resorting to the latter alternative, when they have been taught to believe death either to be an eternal sleep, or a sure entrance into regions of happiness!

How many instances have we on record of persons who have dispatched themselves to avoid falling into the hands of an enemy! The case of the wife of Asdrubal, the Carthaginian general, is a famous instance of the kind. Asdrubal had deserted his post, and had fled to Scipio; and during his absence his wife took shelter with her troops in the temple, which she set on fire. She then attired herself in her richest robes, and holding her two children in her hands, addressed Scipio—who had surrounded the building with his troops—in the following language:—"You, O Roman, are only acting according to the laws of open war; but may the gods of Carthage, and those in concert with them, punish that false wretch who, by such a base desertion, has betrayed his country, his gods, his wife, his children! Let him adorn thy gay triumph; let him suffer in the sight of all Rome those indignities and tortures he so justly merits!"

The case of Nicocles, King of Paphos, in Cyprus, who committed suicide in conjunction with his wife and daughter, on the approach of King Ptolemy, is another in point. Isocrates, the celebrated Athenian orator, starved himself to death, sooner than submit to the dominion of Philip of Macedon. Demosthenes also poisoned himself, when Antipater, Alexander's ambassador, required the Athenians to deliver up their orators, fearful of being subjected to slavery and disgrace.

The persecution to which the Romans subjected Hannibal, after he was oppressed with years and sunk in obscurity, impelled him to have recourse to the poison which he always kept about him in a ring, against sudden emergencies. Mithridates took poison, and administered the same to his wives and daughters, in order to escape being taken prisoner by Pompey, before whose victorious arms he had been compelled to fly.

The case of the inhabitants of the city of Xanthus is another remarkable instance of the determination exhibited by thousands of persons, resolved sooner to die by their own hands than submit to the dominion of a conqueror. Notwithstanding the proffered clemency of Brutus, who not only wept at the dreadful scene he witnessed, but commanded his soldiers to extinguish the fire, and even offered a reward for every inhabitant whose life was saved, the people were so eager for death that they rushed into the flames with exclamations of delight, and forceably drove back the soldiers who were sent by Brutus for the purpose of saving their lives.

The example of Cato is applauded by some writers as a proof of magnanimity; the action was the reverse; it was the effect of pride and timidity. If ever Rome required his experience and patriotic counsels it was at that very period. To desert the duty which Rome had a right to demand by a voluntary death was the meanest conduct in his character. It stamped an indelible stain on his reputation, which only a supposition that his intellect was impaired could rationally excuse. It was not the virtuous Cato who had stemmed the torrent of tyranny, who had crushed the Cataline conspiracy, who had given the most noble examples of virtuous resolution and rectitude in moral conduct, but the enfeebled Cato, sinking under the accumulation of evils, whose soul was depressed with suspense and distracting passions, waiting an opportunity for revenge, or preparing to finish his life on the first disappointment.

If such examples were admitted magnanimous, in any serious quarrel or war, where success could not be commanded, it might be considered laudable to commit suicide. The consequences of such reasoning would be obvious. On such occasions, countries would lose their bravest generals, private families their noblest and most experienced supporters.

"If I cannot acquire what I wish," says Cato, "I will kill myself; I will not live to grace Cæsar's triumph, though I know Cæsar to be the most generous and clement of conquerors; I cannot consent to receive Cæsar's favours. My pride is wounded; my fears destroy all tranquillity; my body is sinking under adversity; I will not dedicate my services to my distressed country under the auspices of successful Cæsar. I will plunge a sword into my bosom, and commit an injustice to myself, which through a long life I never committed to others. From the uniformity of my former patriotic character, writers, without deep reasoning, will paint this concluding action in glowing colours; they will give additional lustre to an immortal reputation." Such, we conceive, were the secret springs of action in Cato's mind; such were the contending passions which excited the delirium. It was not the placid, judicious Cato of former years, but the depressed Cato, *impos mentis*, committing a rash action, contrary to all his former great reasoning, and virtuous persevering conduct. It was, in fact, Cato's act of insanity; it was not dying to serve his country, but to effectually rob Cæsar of his eminent services; it therefore appears more the effect of private pique and despondency than a demonstration of public virtue or courage. Had all others concerned in that civil war followed this extraordinary example, the country would have been robbed of many of its brightest ornaments. Cato could not say with Horace, "Dulce et decorum est pro patria mori," for it was not for his countrymen that he died, but to gratify a selfish caprice, a personal resentment and hatred to Cæsar and his power. Had Cæsar attacked the city while Cato enjoyed a vigour of mind and body, and when the citizens were better disciplined and less corrupt, he would have despised such inglorious conduct; he would rather have hoped for some future opportunity to dispel the dark clouds overwhelming the distracted country.

Physicians have frequent opportunities of observing the diminution of human courage and wisdom from long continued misfortunes, or bodily infirmities. The most lively, spirited, and enterprising, have become depressed from reiterated disappointment; cowardice and despair have succeeded to the most unquestionable bravery and ambition. The man is then changed; his blood is changed; and with these his former sentiments. The timidity is no longer Cato's, but belongs to the miserable *debilitated body* of Cato, which had lost that *vigorous soul* that so eminently distinguished on other important occasions this excellent and divine patriot.

La Motte observes, with reference to Cato's death—

"Stern Cato, with more equal soul, Had bowed to Cæsar's wide control, With Rome, had to her conqueror bowed, But that his spirit, rough and proud, Had not the courage to await A pardoned foe's too humbling fate."

Voltaire, in alluding to the lines quoted above, says, "It was, I believe, because Cato's soul was always equal, and retained to the last its love for his country and her laws, that he chose rather to perish with her than to crouch to the tyrant. He died as he had lived.

"Incapable of surrendering, and to whom? to the enemy of Rome—to the man who had forcibly robbed the public treasury in order to make war upon his fellow citizens, and enslave them by means of their own money. A pardoned foe! It seems as if La Motte Houdart was speaking of some revolted subject who might have obtained his Majesty's pardon by letters in chancery. It seems (continues Voltaire) rather absurd to say that Cato slew himself through weakness. None but a strong mind can thus surmount the most powerful instinct of nature. This strength is sometimes that of frenzy; but a frantic man is not weak."

In forming an estimate of the condition of Cato's mind, we must not look at him as delineated by the dramatist and poet, but as exhibited by the historian and philosopher. Our notions of Cato are too often based on Addison's, and not Plutarch's description of his character. That Cato was one of the most complete and perfect examples in antiquity of private manners and of public spirit cannot be questioned; and therefore, in this respect, worthy to be held up as an example. Sallust thus eulogizes Cato:—"His glory can neither be increased by flattery nor lessened by detraction. He was one who chose to be, rather than to appear good. He was the very image of virtue, and in all points of disposition more like the gods than men. He never did right that he might seem to do right, but because he could not do otherwise. That only seemed to be reasonable which was just. Free from all human vices, he was superior to the vicissitudes of fortune." It was the dignity of Cato's life that stamped a celebrity on the mode of his death.

In forming a judgment of the motives which led this distinguished man to sacrifice his life, we must look at him in connexion with his great enemy, Cæsar. He was not only opposed to him on public, but on private grounds. Cæsar's intimacy with Servilia, Cato's sister, was the ground of much conversation at Rome. During one of the debates concerning the Cataline conspiracy, Cæsar received a letter whilst he was in the senate house. Cato, who had intimated that Cæsar had been privy to Cataline's proceedings, and believing that the letter might refer to the subject, from the manner in which Cæsar endeavoured to conceal it, demanded that it should be handed over to him. The letter was accordingly handed to Cato, when, perceiving that it was a letter from Servilia to Cæsar, full of protestations of love to his deadliest enemy, he threw it at Cæsar in a great rage, and called him a drunkard. This, added to the circumstance of Cæsar's complete triumph over him, induced Cato to put an end to his own life. He did not commit suicide to defeat usurpation, or to preserve the liberties and laws of Rome, but it was done when he despaired of his country. It arose from his horror of tyranny, and the feeling of intolerable shame at the prospect of a long life under an arbitrary master. The superstructure of years was in a moment levelled to the dust. He had to choose between death or slavery. After the defeat at Thapsus, and hearing that Cæsar was marching against him, Lucius Cæsar offered to intercede for Cato. His answer was as follows:—"If I would save my life, I ought to go myself; but I will not be beholden to the tyrant for any act of his injustice; and 'tis unjust for him to pretend to pardon those as a lord over whom he has no lawful power." Although it was evident he was bent upon suicide, he persuaded his son to go to Cæsar, and cautioned his friend Statilius, whom Plutarch calls "a known Cæsar-hater," not to kill himself, but to submit to the conqueror. He then entered into a discussion concerning liberty, which he carried on so violently that his friends were apprehensive that he would lay hands on himself. In consequence of this, his son removed his sword. Cato is then represented as reading Plato's Phædo, and then calling for his sword, which they refused to bring him. He called a second and third time, and in a fit of rage he struck the servant, and wounded him, and by doing so, injured his own hand, which prevented him from effectually killing himself with his weapon. After he had stabbed himself, his wound was dressed; but so determined was he to sacrifice his life, that he tore open the wound forcibly, and pulled his bowels out, and thus effected his purpose.[1]

It has been said that Addison approved of Cato's self-murder. This does not appear to be the fact, if we are to judge from the words which he has put in the mouth of the dying hero—

"I am sick to death; oh, when shall I get loose From this vain world, the abode of guilt and sorrow! And yet methinks a beam of light breaks in On my departing soul. Alas, I fear I have been too hasty! O ye powers that search The heart of man, and weigh his inmost thoughts, If I have done amiss, impute it not: The best may err, but you are good, and—(*dies.*)"

[1] Cæsar's reply on being told of Cato's death was reported to be—"Cato, I envy thee thy death, for thou hast envied me the preservation of thy life;" on which Plutarch remarks, "Had Cato suffered himself to be preserved by Cæsar, it is likely he would not so much have impaired his own honour, as augmented the other's clemency and glory." But Cato's own idea was, that it was an insupportable instance of Cæsar's tyranny and usurpation that he should "pretend" to shew clemency in saving lives over whom he had no legal authority.

Two celebrated instances amongst the Grecians of men who voluntarily sacrificed their lives in order to maintain the dignity and importance of their own institutions, are exhibited in the cases of Charondas and Lycurgus. The former, in order to encourage a proper freedom of debate, had made it death to come armed into the assembly of the states. One day, coming himself in haste to a convention without having first laid aside his sword, he was rebuked by some one present, as a transgressor of his own laws. Stung with the justice of the imputation, he instantly plunged the sword into his own heart, both as a sacrifice to the violated majesty of the law, and a tremendous example of disinterested justice; trusting, moreover, thus to seal with his own blood a strict observance in others of his wholesome institutions.

When Lycurgus had accomplished his great work of legislation in Sparta, he took the following method of rendering his system unchangeable and immortal. He stated that it was necessary that he should consult the Delphian oracle relative to his new laws. He then made all the Spartan magistrates and people take a solemn oath that they would observe and keep his laws inviolate "till his return." He accordingly went to consult the oracle, and having sent back the answer in writing to Sparta, "That the laws were excellent, and would render the people great and happy who should observe them," he resolved never to return himself, in order that the people might never be absolved from their oath. He accordingly starved himself to death. Plutarch considers that Lycurgus reasoned himself into the act, under the belief that a good statesman and patriot should seek to make his death itself in some way useful to his country. The same authority considers that he intended the mode of his death to be a practical illustration of the great principle which pervaded the whole code of his laws, which was—*temperance.*

Alike honourable, in a worldly point of view, was the death of Codrus, King of Athens. The oracle was consulted with reference to the condition of the country. That nation was predicted to be prosperous whose king should be first slain by the enemy. Codrus disguised himself as a private soldier, and entered the enemy's camp, where he contrived to pick a quarrel with the first man he met, whom he permitted to slay him; thus, for the good of his country, courting his own death.

Themistocles is said to have poisoned himself rather than lead on the Persian army against his own countrymen, although fame, wealth, and honour were within his grasp.

The Emperor Otho, to avoid the further sacrifice of life in the imperial contest, resolved to die by his own hands, notwithstanding his troops implored and beseeched him to lead them on to a second engagement in which victory was almost certain. King Otho's answer to the demand of his soldiers is considered to embody the spirit of true Roman heroism—"Deny me not the glory of laying down my own life to preserve yours. The more hope there is left, the more honourable is my early retirement; since it is by my death alone that I can prevent the further effusion of Roman blood, and restore peace and tranquillity to a distracted empire, by being ready to die for its peace and security."[2]

[2] The affection and resolution of an obscure private soldier was very remarkable, who, standing before Otho with his drawn sword, spoke thus—"Behold in my action an

Two of the most distinguished men of antiquity who sacrificed their own lives were Brutus and Cassius. Before their battle with Cæsar on the plains of Philippi, these two warriors had a conversation on suicide. Cassius asked Brutus what his opinions were on the subject of self-destruction, provided fortune did not favour them in the contest in which they were about to be engaged. Brutus replied, that formerly he had embraced such sentiments as induced him to condemn Cato for killing himself; he deemed it an act of irreverence towards the gods, and that it was no evidence of courage. But he continues, "Now, in the midst of dangers, I am quite of another mind." He then proceeds to tell Cassius of his determination to surrender up his life "on the Ides of March." He states no particular reasons for having changed his opinions on the subject of suicide. The issue of the battle is well known. Many things conspired to damp the courage of Cassius and Brutus. In imitation of Cæsar, Brutus made a public lustration for his army in the field, and during the ceremony an unlucky omen is said to have happened to Cassius. The garland he was to wear at the sacrifice was given to him the wrong side outwards; the person, also, who bore the golden image before Cassius stumbled, and the image fell to the ground. Several birds of prey hovered about his camp, and swarms of bees were seen within the trenches. Cassius, believing in the Epicurean philosophy, considered all these circumstances as disheartening omens of his fate. After the defeat of Cassius, he ordered his freedman to kill him, which he did by severing his head from his body.

Plutarch makes Brutus die most stoically. After having taken an affectionate leave of his friends, and having assured them that he was only angry with fortune for his country's sake, since he esteemed himself in his death more happy than his conquerors, he advised them to provide for their own safety. He then retired, and, with the assistance of Strato, he ran his sword through his body. Dion Cassius (Lib. xlvii.) represents Brutus as far from acting the stoic at his last moments. He is said just before his death to have quoted the following passage from Euripides—"O wretched virtue! thou art a bare name! I mistook thee for a substance; but thou thyself art the slave of fortune."

In considering the motives that induced Brutus to destroy himself, we must not forget to take into calculation the effect which the apparition he saw previous to the battle of Philippi must have had on his mind. Brutus was naturally watchful, sparing in his diet, and allowed himself but little time for sleep. He never retired to rest, day or night, until he had arranged all his business. At this time, involved as he was in the operations of war, and solicitous for the event, he only slumbered a little after supper, and spent the remainder of the night in attending to his most urgent affairs. When these were dispatched, he occupied himself in reading till the third watch, when the tribunes and centurions came to him for orders. Thus, a little before he left Asia, he was sitting alone in his tent, by a dim light, at a late hour. The whole army lay in sleep and silence, while Brutus, wrapped in meditation, thought he perceived something enter his tent; turning towards the door,

instance of the unshaken fidelity of all your soldiery. There is not one of us but would strive thus to preserve thee," and immediately he stabbed himself to the heart. Many private soldiers, after Otho's death, gave the same proof of fidelity to their deceased lord.—*Plutarch's Life of Otho.*

he saw a monstrous and horrible spectre standing by the side of his bed. "What art thou?" said he, boldly. The spectre answered, "I am thy evil genius, Brutus! Thou wilt see me at Philippi." To which he calmly replied, "I'll meet thee there." In the morning he communicated to Cassius what he had seen. Cassius, who was an Epicurean, had often disputed with Brutus on the subject of apparitions. He said, when he had heard the statement of Brutus, that the spectre was not a spirit, but a real being; and argued at considerable length on the subject, and induced the general to think that his fate was decided. There can be no doubt but that this singular presentiment co-operated with other circumstances in inducing Brutus to fall by his own hands.[3]

Amongst the ancient suicides, those of Mark Antony and Cleopatra deserve especial consideration. It is not our purpose to enter into an elaborate history of these celebrated characters, but merely to refer to those circumstances that had an immediate connexion with their last moments.

Three circumstances acted powerfully on Antony's mind in inducing him to seek a voluntary death. The first was his having been defeated by Cæsar; the second, the idea that Cleopatra had betrayed him; and the third was the belief in Cleopatra's death.

As soon as Antony was defeated, the unhappy queen fled to her monument, ordered all the doors to be barred, and commanded that Antony should be informed that she was dead. He was overwhelmed with grief, and retiring to his chamber, opened his coat of mail, and ordered his faithful servant Eros (who had been engaged to kill him whenever he should think it necessary) to dispatch him. Eros drew his sword, and, instead of killing his master, ran it through his own body, and fell dead at Antony's feet. Antony then plunged his sword into his bowels, and threw himself on the couch. The wound was not, however, immediately fatal. In a short period after, Diomedes, Cleopatra's servant, came to Antony with a request that he would instantly repair to her chamber. His delight was unbounded when he heard that Cleopatra was alive, and he directly ordered his servant to carry him to her. As she would not allow the doors to be opened, Antony was drawn up to her window by a cord. He was suspended for a considerable time in the air stretching out his hands to Cleopatra. Notwithstanding she exerted all her strength, strained every nerve, and distorted her features in endeavouring to draw him up, it was with the greatest difficulty it was effected. Cleopatra laid him on the bed, and, standing over him, so extreme was her anguish, that she rent her clothes, and beat and wounded her breast. After Antony's death, when Cleopatra heard that Cæsar had dispatched Gallus to take her prisoner, and that he had effected an entrance into the monument, *she attempted to stab herself with a dagger which she always carried about with her for that purpose.* When she heard that it was Cæsar's intention to send her into Syria, she asked permission to visit Antony's tomb, over which she poured forth most bitter lamentations. "Hide me, hide me," she exclaimed, "with thee in the grave; for life, since *thou* hast left it, has been misery to *me.*" After crowning the tomb with flowers, she kissed it, and ordered a bath to be

---

[3] It is said that the night before the battle the same spectre appeared to Brutus, but vanished without saying anything.

prepared. She then sat down to a magnificent supper; after which, a peasant came to the gate with a small basket of figs covered with leaves, which was admitted into the monument. Amongst the figs and under the leaves was concealed the asp, which Cleopatra applied to her bosom. She was found dead, attired in one of her most gorgeous dresses, decorated with brilliants, and lying on her golden bed.

Few of the illustrious men of antiquity have exhibited such philosophic coolness as Petronius, after he had determined to sacrifice his life. The levity which distinguished his voluntary death was in accordance with the gaiety and frivolity of his life. The capricious friendship of a Nero had been withdrawn from him, and in consequence he had determined on his own death. This *arbiter elegantiarum* during life, determined to indulge in a luxurious refinement of that death he was preparing to encounter. Being well aware he could not long escape from the murderous edict, after a fall from the summit of imperial favour, he opened and closed his veins at pleasure. He slept during the intervals, or sauntered about and enjoyed the delights of conversation with his friends; but his discourse was not of so elevated a character as that attributed to Seneca or Socrates.

The poet Lucan exhibited great apparent serenity at the approach of death. After the veins of his arm had been voluntarily opened, and he had lost a large quantity of blood, he felt his hands and his legs losing their vitality. As the hour of death approached, he commenced repeating several lines out of his own Pharsalia, descriptive of a person similarly situated to himself. These lines he repeated until he died.

Cocceius Nerva starved himself to death in the reign of Tiberius. It was said that he was displeased with the state of public affairs, and had made up his mind to die whilst his own integrity remained unsullied.

During the bloody reign of Nero, many singular suicides took place. The particulars attending the deaths of Lucius Vetus, his mother-in-law Sextia, and Pollutia his daughter, are worth recording. After Lucius had distributed all his wealth among his domestics, requesting them to remove everything from his house excepting three couches, he, with his mother-in-law and daughter, retired into the same chamber, opened a vein with the same lancet, and after, reclining each on a separate couch, waited calmly the approach of death. His eyes, and those of his mother-in-law, were both fixed on the daughter, while the daughter's wandered from one to the other. It was the earnest prayer of each of them to die first, and to leave the others in the act of expiring.[4]

When the throne of Sardanapalus was endangered, he conceived a magnificent and truly luxurious mode of committing suicide, quite in character with the extravagance and dissoluteness of his former life. He erected a funeral pile of great height in his palace, and adorned it with the most sumptuous and costly ornaments. In the middle of this building was a chamber of one hundred feet in length, built of wood, in which a number of golden couches and tables were spread. On one of these he reclined with his wife, his numerous concubines occupying the rest. The building was encompassed round at some distance with large beams and

[4] Tac. An. xvi.

thick wood, to prevent all egress from the place. Much combustible matter, and an immense pile of wood were also placed within, together with an infinite quantity of gold and silver, royal vestments, costly apparel, rich furniture, curious ornaments, and all the apparatus of luxury and magnificence. All being arranged, this splendid funeral pile was set on fire, and continued burning until the fifteenth day; during which time Sardanapalus revelled in all kinds of sensualities. The multitude without were in astonishment at the tremendous scene, and at the immense clouds of incense and smoke which issued with the flames. It was stated that the king was engaged in offering some extraordinary sacrifices; while the attendants within alone knew that this dissolute prince was putting such a splendid end to his effeminate life.[5]

There has been some dispute as to the death of Marcus Curtius. Plutarch attributes his death to accident, but Procillius considers that it was voluntary. He says, the earth having opened at a particular time, the Aruspices declared it necessary, for the safety of the republic, that the bravest man in the city should throw himself into the gulf; whereupon Curtius, mounting his horse, leaped armed into it, and the gulf immediately closed. But Livy and Dionysius relate the circumstance in a different manner. They say that Curtius was a Sabine, who, having at first repulsed the Romans, but being in his turn overpowered by Romulus, and endeavouring to make good his retreat, fell into the lake, which from that time bore his name. The lake was situated almost in the centre of the Roman forum. Some writers consider the name was derived from Curtius the Consul, because he caused it to be walled in after it had been struck with lightning.[6]

The death of the celebrated philosopher and poet, Empedocles, of Sicily, was remarkable. Wishing to be believed a god, and that his death might be unknown, he threw himself into the crater of Mount Ætna, and perished in the flames. The mode of his death was not discovered until some time afterwards, when one of his sandals was thrown up from the volcano.

Ancient history affords us many noble examples of individuals who preferred voluntary death to dishonour and loss of character. If ever self-murder could be considered as in the slightest degree justifiable, it would be under such circumstances. Who cannot but honour the conduct of the noble virgins of Macedon, who threw themselves into the wells, and courted death, sooner than submit to the dishonourable proposals of the Roman governor! When Theoxena was pursued by the emissaries of Philip, king of Macedon, who had been guilty of murdering her first husband, she produced a dagger and a box of poison, and placing them before the crew of the ship in which she was endeavouring to make her escape, she said, "Death is now our only remedy and means of vengeance; let each take the

---

[5] At Anchiale, there was a monument erected to the memory of Sardanapalus. It consisted of an image carved in stone work, and having the thumb and the finger of the right hand joined, as if making some sound or noise with them. On the monument was inscribed these words in Assyrian characters: "Sardanapalus, the son of Anacyndarax, founded Anchiale and Tyre in one day. Eat, drink, and be merry. As for the rest, it is not worth the snap of the finger."

[6] Varro *de Ling. Lat.*, lib. iv.

method that best pleases himself of avoiding the tyrant's pride, cruelty, and lust. Come on, my brave companions and family, seize the sword or drink of the cup, as you prefer an instantaneous or gradual death." Some fell on the sword, others drank the poison until death was effected. After Theoxena had accomplished her designs, she threw herself into the arms of her husband, and they both plunged into the sea.

The resistance which Josephus made to the importunities of his soldiers to fall by his own hand sooner than surrender to the enemy, is perhaps the most noble instance of the kind on record. After the success of the Romans in Judæa, Josephus, who commanded the Jewish army, wished to deliver himself up to his conquerors; he was encouraged to this by certain dreams and visions. When Josephus's intention was known, the soldiers flocked round him, and expressed their indignation at his intention. They urged him to fall by his own sword, and to let them follow his example, sooner than abandon the field. To this appeal Josephus replies, "Oh, my friends, why are you so earnest to kill yourselves? why do you set your soul and body, which are such dear companions, at such variance? It is a brave thing to die in war, but it should be by the hands of the enemy. It is a foolish thing to do that for ourselves, which we quarrel with them for doing to us. It is a brave thing to die for liberty; but still it should be in battle, and by those who would take that liberty from us. He is equally a coward who will not die when he is obliged to die. What are we afraid of, when we will not go up and meet the Romans? Is it death? Why then inflict it on ourselves? You say, We must be slaves. Are we then in a clear state of liberty at present? Self-murder is a crime most remote from the common nature of all animals, and an instance of impiety against God our Creator."

Josephus, in the spirit of a true philosopher, urged his soldiers to abandon the notion of suicide; but instead of being calmed by his discourse, they became enraged, and rushed on him. Fearing that the case was hopeless, Josephus prevailed upon them to listen to the following proposal. He persuaded them to draw lots; the man on whom the first lot fell was to be killed by him who had the second, and the second by the third, and so on. In this way no soldier would perish by his own hand, except the last man. Lots were accordingly drawn; Josephus drew his with the rest. He who had the first lot willingly submitted his neck to him who had the second. It happened that Josephus and a soldier were left to draw lots; and as the general was desirous neither to imbrue his own hand in the blood of his countryman, nor to be condemned by lot himself, he persuaded the soldier to trust his fidelity, and to live as well as himself. Thus ended this tragical scene, and Josephus immediately surrendered himself up to Vespasian.

The first instance of suicide recorded in Scripture is that of Samson. After suffering many indignities from the hands of the Philistines, his anger was roused to the highest pitch, and, resting against the pillars that supported the building in which the lords of the Philistines and an infinite number of others were assembled, he offered up the following prayer: "O Lord God, remember me, I pray thee, and strengthen me, I pray thee, only this once, O God, that I may at once be avenged of the Philistines for my two eyes;" and taking hold of the pillars, he said, "Let me die with the Philistines: and he bowed himself with all his might, and the house fell upon the lords and all that were therein; so that the dead which he slew at his death were more than they which he slew in his life."

In Samson's case, there is nothing said in Scripture either to condemn or justify the act; but it appears evident from the whole history of the last events of his life, that he was but an instrument in the hands of God for the accomplishment of his wise purposes. The glory of God had been violated in the person of Samson; he had been subjected by the Philistines to great indignities; and it was to demonstrate the power of God in the destruction of his enemies that Samson's life was sacrificed. Samson is, then, to be considered as a martyr to his religion and his God.

The case of Saul has also been cited. It is thus referred to in Scripture:—"And the battle went sore against Saul, and the archers hit him, and he was sore wounded of the archers. Then said Saul unto his armourbearer, Draw thy sword, and thrust me through therewith, lest these uncircumcised come and thrust me through, and abuse me. But his armourbearer would not, for he was sore afraid; therefore Saul took a sword and fell upon it. And when his armourbearer saw that Saul was dead, he fell likewise upon his sword and died with him."[7]

It must be recollected that the Jews considered that a man was justified in committing suicide to prevent his falling into the enemy's hand, and on this account Saul was commended for killing himself. But there was nothing glorious in Saul's death. His army was defeated by the Philistines, and Saul sounded a retreat; and as he was making his ignominious flight, an arrow from the ranks of the enemy hit him, and it was then that he implored his armourbearer to dispatch him.

Much has been made of the self murder of Ahitophel. Donne has referred to it at some length. He says that in this case there can be "no room for excuse." Ahitophel was considered one of the wisest counsellors of his age. He joined Absalom in his rebellion against his lawful prince, David; and when he saw that it was God's determination to defeat his counsel, and that his advice for the first time was neglected, he became full of secret indignation and disappointment; and in order to avoid the consequences of his own utter despair and ruin, for his perfidy, he hanged himself. Nothing can be urged in justification of this act. The facts are presented to us in biblical history; and we are left to form our own judgment upon the course which this "Machiavellian counsellor," as he has been termed, thought proper to adopt.

Donne has also cited the case of Judas Iscariot.[8] He must have been sadly in

---

[7] 1 Samuel, xxxi.

[8] This is the only case of suicide recorded in the New Testament. Judas's conduct is condemned in the strongest language; he is called in the Gospel of St. John (vi. 70,) "a devil, and the son of perdition;" and in the first chapter of the Acts of the Apostles, at the 25th verse, after the account given of his violent death, he is said to have gone *to his own peculiar place*. (Εἰς τὸν τόπον τὸν ἴδιον)

Virgil thus alludes to the "place of punishment" allotted to those who sacrifice wantonly their own lives:—

"Proxima deinde tenent mæsti loca, qui sibi letum

want of sound illustrations to have brought forward the instance of this traitor as a justification of the act of suicide. Judas has been considered by some writers as a martyr. Petilian said "that Judas, and all who killed themselves through remorse of sin, ought to be accounted martyrs, because they punish in themselves what they grieve to have committed." To whom Augustine replies, "Thou hast said, that the traitor perished by the rope, and has left a rope behind him for such as himself. But we have nothing to do with him. We do not venerate those as martyrs who hang themselves."

The case, mentioned by the same authority, of Eleazar, the brother of Judas Maccabeus, taken from the book of the Maccabees, is said to be one of voluntary suicide, and where self-destruction was laudable. Eleazar sacrificed his own life for the purpose of destroying King Antiochus, and therefore his suicide is to be considered as a voluntary sacrifice for the good of his country.

The self-destruction of Razis is full of horror, and can only be quoted as an evidence of the act of a madman. When the tower in which Razis was fighting against the enemy of Nicanor was set on fire, he fell on his own sword, "Choosing rather," says the text, "to die manfully than fall into the hands of the wicked, to be abused otherwise than beseemed his noble birth; but missing his stroke through haste, the multitude also rushing within doors, he ran boldly up to the wall, and cast himself down manfully among the thickest of them; but they quickly giving back, and a space being made, he fell down in the midst of a void place. Nevertheless, while there was yet breath within him, being inflamed with anger, he rose up; and though his blood gushed out like spouts of water, and his wounds were grievous, yet he ran through in the midst of the throng, and standing on a steep rock, when, as his blood was not quite gone, he plucked out his bowels, and taking them in both his hands, he cast them upon the throng, and calling upon the Lord of life and spirit to restore him them again, he thus died."[9]

Having considered the remarkable suicides of antiquity, we will now briefly

> Insontes peperêre manu, lucemque perosi
> Projecêre animas. Quàm vellent æthere in alto
> Nunc et pauperiem et duros perferre labores!
> Fas obstat. Tristique palus inamabilis undâ
> Alligat, et novies Styx interfusa coërcet."

(ÆNEIS, lib. vi. ver. 434 et seq.)

> "The next in place and punishment are they
> Who prodigally throw their souls away:
> Fools, who, repining at their wretched state,
> And loathing anxious life, suborn their fate:
> With late repentance now they would retrieve
> The bodies they forsook, and wish to live;
> Their pains and poverty desire to bear,
> To view the light of heaven and breathe the vital air.
> But fate forbids, the Stygian floods oppose,
> And with nine circling streams the captive souls inclose."

(DRYDEN.)

[9] Macc. i. 6.

allude to those doctrines and opinions of the celebrated philosophers of ancient times, which must of necessity have tended to create this recklessness of human life.

The doctrines inculcated by the stoical philosophers, or the disciples of Zeno, must have increased the crime of suicide. "A stoical wise man is ever ready to die for his country or his friends. A wise man will never look upon death as an evil; that he will despise it, and be ready to undergo it at any time." "A wise man," says Diog. Laertius, in his life of Zeno, when expounding the stoical philosophy, "will quit life, when oppressed with severe pain, or when deprived of any of his senses, or when labouring under desperate diseases." It is astonishing that a sect of philosophers who inculcated that pain was no evil, should so often have practised suicide. Much as we would condemn such principles, still we must admit that most of the admired characters of antiquity belonged to this celebrated sect—men distinguished for their wisdom, learning, and the strictness of their morals. Cato was a stoic, and he put into practice the principles of the sect to which he belonged.[10]

Among the philosophers of antiquity, Seneca stands preeminently forward as the defender of suicide. He says, "Does life please you? live on. Does it not? go from whence you came. No vast wound is necessary; a mere puncture will secure your liberty. It is a bad thing (you say) to be under the necessity of living; but there is no necessity in the case. Thanks be to the gods, nobody can be compelled to live."[11] These were the principles of the "wise Seneca," and yet he wanted the courage to commit suicide when put to the test. He says, "Being emaciated by a severe illness, I often thought of suicide, but was recalled by the old age of a most indulgent father; for I considered not how resolutely 'I' could encounter death, but how 'he' could bear up under my loss." This is not, however, the only instance in which Seneca yielded his stoical principles to the dictates of natural affection and rational judgment.

Among other distinguished philosophers who advocated suicide was Epictetus. Although a stoic, he did not blindly follow the doctrines of Zeno. Epictetus considered that it was the duty of man to suffer to almost any extent before he sacrificed his own life. "If you like not life, you may leave it; the door is open; get you gone! But a little smoke ought not to frighten you away; it should be endured, and will thereby be often surmounted."

Epictetus followed strictly his own principles: in this respect he was superior to Seneca. Seneca was born in the lap of good fortune; Epictetus was a slave, and had to pass through the rugged paths of adversity, bodily pain, and penury. Seneca was banished from Rome for an intrigue; Epictetus was sent into exile for being a man of learning and a philosopher.

---

[10] There is something sublime in the stern copiousness with which the stoics dwelt particularly on the facility with which suicide may be committed. "Ante omnia cavi, ne quis vos teneret invitos: PATET EXITUS. Si pugnare non vultis, licet fugere. Ideoque ex omnibus rebus, quas esse vobis necessarias volui, nihil feci facilius, quam mori. Attendite modo et videbitis quam brevis ad libertatem et quam expedita ducat via. Non tam longas in exitu vobis quam intrantibus, moras posui," &c.—*Seneca de Providentia*, in fine. Vide epistle lxx.

[11] Epistles xii. and lxx.; and De Irâ, lib. iii.

When Epictetus was beaten unmercifully by his master, he said, with great composure, "You will certainly break my leg." He did so; and the philosopher calmly rejoined, "Did I not tell you you would do it?" This was in the true spirit of stoical philosophy.

Marcus Aurelius Antoninus was, perhaps, one of the brightest ornaments of the sect of stoics. He carried into the minutest concern of life the doctrine of Zeno. "He was," says Gibbon, "severe to himself, indulgent to the imperfections of others, just and beneficent to all mankind."

Zeno, the founder of the sect of stoical philosophers, acted up to the principles which he inculcated to his disciples. His suicide is recorded to be as follows:—As he was going out of his school one day, at the age of ninety-eight, he fell down, put a finger out of joint, went home, and hanged himself.

Cleanthes, also, the successor of Zeno, followed the example of his master in philosophy, by shortening the period of his life in the following manner:—After having used abstinence for two days, by the advice of his physician, for the cure of a trifling indisposition under which he was labouring, he had permission to return to his former diet; but he refused all sustenance, saying, "*that as he had advanced so far on his journey towards death, he would not retreat.*" He accordingly starved himself to death.

Among the most distinguished orators of antiquity who spoke in favour of suicide stands Cicero. During his banishment he would have actually destroyed himself, if it had not been for his natural timidity and want of resolution. He writes to his brother Quintus, "The tears of my friends have prevented me from flying to death as my refuge."

Pliny was an advocate of suicide. In a chapter entitled "On God," he writes thus—"The chief comfort of man in his imperfect state is this, that even the Deity cannot do all things. For instance, he cannot put himself to death when he pleases, which is the greatest indulgence he has given to man amid the severe evils of life." Pliny belonged to the Epicureans, and his notions are in accordance with the doctrines of that sect.

Pliny the younger appears to have had different notions on the subject. When lamenting the death of a dear friend, Corellius Rufus, who had killed himself, he says, "He is dead—dead by his own hand, which agonizes my grief; for that is the most lamentable kind of death which neither proceeds from nature nor from fate." The whole epistle from which the above extract is made indicates a noble and feeling heart.

It appears that the Roman laws respecting suicide were of a fiscal nature. They viewed the act not as a crime abstractedly, but considered how far the circumstance affected the state or treasury. In some portion of the Roman empire the magistrate had the power of granting or refusing permission to commit suicide. If the decision was given against the applicant, and he persisted in sacrificing his life, disgrace and ignominy were heaped upon his body, and it was buried in the most humiliating manner. The tenour of the law relating to suicide laid down in "Justinian's Digests" is to the following effect:—"Those who, being actually accused, or who being caught in any crime, and dreading a prosecution, made way with themselves, were to have their effects confiscated. But this confiscation was no punishment of suicide, *as a crime in itself*, being then only to take place when the crime committed incurred the confiscation of property, and when the person accused of it would have been found guilty. For which reason the heirs-at-law were permitted (if they thought proper) to try the cause as though the accused person, who had put a period to his life, had been still living; and if his innocence could be proved, they were still entitled to his effects. But if any one killed himself, either through weariness of life, or an impatience under pain or ill health, for a load of private debt, or for any other reason not affecting the state or public treasury, the property of the deceased flowed in its natural channel. In the case of an attempted but incomplete suicide, where a man was under no accusation, a distinction was made as to the causes impelling to it, before the question as to its punishment was to be determined. If it proceeded not from weariness of life, or an impatience under the pressure of some calamity, the attempter was to suffer the same punishment as if he had effected his purpose; and for this reason, because he who without reason spared not his own life, would not be likely to spare another man's."[12]

If a prisoner committed suicide, the jailor authorized to protect him was punished very severely. The Roman law made a distinction between soldiers and civilians. If a soldier attempted to take away his life, and it could not be proved that he was suffering at the time from great grief, misfortune, madness, &c., it was deemed a capital offence, and death was the punishment. And even in cases where it was established that the act was the result of mental perturbation, he was dismissed from the service with ignominy and disgrace.

During the pure ages of the Roman Republic, when religion was reverenced, when the gods were looked up to with respect as the disposers of all events, suicide was but little known. But when the philosophy of Greece was introduced into the Roman Empire, and the manners of the people became corrupted and degenerated, the crime increased to an alarming extent. This indifference to life was also augmented by the spread of stoical and epicurean principles. The stoic was taught to believe his life his own; that he was the sole arbiter of his existence; and that he could live or die as he pleased. The same principles were inculcated by the epicurean philosophy. Is it, then, to be wondered at, that suicide should be of common occurrence, when such degrading principles had taken possession of the minds of the people?

By the law of Thebes, the person who committed suicide was deprived of his funeral rites, and his name and memory were branded with infamy. The Athenian law was equally severe: the hand of the self-murderer was cut off, and buried apart from his body, as having been an enemy and traitor to it. The Greeks considered suicide as a most heinous crime. The bodies of suicides, according to the Grecian custom, were not burned to ashes, but were immediately buried. They considered it a pollution of the holy element of fire to consume in it the carcases of those who had been guilty of self-murder. Suicides were classed "with the public or private enemy; with the traitor, and conspirator against his country; with the

---

[12] Corpus Juris Civilis, lib. xlviii. tit. xxi. parag. 3.

tyrant, the sacrilegious wretch, and such grievous offenders whose punishment was impalement alive on a cross."[13]

These laws, however, fell into disuse, as appears evident from the circumstance of there being so many cases of suicide which escaped this treatment.

In the island of Ceos the magistrates had the power of deciding whether a person had sufficient reasons for killing himself. A poison was kept for that purpose, which was given to the applicant who made out his case before the magistracy.

The same custom was followed among the Massilians, the ancient inhabitants of Marseilles. A preparation of hemlock was kept in readiness, and the senate, on hearing the merits of the case, had the power to decide whether the applicant had good and substantial reasons for committing suicide. There was, no doubt, much good effected by this regulation, as it clearly acknowledged the principle that the power of a man over his own life rested not in himself, but in the voice of the magistrate, who alone was to determine how his life or death might affect the state.

Libanius, of Antioch, who flourished towards the end of the fourth century, has very happily ridiculed the practice to which we have alluded. In some imaginary pleadings before the senate, he advocates the cause of a man who wishes to swallow the hemlock draught, that he may be freed from the garrulity of a loquacious wife. "Truly," says he, "if our legislator had not been addicted too much to law making, I should have been under no necessity of proving before you the expediency of my departure, but a rope and the first tree would have given me peace and quiet. But since he, determining we should be slaves, has deprived us even of the liberty of dying when we please, and has enchained us with decrees on this business, I imprecate the author and obey his mandates, in thus laying my complaints and my request before you." He then, with considerable eloquence and humour, advocates the cause of the "envious man," who wishes to taste the "suicidal draught" because his neighbour's wealth had increased beyond his own. "Let the wretch," he says, "recite his calamities, let the senate bestow the antidote, and let grief be dissolved in death."

Libanius then pleads in behalf of Timon, the man hater, who begs permission to dispatch himself because he was bound by profession to hate all mankind, but he could not help loving Alcibiades.

It is a singular circumstance connected with the subject of suicide, that authors who have written in its defence should quote the cases referred to in this chapter in justification of their views. They have not taken into consideration the peculiar customs, habits, and religion of the people, which of course must have greatly influenced their actions. How absurd would it be for us to take the authority of antiquity as an infallible rule of conduct. The Massagetes considered those unhappy who died a natural death, and therefore eat their dearest friends when they grew old. The Libarenians broke their necks down a precipice. The Bactrians were thrown alive to the dogs. The Scythians buried the dearest friends of the deceased with them alive, or killed them on the funeral pile. The Roman people, when sunk in vice and licentiousness, considered it a mark of courage and honour to fall by

[13] Vide Potter's Antiquities.

their own hands, and suicide was a common occurrence with them.

"In the beginning of the spring," says Malt. Brun, "a shocking ceremony takes place at Cola Bhairava, in the mountains between the rivers Taptæ and Nerbuddah. It is the practice of some persons of the lowest tribes in Berar to make vows of suicide, in return for answers which their prayers are believed to have received from their idols. This is the place where such vows are performed in the beginning of spring, when eight or ten victims generally throw themselves from a precipice. The ceremony gives rise to an annual fair, and some trade."[14]

No just distinction can be drawn between these customs. The Indian widow, in obedience to the religion of her country, ascends the funeral pile of her husband, and is burnt to death. Thousands annually sacrifice their lives by throwing themselves under the wheels of their idol Juggernaut. Strong feelings of religion impel them to this; they become excluded from society, they lose caste, and are subjected to all kinds of persecution if they do not bow to the customs of the country. What legitimate argument can be deduced from these facts in favour of suicide? And yet these cases are considered to constitute a justification of the stoical dogma, that we have a right when we please to put an end to our own existence. Desperate indeed must be the circumstances of those who are compelled to found their reasoning on so flimsy a basis.

---

[14] Universal Geography, vol. iii. p. 155.

CHAPTER II.

WRITERS IN DEFENCE OF SUICIDE.

Opinions of Hume—Effect of his writings—Case of suicide caused by—The doctrines of Montesquieu, Rousseau, and Montaigne examined—Origin of Dr. Donne's celebrated work—Madame de Staël's recantation—Robert of Normandy, Gibbon, Sir T. More, and Robeck's opinions considered.

It will be foreign to my purpose to enter elaborately into an examination of the opinions of those who have thought proper to justify the commission of suicide. The arguments which have been advanced by Hume, Donne, Rousseau, Madame de Staël, Montesquieu, Montaigne, Gibbon, Voltaire, and Robeck, are founded on such gross and apparent fallacies, that they carry with them their own refutation.

Hume, whose pen was always ready to support opinions at variance with the precepts of the Christian religion, wrote an essay on the subject of suicide. He has endeavoured to shew that self-murder is consistent with our duty to God, our neighbour, and ourselves. Referring to the first of these three heads, he says—"As, on the one hand, the elements and other inanimate parts of creation carry on their action without regard to the particular interests and situation of men, so men are entrusted to their own judgment and discretion in the various shades of matter, and may employ every faculty with which they are endowed in order to provide for their ease, happiness, or preservation."

If an action be clearly shewn to be an infringement of the laws of God, it certainly cannot be one which he has left us to exercise at discretion. All the laws of religion and morality are so many abridgments of man's liberty, in the exercise of his judgment and discretion for his own happiness. Hume then proceeds to examine whether suicide be a breach of duty to our neighbour and society. He observes—"A man who retires from life does no harm to society,—he only ceases to do good; which, if it be an injury, is of the lowest kind." The man who sacrifices his own life does a *great injury* to society. There are very few men in the world who have no relations or connexions, and he entails upon these the opprobrium that society attaches to the crime of suicide. Independently of this, his example acts injuriously on the minds of others, who may not have such good reasons for suicide as he has. "I believe," continues Hume, "that no man ever threw away life while it was worth keeping. For such is our natural horror of death, that small motives will never be able to reconcile us to it." He might as well have stated that such is our horror of poverty that no man ever threw away *riches* which were worth keeping.

The fallacy consists in drawing a conclusion from a mind supposed in its right state, in which every faculty, propensity, and aversion has its due proportion of strength; and in which the natural horror of death will secure a man from throwing away a life which is worth keeping: and this conclusion is applied to a *depraved* state of mind, in which it can by no means hold.

The same author asserts, "That it would be no crime in me to divert the Nile or Danube from its course, if I could; where, then, is the crime of turning a few ounces of blood out of its natural channel?" The argument is too puerile to merit refutation. He must first establish that no injury would accrue from diverting the course of the Nile and Danube, before any argument can be deduced from it which is worth one moment's consideration.

It has been asserted, and remains uncontradicted, that Mr. Hume lent his "Essay on Suicide" to a friend, who on returning it told him it was a most excellent performance, and pleased him better than anything he had read for a long time. In order to give Hume a practical exhibition of the effects of his defence of suicide, his friend shot himself the day after returning him his Essay.

If, in any one instance, suicide might admit of something like an apology, it would have been in this—if the detestable author of this abominable treatise had, on receiving the melancholy intelligence, committed it to the flames, and terminated his own pernicious existence by a cord. But the cold-blooded infidel was too cowardly to execute summary justice on himself. With a truly diabolical spirit, his delight was to scatter firebrands among the people, and say, "Am I not in sport?"

Mr. Hume is the hero of modern infidels, because he is the only one among them whose life was not disgraced by the grossest of vices; for this, his selfish and avaricious spirit affords, perhaps, the true reason. It is well known that Hume, in more than one instance, sacrificed his principles (if he had any) to views of emolument at the suggestion of the booksellers. It has been said that he was scarcely guilty of a good or benevolent action. His treatment of Rousseau was unfeeling in the extreme; and an intimate friend of the essayist affirms, that "his heart was as hard and cold as marble."

Montesquieu's arguments in favour of suicide appear to border very closely on those advanced by Hume. They will be found in a letter written in the character of a Persian resident in Europe.

Rousseau[15] in his "Nouvelle Heloïse" observes, "The more I reflect upon it

[15] It is generally believed that Rousseau killed himself by taking arsenic; but this has been denied. Judging from the character and disposition of the man, we should feel disposed to credit the statement respecting his voluntary death. Rousseau always maintained that the following stanza of Tasso had a direct application to him, and accurately described his feelings and position in the world—

> "Still, still 'tis mine with grief and shame to rove,
> A dire example of disastrous love;
> While keen remorse for ever breaks my rest,
> And raging furies haunt my conscious breast,
> The lonely shades with terror must I view,
> The shades shall every dreadful thought renew:

(suicide), the more I find that the question reduces itself to this fundamental proposition:—To seek one's own good, and avoid one's own harm in that which hurts not another, is the law of nature." Rousseau must first clearly establish that what he terms "seeking one's own good" will not be productive of injury to others. According to the notion of what the majority of men conceive to be their good, much evil would result from allowing mankind to act under the influence of their own feelings and judgment. What one man considers "good," another considers evil; and what often appears to be very beneficial to ourselves, if examined fairly, will be found to be the very reverse.

Montaigne's arguments are borrowed from ancient writers in defence of suicide. He assumes at the commencement that suicide is not an evil. He says, that pain, and the fear of suffering a worse death, is an excusable incitement to suicide. The whole that he has advanced is but a string of sophistries.

Dr. Donne has entered more fully into the defence of suicide than any other writer. The whole of his work appears to be written for the purpose of demonstrating that it is praiseworthy to shew a contempt of life in the discharge of our duty, and in the execution of noble and beneficent enterprises.

Dr. Donne was probably drawn to the contemplation of this subject by his own sufferings. While he was secretary to Lord Chancellor Egerton, he married a young lady of rank superior to his own, which gave offence to his patron, and he was consequently dismissed from office. He suffered extreme poverty with his wife and children; and in a letter, in which he adverts to the illness of a daughter whom he tenderly loved, he says that he dares not expect relief, even from death, as he cannot afford the expense of a funeral. He afterwards took orders, and was promoted to the deanery of St. Paul's. In the early part of his life, and probably during the period of his sufferings, he wrote his book, entitled, "Βιαθανατος, *A Declaration of that paradox or thesis, that self-homicide is not so naturally sin that it may never be otherwise.*" He did not publish it. He desired *it to be remembered, that it was written by Jack Donne, not by Dr. Donne*; and it was published many years after his death, by his son, a dissipated young man, tempted by his necessities to forget his father's prohibition.

Madame de Staël attempted to justify suicide in her work on the passions, but she, greatly to her honour, published her celebrated "Reflections on Suicide," which was written as a recantation of some opinions on the subject incidentally expressed in the work alluded to. She expresses the change in her sentiments on this subject in the following curious manner:—"J'ai l'acte du suicide, dans mon ouvrage sur l'influence des passions, et je me suis repentie depuis de cétte parole inconsiderée. J'etois alors dans tout l'orgueil et la vivacité de la première jeunesse; mais à quoi servirait-il de vivre, si ce n'était dans l'espoir de s'ameliorer."

Madame de Staël has treated the subject with considerable ingenuity and ability, and with a great deal of eloquence, but she has hardly enforced sufficiently the

> The rising sun shall equal horrors yield,
> The sun that first the dire event revealed;
> Still must I view myself with hateful eye,
> And seek, though vainly, from myself to fly."

arguments against this crime which may be deduced from the use of that portion of existence we pass upon earth. We are wise and good just in proportion as we consider and treat life and all its incidents as moral means to a great end. Upon every moment of time an eternity is dependent; and whenever we sacrifice a moment, we throw away an instrument by which we might have created an eternity of happiness.

All mankind are not placed upon an equality. Some experience pleasure, others pain, privation or suffering; the tools with which we are to work may be inconvenient or burthensome, or light and pleasant; but they must be the most useful and efficacious, or they would not be put into our hands; at any rate, they are all we have. We cannot fix too deeply on our minds the truth that life is not an absolute, but a relative existence, as in its relation to the eternity with which it is connected, consists all its value and importance.

Robert of Normandy, surnamed the Devil, sacrificed his own life, and before doing so he wrote a work in defence of suicide, in which he argued that there was no law that forbids a person to deprive himself of life; that the love of life is to be subservient to that of happiness; that our body is a mean and contemptible machine, the preservation of which we ought not so highly to value; if the human soul be mortal, it receives but a slight injury, but if immortal, the greatest advantage; a benefit ceases to be one when it becomes troublesome, and then surely a man ought to be allowed to resign it; a voluntary death is often the only method of avoiding the greatest crime; and finally, that suicide is justified by the example of most nations in the world. Such is the substance of the arguments in favour of suicide urged by Robert of Normandy, and worthy of his celebrated namesake.

Gibbon and Sir Thomas More are cited as champions in favour of suicide; but there is nothing which these authors have advanced that merits a separate consideration.

CHAPTER III.

SUICIDE A CRIME AGAINST GOD AND MAN.—IT IS NOT AN ACT OF COURAGE.

The sin of suicide—The notions of Paley on the subject—Voltaire's opinion—Is suicide self-murder?—Is it forbidden in Scripture?—Shakspeare's views on the subject—The alliance between suicide and murder—Has a man a right to sacrifice his own life?—Everything held upon trust—Suicide a sin against ourselves and neighbour—It is not an act of courage—Opinion of Q. Curtius on the subject—Buonaparte's denunciation of suicide—Dryden's description of the suicide in another world.

Among the black catalogue of human offences, there is not, indeed, any that more powerfully affects the mind, that more outrages all the feelings of the heart, than the crime of suicide. Our laws have branded it with infamy, and the industry which is exerted by surviving relatives to conceal its perpetration evinces that the shame which is attached to it is of that foul and contagious character, that even the innocent consider themselves infected by its malignity.

Much discussion has taken place as to whether self-murder is expressly forbidden in the Old or New Testament.[16] Paley, who is a high authority on all questions connected with moral philosophy, denies that it is. He considers that the article in the decalogue so often brought forward, "Thou shalt do no murder," is inconclusive. "I acknowledge (he observes) that there is to be found neither any express determination of the question, nor sufficient evidence to prove that the

[16] *Duverger de Haurane*, abbot of St. Cyran, regarded as the founder of Port Royal, wrote, in the year 1608, a treatise on suicide, which has, says Voltaire, become one of the scarcest books in Europe.

He says the decalogue forbids us to kill. In this precept, self-murder seems no less to be comprised than murder of our neighbour. But if there are cases in which it is allowable to kill our neighbour, there likewise are cases in which it is allowable to kill ourselves. We must not make an attempt upon our lives until we have consulted reason. The public authority, which holds the place of God, may dispose of our lives. The reason of man may likewise hold the place of the reason of God,—it is a ray of the eternal light.

Voltaire, disposed as he was to advocate the right of committing suicide whenever a man considered death preferable to a dishonourable life, had sufficient sagacity to see through the glaring sophistry of St. Cyran's reasoning on this point. The same author says, "A man may kill himself for the good of his prince, for that of his country, or for that of his relations."

case of suicide was in the contemplation of the law which prohibits murder. Any inference, therefore, which we deduce from Scripture, can be sustained only by *construction and implication*."

To maintain that God has not forbidden us to destroy the work of his hands, because self-murder is not particularly specified, is to leave us at liberty to commit many other offences which are not named among the prohibitions, but which are included under general heads. When God said to Noah, "Whoso sheddeth man's blood, by man shall his blood be shed, for in the image of God made he man," it is evident that, whatever meaning we may attach to the last words, in whatever sense man is said to be made in the image of God, the reason of the prohibition holds as strong against self-murder as against any other kind of murder. If I am commanded not to shed the blood of another man because he is made in the *image of God*, I am not justified in shedding my own blood, as I stand in the same relation to the Deity as my fellow-men. But there is a particular reason why suicide is not any where expressly forbidden by *name*; that is, that whatever sins and offences God, as a lawgiver, prohibits, he does so with a penalty; he affixes such a punishment to such a crime, and he who transgresses is to undergo the determined punishment in this world or in the next. Neither God nor the magistrate can prohibit self-murder with any penalty that can affect the criminal himself; because of his very crime, he escapes all temporal punishment in person—he has anticipated the operation of the law. In fact, he has, in his own person, acted the part of the criminal, judge, jury, and executioner; he is dead before the law can take any cognizance of his offence. No law can be enacted to any purpose without a penalty; where, therefore, there can be no penalty, there can be no law. Self-murder prevents all penalty, and therefore wants no particular prohibition; it must therefore be included under general commands, and forbidden as a *sin*, which it is only in the power of God to take cognizance of, in another world.

Again, doubtlessly the inspired writer considered suicide of such an atrocious nature that the warnings of conscience were sufficient to prevent its frequency, and because the voice of nature instinctively cries out against it.

That the act of suicide must be most offensive in the sight of God is evident, since it is that which most directly violates those laws by which his providence has formed, and still directs, the universe. If any one principle in man is instinctive and implanted in him by the hand of nature, it is that of self preservation. Different religions and different codes have marked out particular duties, and proscribed particular crimes; in this, every religion unites, every society concurs, and every individual acknowledges within his own bosom the sacred command. If, therefore, to disobey the ordinances of God must be sinful in his sight, if ever the ordinances of men are to be respected, what must be the guilt of that person who violates the first law of nature, who disregards the principle that holds human society together, that fits us for every duty, and prompts us in the performance of them!

But it is not merely against the ordinance of his Creator that the self-murderer offends,[17] he is guilty of a breach of duty to his neighbour. He plants a dagger not

[17] It is evident that the great dramatist considered that suicide was opposed to the divine will.

merely in his own breast, but in that of his dearest, his tenderest connexions. He wantonly sports with the pangs of sensibility, and covers with the blush of shame the cheek of innocence. With a degree of ingratitude which excites our abhorrence, he clouds with sorrow the future existence of those by whom he was most tenderly beloved, and affixes a mark of ignominy on his unfortunate descendants. He disobeys the first of social laws, that order by which God appropriated his labours to the welfare of society, and, because he fancies he can no longer exist with comfort to himself, disregards all the duties which he owes to others.

The alliance between suicide and the murder of others is a closer one than is generally supposed. How many instances are recorded in which suicide and homicide have been conjoined! He who will not scruple to take away his own life, will not require much reasoning to impel him to sacrifice another's. We refer to the cases of Mithridates, king of Pontus, and Nicocles, as illustrative of this position. Many modern instances are recorded of the same character.

It was maintained by Marcus Aurelius, that there was no more of evil in parting from life than in going out of a smoky chamber; and Rousseau asks, "Why should we be permitted to cut off a leg, if we may not equally take away life? has not the will of God given us both?" Madame de Staël very properly observes that the following passage in Scripture replies to this sophism—"If thy hand offend thee, cut it off; if thine eye offend thee, pluck it out and cast it from thee." Temptation is evidently referred to in the above passage, but it may consistently be used in refutation of Rousseau's illogical argument. Although a man may use any means placed in his power for the removal of physical evils, he is distinctly prohibited from destroying his existence.

The interrogatory argument, if it can be so denominated, which is so often used in justification of suicide—"Cannot a man do what he likes with his own?"—is based upon an absurd and gross fallacy. Man, during his residence on this earth, is but a trustee; his wealth, his talents, his time, and his very life, are but trust property. He can call nothing truly his own; he is held accountable for the most apparently trivial action he performs. Life is given to him for noble purposes; it is an emanation from the Deity himself; and no circumstances would justify us in asserting that our very existence is placed at our own disposal. How truly has the noble poet observed, when alluding to the tenure upon which we hold everything during this life—

> "Can despots compass aught that hails their sway,
> Or call one solid span of earth their own,
> Save that wherein at last they crumble bone by bone?"

This life is one of privation. We are born to misery; we are led to expect disap-

---

> "Against self-slaughter
> There is a prohibition so divine,
> That cravens my weak hand."

Again, he says—

> "Or that the Everlasting had not fixed
> His canon 'gainst self-slaughter!"

pointment at every step we take; blighted expectations, ruined hopes, pain, mental and bodily, constitute a part and parcel of our very existence. No man was more overwhelmed with any species of misfortune than Job; he was emphatically styled "*the man of grief;*" and when, prostrated to the earth by the most poignant misery, his wife exhorted him to quit life,—to "curse God, and die,"—he replied, "What, shall I receive good from the hand of God, and not evil?"

No suffering, however acute, could for one moment justify the commission of self-murder. "The concluding scene in the life of Jesus Christ," says Madame de Staël, with a fervid eloquence which does her immortal honour, "seems peculiarly intended to confute those who contend for the right of destroying life to escape misfortune. The dread of suffering seized him who had willingly devoted himself to death for the good of mankind. He prayed a long time to his Father in the Mount of Olives, and his countenance was shaded by the anguish of death. 'My Father,' he cried, 'if it be possible, let this cup pass from me.' Thrice with tears was this prayer repeated. All the sorrows of our nature had passed through his divine mind; like us, he feared the violence of men; like us, perhaps, regretted those whom he cherished and loved, his mother and his disciples; like us, he loved this earth, and the celestial pleasures resulting from active benevolence, for which he incessantly thanked his Father. But, not able to avert the destined chalice, he cried, 'Oh, my Father, let thy will be done,' and resigned himself into the hands of his enemies. What more can be sought for in the gospel respecting resignation to grief, and the duty of supporting it with fortitude and patience." Poets and orators have entered into a chivalrous rivalry to celebrate the character of the "bold man struggling with the storms of fate." That adversity refines and ennobles our nature there cannot be a doubt. The most beautiful features of the human mind are developed in suffering; the ordeal through which we pass, however repugnant and abhorrent it may be to our feelings, produces a moral regeneration in the character. We come out of the "fiery furnace," like gold and silver, deprived of much of our dross; and life, youthful and innocent life, again dawns upon us and gladdens our hearts.

Suicide is an injury to our neighbour and to society. As long as life lasts,—no matter what amount of misery a person may suffer,—he has it in his power to contribute to the happiness of others. By mitigating the distresses of others, his own will be subdued. Let a man writhing under the torture of the gout be brought into contact with a person suffering from the intense agony of tic douloureux, and he will have a practical illustration of the fact, that there are others in the world worse off than himself.

Suicide has been defended as an act of courage. Courage, forsooth! If ever there is an act of cowardice, it is that exhibited by the person who, to escape from the disappointments and vexations of the world, wantonly puts an end to his existence. The man of courage will defy the opinions and scorns of the world, when he knows himself to be in the right; will be above sinking under the petty misfortunes that assail him; will make circumstances bow to him; will court difficulties and dangers, in order to shew that he is able to master them.

It was a noble sentiment which Q. Curtius put into the mouth of Darius, after every ray of hope had abandoned him:—"I will wait," cried the king, addressing his attendants, "the issue of my fate. You wonder, perhaps, that I do not terminate my own life; but I choose rather to die by another's crime than by my own." The sentiments of Cleomenes, king of Sparta, expressed when his fortunes appeared most desperate, are equally noble and magnanimous. Being much urged by a friend to dispatch himself, he replied—"By seeking this easy and ready kind of death, you think to appear brave and courageous; but better men than you and I have been oppressed by fortune, and borne down by multitudes. He that sinks under toil, or yields to affliction, or is overcome by the opinions and reproaches of men, gives way, in fact, to his own effeminacy and cowardice. A voluntary death is never to be chosen as a relief from action, but as exemplary in itself, it being base to live or die only for ourselves. The death to which you now invite us is only proposed as a release from present misery, but conveys with it no signs of bravery or prospects of advantage."

Euripides put the following words in the mouth of Hercules: "I have considered, and, though oppressed with misfortunes, I have determined thus: Let no one depart out of life through fear of what may happen to him; for he who is not able to resist evils will fly, like a coward, from the darts of the enemy."

When Buonaparte was told of the prevalent opinion, that he ought not to have survived his political downfall, he calmly replied—"No, no; I have not enough of the Roman in me to destroy myself." After reasoning, with considerable ingenuity, on the subject of suicide, he concluded by giving expression to this decided opinion:—"Suicide is a crime the most revolting to my feelings; nor does any reason present itself to my understanding by which it can be justified. It certainly originates in that species of fear which we denominate cowardice, (*poltronnerie*.) For what claim can that man have to courage who trembles at the frowns of fortune? True heroism consists in becoming superior to the ills of life, in whatever shape they may challenge him to the combat." He might have added—"Tu ne cede malis, sed contrà audentior ito." On another occasion, when talking on the subject of suicide, Buonaparte observed, "If Marius had slain himself in the marshes of Minturnæ, he never would have stood the seventh time for consul." After having been some time at St. Helena, he one day spoke further on the subject of suicide. He observed:—"With respect to the English language, I have been very diligent. I now read your newspapers with ease; and must own that they afford me no inconsiderable amusement. They are occasionally inconsistent, and sometimes abusive. In one paper I am called a *Lear*; in another, a *tyrant*; in a third, a *monster*; and in one of them—which I really did not expect—I am described as a *coward*. But it turned out, after all, that the writer did not accuse me of avoiding danger in the field of battle, or flying from an enemy, or fearing to look at the menaces of fate and fortune. It did not charge me with wanting presence of mind in the hurry of battle, and in the suspense of conflicting armies; no such thing. I wanted courage, it seems, because I did not coolly take a dose of poison, or throw myself into the sea, or blow out my brains. The editor most certainly misunderstands me; I have, at least, too much courage for that."[18]

We think it has decidedly been established in the preceding observations that

___

[18] Warder's "Letters from the Northumberland."

suicide is a crime clearly prohibited in the Bible; that it is, in every sense of the term, self-murder; and that our duty to our Creator, to ourselves, and to society, loudly calls upon us to denounce it, and hold it up to the scorn and reprobation of mankind. How terrifically has Dryden, in his Fables, portrayed the condition of the unfortunate suicide in another world:—

> "The slayer of himself, too, saw I there:
> The gore, congealed, was clotted in his hair.
> With eyes half closed, and mouth wide ope, he lay,
> And grim as when he breathed his sullen soul away."

CHAPTER IV.

ON THE INFLUENCE OF CERTAIN MENTAL STATES IN INDUCING THE DISPOSITION TO SUICIDE.

Moral causes of disease—Neglect of psychological medicine—Mental philosophy a branch of medical study—Moral causes of suicide—Tables of Falret, &c.—Influence of remorse—Simon Brown, Charles IX. of France—Massacre of St. Bartholomew—Terrible death of Cardinal Beaufort, from remorse—The Chevalier de S——. Influence of disappointed love—Suicide from love—Two singular cases—Effects of jealousy—Othello—Suicide from this passion—The French opera dancer—Suicide from wounded vanity—False pride—The remarkable case of Villeneuve, as related by Buonaparte—Buonaparte's attempt at suicide—Ambition—Despair, cases of suicide from—The Abbé de Rancé—Suicide from blind impulse—Cases—Mathews, the comedian—Opinion of Esquirol on the subject—Ennui, birth of—Common cause of suicide in France—Effect of speculating in stocks—Defective education—Diffusion of knowledge—"Socialism" a cause of self-destruction—Suicide common in Germany—Werter—Goëthe's attempt at suicide—Influence of his writings on Hackman—Suicide from reading Tom Paine's "Age of Reason"—Suicide to avoid punishment—Most remarkable illustrations—Political excitement—Nervous irritation—Love of notoriety—Hereditary disposition—Is death painful? fully considered, with cases—Influence of irreligion.

In our voyage through life, the passions are said to be the gales that swell the canvass of the mental bark; they obstruct or accelerate its course, and render the passage favourable or full of danger, in proportion as they blow steadily from a proper point, or are adverse or tempestuous. Like the wind itself, the passions are engines of mighty power and of high importance. Without them we cannot proceed, and with them we may be shipwrecked and lost. Curbed in and regulated, they constitute the source of our most elevated happiness; but when not subdued, they drive the vessel on the rocks and quicksands of life, and ruin us.

> "How few beneath auspicious planets born
> With swelling sails make good the promis'd port,

> With all their wishes freighted."

Young.

"In this country," Dr. J. Johnson justly observes, "where man's relations with the world around him are multiplied beyond all example in any other country, in consequence of the intensity of interest attached to politics, religion, amusement, literature, and the arts; where the temporal concerns of an immense proportion of the population are in a perpetual state of vacillation; where spiritual affairs excite in the minds of many great anxiety; and where speculative risks are daily involving in difficulties all classes of society,—the operation of physical causes in the production of disease dwindles into complete insignificance when compared with that of anxiety and perturbation of mind."

"Mens conscia recti in corpore sano," is Horace's well-known description of the happy man. Lucretius appears to have formed a correct estimate of the most important bodily and mental conditions on which our happiness depends:—

> "O wretched mortals! race perverse and blind!
> Through what dread, dark, what perilous pursuits
> Pass ye this round of being! Know ye not,
> Of all ye toil for, Nature nothing asks,
> But for the *body* freedom from disease,
> And sweet unanxious quiet for the mind?"

Like human beings, the sciences are closely connected with, and are mutually dependent upon, one another. The link in the chain may not be apparent, but it has a real and palpable existence. Medical and moral science are more nearly allied than we should, *à priori*, conclude. We speak of the science of medicine, not the practice of it; for, like judgment and wit, or, as the author of the School for Scandal ironically observes, like *man and wife*, how seldom are they seen in happy union. Garth feelingly alludes to this unnatural divorce:—

> "The healing art now, sick'ning, hangs its head,
> And, once a *science*, has become a *trade*."

Psychological medicine has been sadly neglected. We recoil from the study of mental philosophy as if we were encroaching on holy ground. So great is the prejudice against this branch of science, that it has been observed, that to recommend a man to study metaphysics was a delicate mode of suggesting the propriety of confining him in a lunatic asylum!

In order to become a useful physician, it is necessary to become a good metaphysician; so says a competent authority. It was not, however, Dr. Cullen's intention to recommend that species of philosophy which confounds the mind without enlightening it, and which, like an *ignis fatuus*, dazzles only to lead us from the truth. To the medical man we can conceive no preliminary study more productive of advantage than that which tends to call into exercise the latent principle of thought, and to accustom the mind to close, rigid, and accurate observation. The science of mind, when properly investigated, teaches us the laws of our mental frame, and shews us the origin of our various modes and habits of thought and feeling—how they operate upon one another, and how they are cultivated and repressed; it disciplines us in the art of induction, and guards us against the many sources of fallacy in the practice of making inferences; it gives precision and accuracy to our investigations, by instructing us in the nicer discriminations of truth and falsehood.

The value of mental philosophy as a branch of education will be properly appreciated when we consider that this ennobling principle was given to us for the purpose of directing and controlling our powers and animal propensities, and bringing them into that subjection whereby they become beneficial to the individual and to the world at large, enabling him to exchange with others those results which the power of his own and the gigantic efforts of other minds have developed; maintaining and perpetuating the most dignified and exalted state of happiness, the attribute of social life; unfolding not only treasures which the concentrated powers of individuals are enabled to discover, but developing those more quiet and unobtrusive characteristics of virtuous life, those social affections, which are alone calculated to make our present state of being happy.

Independently of the utility of the study, what a world of delight is open to the mind of that man who has devoted some portion of his time to the investigation of his mental organization! In him we may truly behold—

> "Nature, gentle, kind,
> By culture tamed, by liberty refreshed,
> And all the radiant fruits of truth matured."

When we take into consideration the tremendous influence which the different mental emotions have over the bodily functions, when we perceive that violent excitement of mind will not only give rise to serious functional disorder, but actual organic disease, leading to the commission of suicide, how necessary does it appear that he to whose care is entrusted the lives of his fellow-creatures, should have made this department of philosophy a matter of serious consideration! It is no logical argument against the study of mental science, to urge that we are in total ignorance of the nature or constitution of the human understanding. We know nothing of the nature of objects which are cognizable to sense, and which can be submitted to actual experiment, and yet we are not deterred from the investigation of their properties and mutual influences. The passions are to be considered, in a medical point of view, as a part of our constitution. They stimulate or depress the mind, as food and drink do the body. Employed occasionally, and in moderation, both may be of use to us, and are given to us by nature for this purpose; but when urged to excess, the system is thrown off its balance, and disease is the result.

To the medical philosopher, nothing can be more deeply interesting than to trace the reciprocity of action existing between different mental conditions, and affections of particular organs. Thus the passion of fear, when excited, has a sensible influence on the action of the heart; and when the disease of this organ takes place independently of any mental agitation, the passion of fear is powerfully roused. Anger affects the liver and confines the bowels, and frequently gives rise to an attack of jaundice; and in hepatic and intestinal disease, how irritable the temper is!

Hope, or the anticipation of pleasure, affects the respiration; and how often do we see patients, in the last stage of pulmonary disease, entertaining sanguine expectations of recovery to the very last!

As the passions exercise so despotic a tyranny over the physical economy, it is natural to expect that the crime of suicide should often be traced to the influence of mental causes. In many cases, it is difficult to discover whether the brain, the seat of the passions, be primarily or secondarily affected. Often the cause of irritation is situated at some distance from the cerebral organ; but when the fountain-head of the nervous system becomes deranged, it will react on the bodily functions, and produce serious disease long after the original cause of excitement is removed. It is not our intention to attempt to explain the *modus operandi* of mental causes in the production of the suicidal disposition. That such effects result from an undue excitement of the mind cannot for one moment be questioned. Independently of mental perturbation giving rise to maniacal suicide, there are certain conditions of mind, dependent upon acquired or hereditary disposition, or arising from a defective expansion of the intellectual faculties, which originate the desire for self-destruction. These states will all be alluded to in the course of the present inquiry.

Some idea of the influence of certain mental states on the body will be obtained by an examination of the various tables which have been published, in this and other countries, respecting the causes of suicide, as far as they could be ascertained.

The following suicides were committed in London, between the years 1770 and 1830:[19] —

Indication of Causes.	*Men.*	*Women.*
Poverty	905	511
Domestic grief	728	524
Reverse of fortune	322	283
Drunkenness and misconduct	287	208
Gambling	155	141
Dishonour and calumny	125	95
Disappointed ambition	122	410
Grief from love	97	157
Envy and jealousy	94	53
Wounded self-love	53	53
Remorse	49	37
Fanaticism	16	1
Misanthropy	3	3
Causes unknown	1381	377
Total	4337[20]	2853

---

[19] London Medical and Surgical Journal, vol. v. p. 51.

[20] In a table given by Professor Caspar, of Berlin, one hundred and three cases of suicide are attributed to mental affections; thirty of these may be classed under this head, and thirty-two under that of fear and despondency combined.

According to a table formed by Falret of the suicides which took place between 1794 and 1823, the following results appear:—Of 6782 cases, 254 were from disappointed love, and of this number 157 were women; 92 were from jealousy; 125 from being calumniated; 49 from a desire, without the means, of vindicating their characters; 122 from disappointed ambition; 322 from reverses of fortune; 16 from wounded vanity; 155 from gambling; 288 from crime and remorse; 723 from domestic distress; 905 from poverty; 16 from fanaticism.

In preparing the present work, we have endeavoured to obtain access to documents which would throw some light on the probable origin of the many cases of self-destruction which have taken place within the last four or five years. In many cases we could obtain no insight into the motives of the individuals; but in nine-tenths of those whose histories we succeeded in making ourselves somewhat conversant with, we found that mental causes played a very conspicuous part in the drama. Our experience on this point accords with that of many distinguished French physicians who have devoted their time and talents to the consideration of the subject.

In considering the influence of mental causes, we shall in the first instance point out the effects of certain passions and dispositions of the individual on the body; then investigate the operation of education, irreligion, and certain unhealthy conditions of the mind which predispose the individual to derangement and suicide.

There is no passion of the mind which so readily drives a person to suicide as remorse. In these cases, there is generally a shipwreck of all hope. To live is horror; the infuriated sufferer feels himself an outcast from God and man; and though his judgment may still be correct upon other subjects, it is completely overpowered upon that of his actual distress, and all he thinks of and aims at is to withdraw with as much speed as possible from the present state of torture, totally regardless of the future.

> "I would not if I could be blest,
> I want no other paradise but rest."

The most painfully interesting and melancholy cases of insanity are those in which remorse has taken possession of the mind. Simon Brown, the dissenting clergyman, fancied that he had been deprived by the Almighty of his immortal soul, in consequence of having accidentally taken away the life of a highwayman, although it was done in the act of resistance to his threatened violence, and in protection of his own person. Whilst kneeling upon the wretch whom he had succeeded in throwing upon the ground, he suddenly discovered that his prostrate enemy was deprived of life. This unexpected circumstance produced so violent an impression upon his nervous system, that he was overpowered by the idea of an involuntary homicide, and for this imaginary crime fancied himself ever afterwards condemned to one of the most dreadful punishments that could be inflicted upon a human being.

A young lady was one morning requested by her mother to stay at home; notwithstanding which, she was tempted to go out. Upon her return to her domestic roof, she found that the parent whom she had so recently disobliged had expired in her absence. The awful spectacle of a mother's corpse, connected with the filial disobedience which had almost immediately preceded, shook her reason from its seat, and she has ever since continued in a state of mental derangement.

It is said that the solitary hours of Charles the Ninth of France were rendered horrible by the repetition of the shrieks and cries which had assailed his ears during the massacre of St. Bartholomew.[21]

The death of Cardinal Beaufort is represented as truly terrible. The consciousness of having murdered the Duke of Gloucester is said to have rendered Beaufort's death one of the most terrific scenes ever witnessed. Despair, in its worst form, appeared to take possession of his mind at the last moment. His concluding words, as recorded by Harpsfield,[22] were—"And must I then die? Will not all my riches save me? I could purchase the kingdom, if that would save my life. What! is there no bribing of death? When my nephew, the Duke of Bedford, died, I thought my happiness and my authority greatly increased; but the Duke of Gloucester's death raised me in fancy to a level with kings, and I thought of nothing but accumulating still greater wealth, to purchase at last the triple crown. Alas! how are my hopes disappointed! Wherefore, O my friends, let me earnestly beseech you to pray for me, and recommend my departing soul to God!" A few minutes before his death, his mind appeared to be undergoing the tortures of the damned. He held up his two hands, and cried—"Away! away!—why thus do ye look at me?" It was evident he saw some horrible spectre by his bed-side. This last scene in the Cardinal's life has been most ably delineated by the immortal Shakspeare:—

SCENE—The Cardinal's Bed-chamber.

Enter KING HENRY, SALISBURY, and WARWICK.

King Hen.	How fares my Lord? Speak, Beaufort, to thy sovereign.
Cardinal.	If thou be'st Death, I'll give thee England's treasure, Enough to purchase such another island, So thou wilt let me live, and feel no pain.
King Hen.	Ah! what a sign it is of evil life When death's approach is seen so terrible.
Warwick.	Beaufort, it is thy sovereign speaks to thee.

---

[21] The massacre of St. Bartholomew lasted seven days, during which more than 5000 persons were slain in Paris, and from 40 to 50,000 in the country. During the execution, the king betrayed neither pity nor remorse, but fired with his long gun at the poor fugitives across the river; and on viewing the body of Coligni on a gibbet, he exulted with a fiendish malignity. In early life, this monster had been noted for his cruelty: nothing gave him greater pleasure than cutting off the heads of asses or pigs with a single blow from his *couteau de chasse.* After the massacre, he is said to have contracted a singularly wild expression of feature, and to have slept little and waked in agonies. He attributed his thirst for human blood to the circumstance of his mother having at an early period of his life familiarized his mind with the brutal sport of hunting bullocks, and with all kinds of cruelty. It is recorded that, when dying, he actually sweated blood.

[22] Hist. Eccles. edit. Duaci, 1622, pp. 643-4.

Cardinal.	Bring me unto my trial when you will.
	Died he[23] not in his bed? Where should he die?
	Can I make men live whe'er they will or no?
	O, torture me no more, I will confess—
	Alive again? then shew me where he is:
	I'll give a thousand pound to look upon him—
	He hath no eyes, the dust hath blinded them.—
	Comb down his hair; look! look! it stands upright,
	Like lime-twigs set to catch my winged soul.—
	Give me some drink, and bid the apothecary
	Bring the strong poison that I bought of him.
King Hen.	O thou eternal Mover of the Heav'ns,
	Look with a gentle eye upon this wretch.
	O, beat away the busy meddling fiend,
	That lays strong siege unto this wretch's soul,
	And from his bosom purge this black despair.
Warwick.	See how the pangs of death do make him grin!
Salisbury.	Disturb him not; let him pass peaceably.
King Hen.	Peace to his soul, if God's good pleasure be!
	Lord Cardinal, if thou think'st on heaven's bliss,
	Lift up thy hand, make signal of thy hope.—
	He dies, and makes no sign—O God, forgive him!
Warwick.	So bad a death argues a monstrous life.
King Hen.	Forbear to judge, for we are sinners all.—
	Close up his eyes, and draw the curtain close,
	And let us all to meditation.[24]

M. Guillon relates the following remarkable case:—"The Chevalier de S——had been engaged in seventeen 'affairs of honour,' in each of which his adversary fell. But the images of his murdered rivals began to haunt him night and day; and at length he fancied he heard nothing but the wailings and upbraidings of seventeen families—one demanding a father, another a son, another a brother, another a husband, &c. Harassed by these imaginary followers, he incarcerated himself in the monastery of La Trappe; but the French revolution threw open this asylum, and turned the chevalier once more into the world. He was now no longer able to bear the remorse of his own conscience, or, as he imagined, the sight of seventeen murdered men, and therefore put himself to death. It is evident that insanity was the consequence of the remorse, and the cause of the suicide.

"No disease of the imagination is so difficult to cure as that which is complicated with the idea of guilt: fancy and conscience then act interchangeably upon us, and so often shift their places, that the illusions of one are not distinguished from the dictates of the other. If fancy presents images not moral or religious, the

---

[23] Meaning the Duke of Gloucester.
[24] King Henry, Act 3.

mind drives them away when they give pain; but when melancholy notions take the form of duty, they lay hold on the faculties without opposition, because we are afraid to exclude or banish them."[25]

How accurately has the poet depicted the tortures, the sleeplessness, of a guilty conscience:—

> "Though thy slumber may be deep,
> Yet thy spirit shall not sleep;
> There are shades which will not vanish,
> There are thoughts thou canst not banish;
> By a power to thee unknown,
> Thou canst never be alone;
> Thou art wrapt as with a shroud,
> Thou art gathered in a cloud;
> And for ever shalt thou dwell
> In the spirit of this spell."

A woman with her husband had been employed in a French hospital as servants for a considerable time. Having left their situations, the wife, *thirty years* afterwards, declared she heard a voice within, commanding her to repair instantly to the chief commissioner of police, and confess the thefts she had committed during the time she was at the hospital. The fact was, that she had been guilty of appropriating occasionally to her own use a portion of the food supplied for the patients attached to the Institution. The commissioner listened to the woman's story, and her demand that she should be punished, but refused to take any cognizance of the offence. She returned home, and for some time was extremely dejected. She became so miserable that existence was no longer desirable; and as the legal tribunals refused to punish her, she determined on suicide, which she committed at the age of fifty-one.

It is admitted, by almost universal consent, that there is no affection of the mind that exerts so tremendous an influence over the human race as that of love.

> "To love, and feel ourselves beloved,"

is said to constitute the height of human happiness. This sacred sentiment, which some have debased by the term passion, when unrequited and irregulated, produces the most baneful influence upon the system.

"A youthful passion, which is conceived and cherished without any certain object, may be compared to a shell thrown from a mortar by night: it rises calmly in a brilliant track, and seems to mix, and even to dwell for a moment with the stars of heaven; but at length it falls—it bursts—consuming and destroying all around, even as itself expires."[26]

From the constitution of woman, from the peculiar position which she of necessity holds in society, we should, *à priori*, have concluded that in her we should see manifested this sentiment in all its purity and strength. Such is the fact. A

---

[25] Dr. Johnson's Rasselas.
[26] Goëthe, in allusion to one of his own early attachments.

woman's life is said to be but the history of her affections. It is the soul within her soul; the pulse within her heart; the life blood along her veins, "blending with every atom of her frame." Separated from the bustle of active life—isolated like a sweet and rare exotic flower from the world, it is natural to expect that the mind should dwell with earnestness upon that which is to constitute almost its very being, and apart from which it has no existence.

> "Alas! the love of woman, it is known
> To be a lovely and a fearful thing;
> For all of theirs upon that die is thrown;
> And if 'tis lost, life hath no more to bring
> To them, but mockeries of the past alone."
>
> BYRON.

The term "broken heart" is not a mere poetical image. Cases are recorded in which that organ has been ruptured in consequence of disappointed hope. Let those who are sceptical as to the fact that physical disease so often results from blighted affection, visit the wards of our public and private asylums. In those dreary regions of misery they will have an opportunity of witnessing the wreck of many a form that was once beauteous and happy. Ask their history, and you will be told of holy and sincere affection nipped in the bud—of wild and passionate love strangled at its birth—of the death of all human hopes, of a severance from those about whom every fibre of the soul had entwined itself. Silent and sullen grief, black despair,

> "And laughter loud, amidst severest woe,"

are the painful images that meet the eye at every step we take through these "hells upon earth."[27]

In this country, the great majority of the cases of insanity among women, in our establishments devoted to the reception of the insane, can clearly be traced to unrequited and disappointed affection. This is not to be wondered at, if we consider the present artificial state of society. We make "merchandize of love;" both men and women are estimated, not by their mental endowments, not by their moral worth, not by their capacity of making the domestic fire-side happy, but by the length of their respective purses. Instead of seeking for a heart, we look for a dowry. Money is preferred to intellect; pure and unadulterated affection dwindles into nothingness when placed in the same scale with titles and worldly honours,

> "And Mammon wins his way
> Where seraphs might despair."

How little do those who ought to be influenced by more elevated motives calculate the seeds of wretchedness and misery which they are sowing for those who, by nature, have a right to demand that they should be actuated by other principles!

---

[27] Love, it is said, often turns the brains of the Italians, even the men. M. Esquirol says, "Frenchmen seldom go mad from love. A Frenchman often kills himself in a sally of passion and feeling, but is seldom in love long enough to go mad about it."

"Shall I be won
Because I'm valued as a *money-bag*?
For that I bring to him who winneth me,"[28]

says Catherine, in the spirit of honest indignation. It should be remembered that "wedlock joins nothing, if it joins not hearts."

How many melancholy cases of suicide can clearly be traced to this cause! Death is considered preferable to a long life of unmitigated sorrow. When the heart is seared, when there exists no "green spot in memory's dreary waste,"—when all hope is banished from the mind, and wretched loneliness and desolation take up their residence in the heart, need it excite surprise that the quiet and rest of the grave is eagerly longed for! If a mind thus worked upon be not influenced by religious principles, self-destruction is the idea constantly present to the imagination.

Of all the sufferings, however, to which we are exposed during our sojourn below, nothing is so truly overwhelming and irreparable as the death of one with whom all our early associations are inseparably linked—one endeared to us by the most pleasing recollections. Death leaves a blank in our existence; a cold shuddering shoots through the frame, a mist flits before our eyes, darkening the face of nature, when the heart that mingled all its feelings with ours lies, cold and insensible, in the silent grave.

As long as life lasts, there is hope; but death snatches every ray of consolation from the mind. The only prop that supported us is removed, and the mansion crumbles to the dust; the mind becomes utterly and hopelessly wrecked. To say that this is but the effect on understandings constitutionally weak, is to say what facts will not establish. The most elevated and best cultivated minds are often the most sensitively alive to such impressions.

The following case made considerable noise at Lyons, in 1770. A young gentleman of rank, of handsome exterior, possessing considerable mental endowments, and most respectably connected, fell in love with a young lady, who, like himself, possessed a handsome person, in union with accomplishments of a high order. They met; the passion was reciprocal, and the gentleman accordingly made an application to her parents to be allowed to consummate their bliss by marriage. The parents, as parents sometimes do under these circumstances, refused compliance. The gentleman took it greatly to heart; it preyed much upon his mind, and in the midst of his grief he burst a blood-vessel. His case was given over by the medical men. The young lady, on being made acquainted with his condition, paid him a clandestine visit, and they then agreed to destroy themselves. Accordingly the lady brought with her, on her next visit, two pistols and two daggers, in order that, if the pistols missed, the daggers might the next moment pierce their hearts. They embraced each other for the last time. Rose-coloured ribbons were tied to the triggers of the pistols; the lover holding the ribbon of his mistress' pistol, while she held the ribbon of his; both fired at a given signal, and both fell at the same instant dead on the floor!

---

[28] "Love."

The case now about to be recorded presents some peculiarly interesting features. An English lady, moving in the first circles of society, went, in company with her friends, to the opera at Paris. In the next box sat a gentleman, who appeared, from the notice he took of the lady, to be enamoured of her. The lady expressed herself annoyed at the observation which she had attracted, and moved to another part of the box. The gentleman followed the carriage home, and insisted upon addressing the lady, declaring that he had had the pleasure of meeting her elsewhere, and that one minute's conversation would convince her of the fact, and do away with the unfavourable impression which his apparent rudeness might have made upon her mind. As his request did not appear at the moment unreasonable, she consented to see him for a minute by herself. In that short space of time he made a fervent declaration of his affection; acknowledged that desperation had compelled him to have recourse to a *ruse* to obtain an interview, and that, unless she looked favourably on his pretensions, he would kill her and then himself. The lady expressed her indignation at the deceit he had practised, and said, with considerable firmness, that he must quit the house. He did so, retired to his home, and with a lancet opened a vein in his arm. He collected a portion of blood in a cup, and with it wrote a note to the lady, telling her that his blood was flowing fast from his body, and it should continue to flow until she consented to listen to his proposals. The lady, on the receipt of the note, sent her servant to see the gentleman, and found him, as he represented, actually bleeding to death. On the entreaty of the lady, the arm was bound up and his life saved. On writing to the lady, under the impression that she would now accept his addresses, he was amazed on receiving a cool refusal, and a request that he would not trouble her with any more letters. Again driven to desperation, he resolved effectually to kill himself. He accordingly loaded a pistol and directed his steps towards the residence of his fair amorosa, when, knocking at the door, he gained admission, and immediately blew out his brains. The intelligence was communicated to the lady, she became dreadfully excited, and a severe attack of nervous fever followed. When the acute symptoms subsided, her mind was completely deranged. Her insanity took a peculiar turn. She fancied she heard a voice commanding her to commit suicide, and yet she appeared to be possessed of sufficient reason to know that she was desirous of doing what she ought to be restrained from accomplishing. Every now and then she would exclaim, "Take away the pistol! I won't hang myself! I won't take poison!" Under the impression that she would kill herself, she was carefully watched; but notwithstanding the vigilance which was exercised she had sufficient cunning to conceal a knife, with which, during the temporary absence of the attendant, she stabbed herself in the abdomen, and died in a few hours. It appears that the idea that she had caused the death of another, and that she had it in her power to save his life by complying with his wishes, produced the derangement of mind under which she was labouring at the time of her death; and yet she did not manifest, and it was evident to everybody that she had not, the slightest affection for the gentleman who professed so much to admire her. Possessing naturally a sensitive mind, it was easily excited. The peculiar circumstances connected with her mental derangement were sufficient to account for the delusions under which she laboured. Altogether the case is full of interest.

Few passions tend more to distract and unsettle the mind than that of jealousy. Insanity and suicide often owe their origin to this feeling. One of the most terrific pictures of the dire effects of this "green-eyed monster" on the mind is delineated in the character of Othello. In the Moor of Venice we witness a fearful struggle between fond and passionate love and this corroding mental emotion. Worked upon by the villainous artifices of Iago, Othello is led to doubt the constancy of Desdemona's affection; the very doubt urges him almost to the brink of madness; but when he feels assured of her guilt, and sees the gulf into which he has been hurled, and the utter hopelessness of his condition, he abandons himself to despair. Nothing which the master spirit of Shakspeare ever penned can equal the exquisitely touching and melting pathos of the speech of the Moor when he becomes perfectly conscious of the wreck of one around whom every tendril of his heart had indissolubly interwoven itself. To be forcibly severed from one dearer to us than our own existence is a misfortune that requires much philosophy to bear up against; to be torn from a beloved object by death, to feel that the earth encloses in its cold embrace the idol of our affections, freezes the heart; but to be separated from one who has forfeited all claim to our affection and friendship, and who still lives, but lives in dishonour, must be a refinement of human misery. Need we then wonder that, when influenced by such feelings, Othello should thus give expression to the overflowings of his soul:—

> "Oh now, for ever,
> Farewell the tranquil mind! farewell content!
> Farewell the plumed troop, and the big wars,
> That make ambition virtue! Oh, farewell!
> Farewell the neighing steed, and the shrill trump,
> The spirit-stirring drum, th' ear-piercing fife,
> The royal banner, and all quality,
> Pride, pomp, and circumstance of glorious war!
> And, oh, you mortal engines, whose rude throats
> Th' immortal Jove's dread clamours counterfeit,
> Farewell! Othello's occupation's gone!"

It is under the infliction of such a concentration of misery that many a mind is shattered, and that death is courted as the only relief within its grasp. Othello, having discovered when it was too late that he had wrongly suspected Desdemona, and had sacrificed the life of the sweetest creature on earth, a combination of passions drives him to distraction, and under their influence he plunges the dagger into his heart. Jealousy was not, as some have supposed, the exclusive cause of Othello's suicide.

The following singular case attracted considerable notice fifteen years ago. A woman was subjected to much maltreatment by her husband. She was jealous of his attentions to one of the servants, and she had frequently declared, that if he persisted in insulting her under her own roof she would either cause his or her own death. On one occasion she was more than usually violent, and expressed her determination to ruin him. Fearful that she would carry her threat into execution, he had her placed in a room where there was no furniture, and nothing that she could use for the purpose of self-destruction. Her rage was greatly increased by this barbarous treatment, and her screams were sufficiently loud to alarm the whole neighbourhood. As her husband refused to release her from confinement, she determined no longer to submit to his brutal control, and resolved to commit suicide. Having no instrument that she could use, she felt some difficulty in effecting her purpose. She held her breath for some time, but that did not succeed. She then tried to strangle herself with her hands, but that mode was equally unsuccessful. Her determination was so resolutely fixed, that in desperation she tore her hair out by the roots. Still death did not come to her relief. In vain she searched in every corner of the room for something with which she might effectually take away her life. Just as she was beginning to give up the idea as hopeless, her eye caught a sight of the glass in the window; she instantly broke a pane, and with a piece of it endeavoured to cut her throat; and yet she could not succeed in effecting her horrid purpose. At last, as a dernier resort, she resolved to swallow a piece of the broken glass, hoping by this means to choke herself. She did so, and the glass stuck in her throat, and produced the most excruciating agony. Her groans became audible; the husband became alarmed, and opened the door, when he found his wife apparently in the last struggles of death. Medical relief was immediately obtained, and although everything that surgical ingenuity could suggest was had recourse to, she died, a melancholy spectacle of the effects of unsubdued passion.

The two following cases shew how trifling a cause often incites to self-destruction:—

Madame N——, a once famous dancer at the French opera-house, was taken to task by her husband for not acquitting herself so well in the ballet as she usually did. She exhibited indications of passion at the, as she thought, unmerited reproof. When she arrived home, she resolved to die, but was much puzzled to effect her purpose. The next morning, she purchased a potent poison, but when she returned to her home she found that her husband looked suspiciously at her, and appeared to watch her movements. She then made up her mind to take the fatal draught in the evening, as she was going in the carriage to the opera. She accordingly did so; the poison did not have an immediate effect. The ballet commenced, and Madame N—— was led on the stage; and it was not until she had commenced dancing that she began to feel the draught producing the desired effect. She complained of illness, and was removed to her dressing-room, where she expired in the arms of her husband, confessing that she had, in a fit of chagrin at his rebuke, swallowed poison!

A young gentleman, of considerable promise, of high natural and acquired attainments, had been solicited to make a speech at a public meeting, which was to take place in the town in which he resided. As he had never attempted to address extemporaneously a public body, he expressed himself extremely nervous as to the result, and asked permission to withdraw his name from the published list of speakers. This wish was not, however, complied with, as it was thought that when the critical moment arrived he would not be found wanting even in the art of public speaking. He had prepared himself with considerable care for the attempt. His name was announced from the chair; when he rose for the purpose of delivering his sentiments. The exordium was spoken without any hesitation; and his friends felt assured that he would acquit himself with great credit. He had not, however, advanced much beyond his prefatory observations, when he hesitated, and found himself incapable of proceeding. He then sat down, evidently excessively mortified. In this state he retired to a room where the members of the committee had previously met, and cut his throat with his penknife. He wounded the carotid artery, and died in a few minutes.

A case of suicide from mortified pride, somewhat similar to the last, occurred some years ago in London. A gentleman, whose imagination was much more active than his judgment, conceived that he was possessed of histrionic powers equal to those which were exhibited by the immortal Garrick. A manager of a London theatre, to whom he was introduced, allowed him to make his début at his theatre. As is often the case, the public formed a different estimate of his abilities to that which the vanity of the young aspirant had induced him to form; and the consequence was, that he was well hissed and hooted for his presumption in attempting a character for which his talents so little adapted him. Being naturally sensitive, his failure preyed on his mind; and under the influence of the mortification, he hung himself, leaving in his room the following laconic epistle, addressed to his mother:—

"MY DEAR MOTHER,—All my hopes have been ruined. I fancied myself a man of genius; the reality has proved me to be a fool. I die, because life is no longer to be supported. Look charitably on this last action of my life. Adieu!"

A common cause of suicide is the feeling of false pride. The only reason assigned for the desperate act of Elizabeth Moyes, who threw herself from the Monument, was, that, owing to the reduced circumstances of her father, (a baker,) it was determined that she should procure a situation at a confectioner's, and support herself. This she allowed to prey upon her mind, although she expressed a concurrence in the propriety of the course suggested. How true it is—

"Abstract what others feel, what others think,
All pleasures sicken, and all glories sink."

POPE.

Owing to the fictitious notions abroad in society, the ridiculously false views which are taken of worldly honours, the ideas which a sickly sentimentality infuses into the mind, this feeling is engendered, to an alarming extent, through the different ranks of society. This constitutes one great element which is undermining and disorganizing our social condition. A fictitious value is affixed to wealth and position in the world; it is estimated for itself alone, all other considerations being placed out of view.

"None think the great unhappy but the great."

Vatel committed suicide because he was not able to prepare as sumptuous an entertainment as he wished for his guests.

We cannot conceive how this evil is to be obviated, unless it be possible to revolutionize the ideas which are generally attached to fame and worldly grandeur. It is difficult to persuade such persons that the end of fame is merely

> "To have, when the original is dust,
> A name, a wretched picture, and worse bust."

There is a nameless, undefinable something, that the world is taught to sigh after—is always in search of; a moral *ignis fatuus*, which is dazzling to lead it from the road which points to true and unsophisticated happiness.

Persons naturally proud are less able than others to bear up against the distresses of life; they are more severely galled by the yoke of adversity; and hence this passion often produces mental derangement. Such characters exhibit a morbid desire for praise; it acts like moral nourishment to their souls; it is a stimulus that is almost necessary to their very being, forgetting that

> "Praise too dearly loved, or warmly sought,
> Enfeebles all eternal weight of thought;
> 'Till the fond soul, within itself unblest,
> *Leans for all pleasure on another's breast.*"

Dr. Reid justly observes, that "he who enters most deeply into the misfortunes of others, will be best able to bear his own. A practical benevolence, by habitually urging us to disinterested exertion, tends to alienate the attention from any single train of ideas, which, if favoured by indolence and self contemplation, might be in danger of monopolizing the mind, and occasions us to lose a sense of our personal concerns in an enlarged and liberal sympathy with the general good."

Villeneuve, the celebrated French admiral, when he was taken prisoner and brought to England, was so much grieved at his defeat that he studied anatomy in order to destroy himself. For this purpose he bought some anatomical plates of the heart, and compared them with his own body, in order to ascertain the exact situation of that organ. On his arrival in France, Buonaparte ordered that he should remain at Rennes, and not proceed to Paris. Villeneuve, afraid of being tried by a court-martial for disobedience of orders, and consequently losing his fleet, (for Napoleon had ordered him not to sail or to engage the English,) determined to destroy himself; and accordingly took his plates and compared them with the position of his heart. Exactly in the centre he made a mark with a large pin; then fixed it, as near as he could judge, in the same spot in his own breast, and shoved it on to its head; it penetrated his heart, and he expired. When the room was opened, he was found dead, the pin through his breast, and a mark in the plate corresponding with the wound.[29]

It has been said that after the death of Josephine, and when Buonaparte was overwhelmed with misfortunes, he attempted suicide. Those who consider Napoleon immaculate deny the accuracy of the charge. But in order to give the reader an opportunity of judging for himself, we lay before him Sir Walter Scott's account of the transaction referred to. "Buonaparte," he observes, "belonged to the Roman school of philosophy; and it is confidently reported by Baron Fane, his secretary—though not universally believed—that he designed to escape from life by an act of suicide. The Emperor, according to this account, had carried with him,

[29] O'Meara's "Voice from St. Helena," vol. i. p. 57.

ever since his retreat from Moscow, a packet containing a preparation of opium, made up in the same manner with that used by Condorcet, for self-destruction. His valet-de-chambre, in the night of the 12th or 13th of April, heard him arise, and pour something into a glass of water, drink, and return to bed. In a short time afterwards the man's attention was called by sobs and stifled groans; an alarm took place in the chateau; some of the principal persons were roused, and repaired to Napoleon's chamber. Yvan, the surgeon who had procured him the poison, was also summoned; but hearing the Emperor complain that the operation of the potion was not quick enough, he was seized with a panic of terror, and fled from the palace at full gallop. Napoleon took the remedies recommended, and a long fit of stupor ensued, with profuse perspiration. He awakened much exhausted, and surprised at finding himself still alive. He said aloud, after a few moments' reflection, 'Fate will not have it so;' and afterwards appeared reconciled to undergo his destiny without similar attempts at personal violence." Napoleon's illness was, at the time, imputed to indigestion. A general of the highest distinction transacted business with Napoleon on the morning of the 13th of April. He seemed pale and dejected, as from recent and exhausting illness. His only dress was a night-gown and slippers; and he drank, from time to time, a quantity of ptisan, or some such liquid, which was placed beside him, saying he had suffered severely during the night, but that his complaint had left him.[30]

We cannot conceive a more piteous condition than that of a man of great ambition without the powers of mind which are indispensable for its gratification. In him a constant contest is going on between an intellect constitutionally weak, and a desire to distinguish himself in some particular department of life. How often a man so unhappily organized ends his career in a mad-house, or terminates his miserable existence by suicide! Let men be taught to make correct estimates of their own capabilities, to curb in the imagination, to cease "building castles in the air," if we wish to advance their mental and bodily health. "*Ne sutor ultra crepidam*," said Apelles to the cobbler. A young man who "penned a stanza when he ought to engross," blew out his brains because he had failed in inducing a London publisher to purchase an epic poem which he had written, and which he had the vanity to conceive was equal to Paradise Lost, forgetting that, in order to be a poet,—

> "Nature's kindling breath
> Must fire the chosen genius; nature's hand
> Must string his nerves and imp his eagle wings."

That this state of mind predisposes and often leads to the commission of suicide, numerous cases testify.

Despair often drives men to suicide. The dread of poverty and want; the hopes in which we often injudiciously place too much of our happiness entirely blasted; either honest or false pride humbled by public or private contempt; ambitious views suddenly and unexpectedly disappointed; pains of the body, the loss of those dear and near to us,—tend to originate this feeling, and induce the unhappy person to seek relief in self-murder.

---

[30] "Life of Napoleon." vol. viii. p. 244.

How terrible is the situation of the man exposed to the influence of this passion, and deprived of the cheering and elevating influence of hope! We had an opportunity, some years back, of witnessing the case of a maniac, whose derangement of mind consisted in his having abandoned himself completely to despair. He laboured under no distinct or prominent delusion, but his mental alienation consisted in the total absence of all prospect of relief. The iron had entered his very soul; he appeared as if the hand of a relentless destiny had written on the threshold of his door, as on the gate of the Inferno of Dante, the heart-rending sentence, "Abandon all hope!"

A woman is seduced by some heartless and profligate wretch; she is in a short time forsaken and left to her fate. Her mind recurs to the past; she recalls to recollection her once happy state of innocence and peace. Scorned by the world, shunned by her relations and friends, she is driven to a state of agonizing distraction. Despair, in its worst features, takes possession of her mind, and under this feeling she puts an end to her existence. A man under the operation of this passion wrote as follows:—

"It has pleased the Almighty to weaken my understanding, to undermine my reason, and to render me unfit for the discharge of my duty. My blood rolls in billows and torrents of despair. It must have vent. How? I possess a place to which I am a dishonour, inasmuch as I am incapable of discharging it properly; I prevent some better man from doing it more justice. This piece of bread which I lament is all that I have to support myself and family; even this I do not merit; I eat it in sin, and yet I live. Killing thought! which a conscience hitherto uncorrupted inspires. I have a wife, also, and my child reproaches me with its existence. But you do not know, my dear friends, that if my unhappy life is not speedily ended, my weak head will require all your care, and I shall become a burthen rather than an assistance to you. It is better that I yield myself a timely sacrifice to misfortune, than, by permitting the delusion to continue longer, I consume the last farthing of my wife's inheritance. It is a duty of every person to do that which his situation requires; reason commands it, religion approves. My life, such as it is, is a mere animal life, devoid of reason; in my mind, a life which stands in opposition to duty is moral death, and worse than that which is natural. In favour of the few whose life I cannot render happy, it is at least my duty not to become an oppression. I ought to relieve them from a weight which sooner or later cannot fail to crush them."

This unfortunate man, after penning the above account of his morbid feelings, sent his wife to church on Sunday, May 13th, 1783; and after writing an addition to his journal, took a pair of scissors and attempted, although unsuccessfully, to terminate his life by cutting his throat. He then opened the arteries at the wrists, and again failed in destroying himself; he staggered to the window, and saw his wife returning home, upon which he seized a knife used for killing deer, and stabbed himself in the heart. He was lying weltering in his blood when his wife came in, but was not quite dead. M. le Clarc, who relates the case, observes, that he was a man of understanding, and of a lively wit. He possessed a great deal of theoretical learning; his heart was incorruptibly honest. Like every calm and determined self-murderer, he was proud; but his pride was not the pride of rank, of riches, or of learning, but that divine pride which arises from a consciousness of incorrupt-ible honesty, and of being possessed of good powers of mind. The office he held was that of an assistant judge in a small college of justice at Insterberg. His mother had been once deranged in her mind.

Few persons have given a more striking example of this passion than the Abbé de Rancé, when first touched with remorse for the enormity of his past life, and before the disturbed state of his mind had settled into that turn for religious seclu-sion and mortification which produced the appalling austerities of La Trappe. "To a state of frantic despair," says Don Lancelot, in his letter to La Mère Angelique of Port Royal, "succeeded a black melancholy. He sent away all his friends, and shut himself up in his mansion at Veret, where he would not see a creature. His whole soul, nay, even his bodily wants, seemed wholly absorbed in a deep and settled gloom. Shut up in a single room, he even forgot to eat and drink; and when the servant reminded him that it was bed-time, he started as from a deep reverie, and seemed unconscious that it was not still morning. When he was better, he would often wander in the woods for the entire day, wholly regardless of the weather. A faithful servant, who sometimes followed him by stealth, often watched him standing for hours together in one place, the snow and the rain beating on his head, whilst he, unconscious of his position, was wholly absorbed in painful rec-ollections. Then, at the fall of a leaf, or the noise of the deer, he would awake as from a slumber, and, wringing his hands, hasten to bury himself in a thicker part of the wood, or else throw himself prostrate, with his face in the snow, and groan bitterly."[31]

How many commit suicide from what is termed a *blind impulse*! They fancy that an internal voice tells them to kill themselves; and considering it impossible to resist what they term a destiny, they do so. A gentleman, a merchant of the city of London, had been exposed to great mental perturbation; his nervous system had received a severe shock. He suffered extremely from a dread of going mad. As he was walking home one afternoon, he heard a voice say, "Kill thyself!" "Commit suicide!" and from that moment he could not banish the idea from his mind. Two or three times he was on the eve of obeying the mandate of this internal voice; but he fortunately possessed sufficient resolution to resist the temptation. In this state of mind he consulted a physician, who ordered him to be cupped in the neigh-bourhood of the head. His bowels were attended to, and he was recommended to visit some friends in the north of Scotland, and to banish from his mind all ideas connected with business. He followed the advice of his judicious physician, and in a short time he completely recovered.

In the midst of health apparently perfect and uniform, a man was attacked

[31] It is worthy of remark that the judge who condemned, as well as the disciple who betrayed, our Saviour, were both driven by despair to suicide. The fate of Judas is recorded in the Gospel; the concluding scenes in the life of Pontius Pilate are related by two learned historians (*Josephus* and *Eusebius*.) The former says that "Pontius Pilate, after having exer-cised great cruelties in his government of Judæa, was, before the Roman Emperor (Caligu-la), stripped of all his dignities and fortunes, and banished to Gaul, where it is said he suffered such extreme hardships of body and despair of mind, that, after lingering for two years, he became his own executioner."

with a sudden disposition to destroy. He seized a stick, raised it, struck indiscriminately and broke everything that presented itself to him. After some seconds, the stick fell from his hands, and he appeared restored to himself. The man knew nothing of what he had just done. He was reproached, he was shewn the remnants of the things that he had broken; he thought they were ridiculing him, and he was greatly irritated. He was again seized with frenzy, and killed a person. He was taken before a court of justice, acquitted on the ground of insanity, and placed in an hospital. This disposition to destroy returned at distant intervals; it then came on more frequently; and finally, changed into fits of epilepsy. A person seized with this morbid desire is not always unconscious of the approach of the disposition; he has sometimes a presentiment of it, perceives its danger, seeks to combat it, and frequently succeeds in effecting his purpose.

A labourer, at the end of his day's work, felt himself seized with an irresistible desire of running; he rushed upon the quay, which goes from the Louvre to the Grève: every obstacle was overcome. An attempt was made to stop him, but it was not successful. At last he dexterously engaged one of his arms in the wheel of a carriage, which happened to be within his reach. Thus withheld, he recovered his breath, became calm, and appeared to have no idea of what had occurred. This feeling was again manifested, and he was properly sent by his friends to an hospital, when it was discovered that he had a disease of the spinal marrow.

A man arrived upon the Pont Neuf; he rushed violently to the parapet, and precipitated himself into the Seine. He was seen by some of the bystanders, who drew him out of the water and saved his life. After some days of complete restoration, his friends asked him the reason of his strange conduct. He replied, "I cannot give any account. I am in the happiest situation in the world. I have only to play with fortune and with men. I have never been ill. I do not know what troubles may come upon me. I can only recollect my arrival on the Pont Neuf, and my recall to life."

The particulars of the following fact are recorded in Mrs. Mathews' life of her husband. Mathews the comedian had lived for some days a vapid and inactive life. His spirit had been pressed down, "cabin'd, cribb'd, confin'd." In this state of mind, a party of gentlemen called upon him, and proposed a day's excursion. Accordingly, they all mounted their horses. Mrs. Mathews says—"My husband's depressed spirits were exhilarated by the beauty of the weather, and the prospect of a day's pleasure (free from the restraint of a room, listening to truisms) in the open air, where he would have uncontrolled power to gaze upon his idol, Nature, in her most beautiful form. He had not ridden out of the city for some weeks, and was in a state of childish delight and excitement. At this moment his eyes turned upon one of the party, a very little man, who was perched on a very tall horse, and who seemed unusually grave and important. Mr. Mathews looked at him for a moment; and the next, knocked him off with a smart blow, felling him to the ground. The whole party were struck with horror; but no one felt more shocked than he who had committed the outrage. He dismounted, picked up the little victim to his unaccountable freak, declared himself unable to give any motive for the action, but that it was an impulse he could not resist; and afterwards, in relating this extraordinary incident, he declared his conviction that it was done in a moment of frenzy, induced by the too sudden reaction from previous stagnation of all freedom and amusement."

A young woman, about twenty years of age, who had been insane but a short time, and appeared to be recovering, after having assisted to whitewash and clean a ward in an asylum in which she was confined, was sitting, in the evening, taking tea with the nurse and several other inmates. She took advantage of the opportunity when the nurse went to the cupboard for some sugar to seize a knife with which some bread had just been cut; and in the presence of the whole party, in an instant, before her hand could be arrested, cut her throat in so dreadful a manner that she died almost immediately.

A patient in the Asylum at Wakefield, the wife of a labourer, a kind-hearted and clever woman, was afflicted with such a propensity to destroy that she was almost constantly obliged to be kept in confinement; and when at liberty, she could not resist the pleasure of breaking anything she met with. In one instance, she saw some tea-cups on a table, and for some time walked backwards and forwards, and checked the inclination; but eventually the temptation proved too strong, and she swept them at once on to the floor. She afterwards regretted the circumstance; but the impulse was too powerful to be resisted.

A monomaniac (says Esquirol) heard a voice within him repeat these words— *"Kill thyself! kill thyself!"* He therefore committed suicide, in obedience to this superior power, whose order he dare not withstand.

A man, under a religious hallucination, believed himself to be in communication with the Deity. He fancied he heard a celestial voice saying—*"My son, come and seat thyself by my side."* He opened the window to obey the invitation, fell down, and fractured his leg. When he was carried to his bed, he expressed the greatest astonishment on finding that he had precipitated himself from the window.

A young lady of considerable beauty was accosted in the street by a strange gentleman. She took no notice at first of the unwarrantable liberty; but on finding that he persisted in following her, she attempted, by quickening her pace, to escape. Being extremely timid, and having naturally a very nervous temperament, she was much excited. The person in the garb of a gentleman followed her for nearly a mile, and when he saw that she was home, he suddenly turned down a street, and disappeared. The young lady expressed herself extremely ill soon after she entered the house. A physician was sent for, who declared his astonishment at her severe illness from a cause so trifling. During the following night she manifested indications of mental derangement, with a disposition to commit suicide. A strait-waistcoat was procured, and all apprehensions of her succeeding in gratifying the propensity of self-destruction was removed. Some weeks elapsed before she recovered. To all appearance she was perfectly well. She had no recollection of what had transpired, and expressed herself amazed when she was told that she had wished to kill herself. Two months after she left her bed she was missed. Search was made in every direction, but in vain. After the lapse of two days, she was discovered floating in a pond of water several miles from her home. In her pocket was discovered a piece of paper, on which were written the following lines:—"Oh, the misery and wretchedness I have experienced for the last month no one but myself can tell. A demon haunts me—life is insupportable. A voice tells me that I am destined to fall by my own hands. I leave this world for another, where I hope to enjoy more happiness. Adieu."

We have no doubt that in this case, although the acute symptoms of insanity had subsided, she had not recovered completely her sane state of mind. None but those conversant with the subject of mental derangement would believe that so trifling a circumstance as that of being spoken to in the street would have produced so violent an attack of maniacal delirium as was witnessed in the case of this poor girl.

M. Esquirol states that he has never seen an unequivocal instance of any individual drawn to the commission of suicide by a kind of irresistible impulse, independently of any secret grievance, real or imaginary. Could the secret feelings of these suicides be accurately ascertained, there would generally, if not always, be found some lurking source of discontent, real or fanciful, in the breast, which serve as motives to their suicidal propensity. Many instances are on record, it is true, where men have put a period to their existence without any apparent visible cause or motive; but as Rousseau has justly observed, *Le bonheur n'a point d'enseigne exterieur: pour en juger, il faudrait lire dans le c[oe]ur de l'homme heureux.*"

"Individuals," says Esquirol, "who appear outwardly the residence of happiness, are often inwardly the focus of chagrin, and tortured with distracting passions. That man can destroy his own life, being at the same time happy in his mind, is a phenomenon which human reason cannot comprehend."

A diseased temperament, a serious lesion of one or more of the viscera, a gradual exhaustion of the energies of the system, may so aggravate the miseries of life as to hasten the period of voluntary death. But how are we to account for the irresistible propensity to suicide which sometimes exists, independent of any apparent mental or physical ailments? A melancholic, whose case was published in Fourcroy's Medical Journal of 1792, once said, "I am in prosperous circumstances; I have a wife and a child who constitute my happiness; I cannot complain of bad health, and still I feel a horrible propensity to throw myself into the Seine." His declaration was too fatally verified in the event. Crichton was once consulted upon the case of a young man, twenty-four years of age, in full vigour and health, who was tormented by periodical accessions of these gloomy feelings and propensities. At those times he meditated his own destruction. But on a nearer view of the fatal act, he shrunk back into himself, and recoiled with horror from its execution. Without relinquishing his project, he never had the courage to accomplish it. "It is in cases like these," says Crichton, "that energetic measures of coercion, and the effectual excitement of terror, should lend their aid to the powers of medicine and regimen."

In many cases of suicide, the act is preceded by a long train of perverted reasoning. These individuals become taciturn, morose, pusillanimous, and distrustful. The future presents itself to their view under the most unfavourable aspect, and despair becomes painted on their countenances. Their eyes become hollow; they complain of sleeplessness, and are disturbed by frightful dreams. The bowels are in an inactive state; the functions of the liver become to a certain extent suspended. It is in this state that they contemplate the idea of suicide; and the diaries which some have kept of their sensations and thoughts disclose the various kinds of death which they have contemplated and rejected, one after another, often for reasons the most preposterous and ridiculous. It is singular that in these journals they generally endeavour to hide their despondency and their mental aberration, while their moral and intellectual weakness is sure to be betrayed. They often accuse themselves of insanity, and bewail their unhappy lot; others argue most ingeniously in favour of their meditated suicide. Others again, subdued as it were by the force of the moral and religious principles which they have imbibed, represent to themselves that the act they contemplate is contrary to the moral end for which man was created—fatal to the welfare and happiness of their families. Then ensues a conflict in their breasts. If reason and religion prevail, the project is abandoned,—sometimes abandoned altogether. If otherwise, the suicide is committed. Falret knew the case of a woman who exhibited a tendency to suicide, but who was delivered for a period from the commission of the crime by the principles of religion in which her mind had been educated. A long period elapsed before she could reconcile herself to the act of suicide, and then she argued herself into it by the following piece of sophistry:—"There are no general rules without exceptions; and I am the precise exception in this case: therefore I may commit suicide without violating my religious principles."

Having once conceived the idea of suicide, the mind is often rendered so miserable in consequence of it, that the person rushes into the arms of death in order to escape from the terrible state of anticipation. Others meditate on the bloody deed for years. Rousseau, after drawing a piteous portrait of his proscribed and solitary condition, and of the state of his health, adds, *"Puisque mon corps n'est plus pour moi qu'un embarras, un obstacle à mon repos, cherchons donc à m'en degager le plus tôt que je pourrai."*

Tedium vitæ, or *ennui*, is said to be a frequent cause of suicide. We have heard of an Englishman who hanged himself in order to avoid the trouble of pulling off and on his clothes. Goëthe knew a gardener, and the overseer of some extensive pleasure-grounds, who once splenetically exclaimed, "Shall I see these clouds for ever passing, then, from east to west?" So singularly developed was this weariness of life, this feeling of satiety, in one of our distinguished men, that it is said of him that he viewed with dissatisfaction the return of spring, and wished, by way of change, that everything would, for once, be red instead of green.[32]

> "— — Within that ample nich,
> With every quaint device of splendour rich,
> Yon phantom, who, from vulgar eyes withdrawn,
> Appears to stretch in one eternal yawn:
> Of empire here he holds the tottering helm,
> Prime-minister in Spleen's discordant realm,

---

[32] Lessing.

> The pillar of her spreading state, and more,
> Her darling offspring, whom on earth she bore.
> For, as on earth his wayward mother strayed,
> Grandeur, with eyes of fire, her form surveyed,
> And with strong passion starting from his throne,
> Unloos'd the sullen queen's reluctant zone.
> From his embrace, conceived in moody joy,
> Rose the round image of a bloated boy:
> His nurse was, Indolence; his tutor, Pomp,
> Who kept the child from every childish romp.
> They rear'd their nursling to the bulk you see,
> And his proud parents called their imp—*Ennui*."
>
> *Hayley's Triumphs of Temper.*

It is rare for an Englishman to commit suicide from ennui. The English are different in this respect from the French people. The causes which lead to suicide in this country, are those connected with sudden reverse of fortune, or grievous disappointments, which are allowed to prey upon the mind until the individual seeks relief in the arms of death. In great commercial communities, where men may be reduced, in a few minutes, from affluence to beggary; where the hopes and aspirations of years are levelled in a moment to the dust, and the individual finds himself exposed to the insulting pity of friends, and the searching curiosity of the public, we need not feel surprise, when all these circumstances rush upon a man's mind in the sudden convulsion and turbulence of its elements, that he should welcome the only escape from the abyss into which he has been hurled.

It has been stated, by a competent authority, that the week following the drawing of the last lottery in England, no less than fifty suicides were committed!

M. Gase, in a memoir read before the *Academie Royale de Médecine*, traces the increase of suicide in Paris to the spirit of gambling which the Parisians so passionately indulge in. The extended system of speculation in this country approximates in its pernicious effects on the constitution to those which have been considered to result from gambling. The following case, which was communicated to a popular journal, by Dr. J. Johnson, forcibly illustrates how the constitution may be undermined by rash, inconsiderate conduct, during the excitement arising from temporary circumstances:—

One day, on the Stock Exchange, when the rumours of failings at home and commotions abroad were producing such alarming vacillations in the public funds that the whole property of a gentleman of high probity, temperance, and respectability, was in momentary jeopardy, he found himself in so terrible a state of nervous agitation that he was obliged to leave the scene of confusion, and apply to wine, though quite unaccustomed to more than a glass or two after dinner. To his utmost surprise, the wine had no apparent effect, though he drank glass after glass, in rapid succession, until he had finished a whole bottle. Not the slightest inebriating influence was induced by this unusual quantity taken before dinner. His nervous agitation was, however, calmed, and he went back to the Exchange, and transacted business with steadiness, composure, and equanimity. None of the ordinary effects of wine were produced at the time, but a few days afterwards he was seized with a severe attack of indigestion, a malady by which he had never been previously affected. This case shews that although mental agitation masks, or even prevents, the usual effects of wine, and other stimulants, at the time, and thus enables, and indeed induces, men to take more than under ordinary circumstances, yet the ulterior effects are greatly worse on the constitution than if the stimulants had produced the usual excitement at the moment of their reception into the stomach. It is thus, we have no doubt, that the nervous system of thousands in this country is ruined, and, in numerous cases, the seeds of suicidal derangement sown, and that without the victims being conscious of the channel through which they have been poisoned.

Defective education is a frequent cause of suicide. At the present day, the ornamental has taken the place of the substantial; the showy and specious, the situation of the solid and virtuous. The endowments of the mind and cultivation of the heart are forced to yield to the external accomplishments and graces of the body, and polished manners are too generally preferred to sound morals. The importance of fashion is inculcated in opposition to reason; religion is made to bow down before the shrine of honour; and the fear of the world is taught to supersede the fear of God. But what superstructure can be raised on so sandy a foundation? It can support no incumbent weight; and, in consequence, it cannot be deemed surprising that an inundation of folly and vice, like a sweeping torrent, should bear down all before it. The dignity of personal worth and character is a point too little considered. Brilliant parts supersede sound judgment; and disinterested virtue, integrity, and public spirit, are out of character in a nation immersed in voluptuousness. Education of a light and frivolous character leads to a vacuity of serious thoughts and solid principles of conduct. Luxury and profligacy, in all ages, have operated injuriously on the human mind. Cato the elder observes that there could be no friendship in a man whose palate had quicker sensations than his brain and heart. The man who has no internal sources of enjoyment to fly to when others fail,—he whose happiness consists in an indulgence in the pleasures of the senses, when these ephemeral sources of gratification are removed, will, to avoid the vacuum which is made in his existence, readily terminate his own life.

There cannot be a doubt but that the general diffusion of knowledge, and the desire to place within the command of the humblest person the advantages of education, have not a little tended to promote the crime of suicide. It may be opposed to all our *à priori* reasoning to suppose that, in proportion as the intellect becomes expanded, knowledge and civilization diffused, the desire to commit self-murder would be engendered. It is an indisputable fact, that insanity, in all its variations, is in a ratio to the refinement and civilization of a country. "It is clearly proved," says Brown, "that in Finéstre, where the people are in a deplorable state of ignorance, and education is entirely neglected, only twelve in a hundred of the inhabitants being able to write or read, few suicides occur, at least only in the proportion of one in 25,000. In Paris, that focus of all that is brilliant and imposing in science and literature, the crime is of common occurrence. In Coréze, where only twelve in the hundred can read or write, one suicide in 47,000 occurs; and in the High Loire one in 163,000. On the other hand, in Oise and Lower Seine, both places in possession of the highest degree of general instruction, and of the means of advancing in improvement, suicides occur in every 5000 or 9000 inhabitants. In the north of France, Catholicism has been nearly extirpated, and there suicide and crime predominate; south of the Loire, on the contrary, it still retains a strong hold of the affections of the people, and there suicide, and its sinister crimes or maladies are comparatively rare. This affords a noble proof that the effects of Christianity, in whatever form and under whatever circumstances, are peace and joy."[33]

It is our firm belief that the increase of suicide in this country is to a certain extent to be traced to the atrocious doctrines promulgated with such zeal by the sect of modern infidels, who falsely denominate themselves *Socialists*; a class whose opinions are subversive of all morality and Christianity, and which sap the foundation of society itself. It is natural to expect when such principles of infidelity are inculcated, when men are taught to believe in the non-existence of a God, and to consider they are not accountable agents, and are under the operation of an organization over which they have no control, that they should look with philosophic indifference on suicide, and consider it as a justifiable mode of putting an end to the misery and wretchedness engendered by their own opinions. Such doctrines must of necessity be productive of great evil to society; and it becomes the duty of every Christian and well-wisher to his fellow-men to hold them up to reprobation. The opinions of Owen strike at the root of all order, and of all virtue, social and public, and break down every barrier of law and restraint, making the passions the only standard of right and wrong—the animal appetites the only test of virtue and vice.

In the Bishop of Exeter's able speech in the House of Lords, on the subject of Socialism, he stated that cases of suicide under circumstances of the most dreadful suffering had occurred, which had been brought about by Mr. Owen's pernicious doctrines. The learned prelate related the particulars of the following case:—Mr. Parke, a most respectable inhabitant of Wolverhampton, had an apprentice, who had been in the habit of attending Socialists' meetings, and hearing their lectures. He purchased all their publications, and his master's shop not being of that kind to furnish them, he was obliged to go elsewhere to obtain them. He dined and drank tea as usual with Mr. Parke on the Sunday, and left after tea to attend St. George's Church. Not coming home at the usual hour, his master sat up for him until 12 o'clock, when, as he had not returned, he concluded that his relations had detained him. He was, however, found dead, in a sort of lumber room, the next morning. Two bottles of poison were lying by his side; the one which occasioned his death contained prussic acid; the other, nux vomica: near him were lying four letters, one addressed to his father, another to Mr. Parke, a third to the jury, and a fourth containing his creed; in all of which he expressed his disbelief in the Bible, considering it "the most dangerous book that ever was written," and if ever such a person as Jesus Christ lived, he was the weakest man he ever heard of. In one of the letters he also stated that he had been nurtured in superstition, (meaning, that

---

[33] On Lunatic Asylums.

he had been brought up as a member of the church of England,) and that when he read Owen's works he "shuddered at their common sense." He denied all belief in a future state of retribution; and as he considered apprenticeship slavery, he thought it more prudent to suffer pain for a moment than to endure six years' servitude. He earnestly entreated the jury not to bring in a verdict of insanity.

It appears from a letter to the Bishop of Exeter, written by the unfortunate youth's uncle, that he had been from infancy an exceedingly lively boy; between him and his parents the most glowing affection, as well as the most boundless confidence, existed; but the fatal poison of Socialism changed a confiding heart into a cold concentration of selfishness. After the verdict of the jury, the uncle declared aloud, before a crowded room, in a most vehement manner, that, were he in the presence of the Queen, he would proclaim Owen as the murderer of his nephew.

The indifference with which self-murder is looked at in Germany is to be ascribed in a great measure to the popular productions of that country. We are reluctant to denounce as undoubted causes of suicide the works of men of splendid talents; but in such a case it would be wrong, it would be criminal, to mince the matter, and plead any excuse for so detestable a work as Werter, which has unhinged the minds of thousands, before they were aware of its impoisoned and insidious tendency. That it is the work of a man of genius only makes its blackening influence the stronger; as the fascination of the style, and the intense interest of the narrative, operate like an infernal spell to smooth the road to self-destruction. Its leading theme is, that human passions, and particularly love, are immediately inspired by Heaven; and that it would be wrong—nay, that it is impossible—to resist them; and consequently, if a lover meets with disappointment, his only virtuous course is suicide, which is triumphantly catalogued among the virtues, as it was by the heathen morality of the ancients.

This work, together with Foscolo's imitation of it, the "*Ultime Lettere di Jacopo Ortis*," and all publications of a similar character, ought to be repudiated by every sound thinking man. Resistance to the dictates of passion, when it prompts to crime and suicide, is a most deadly sin against Werterism; whilst, obeying the passions to the letter, even if they incite to criminal love or self-murder, gives to its disciple the stamp of one of the virtuous who have courageously braved the laws of good order, fearlessly dared to trample under foot all the commands of God and man, and stood forth as the redoubted champions of human supremacy and the glorious right of self-destruction. Such are the principles of the miscreants who wish to prove that suicide is a virtue; and, with the sentiments found in the pages of Werter, they rush headlong and unthinkingly into a deep and awful futurity.

It is not generally known that Goëthe, the author of the work alluded to, attempted suicide. He considered the death of the Emperor Otho as worthy of imitation. In contemplating the feelings which influenced that monarch, he says he convinced himself that if he could not proceed as Otho had done, he was not entitled to resolve on renouncing life. He adds, "By this conviction, I saved myself from the purpose, or indeed, more properly speaking, from the whim, of suicide. Among a considerable collection of arms, I possessed a costly well-ground dagger. This I laid down nightly by my side; and, before extinguishing the light, I tried whether

I could succeed (*à la Otho*) in sending the sharp point an inch or two deep into my heart. But as I truly never could succeed, I at last took to laughing at myself, threw away all these hypochondriacal crotchets, and determined to live."

In the melancholy case of Hackman and Miss Ray, the following is the substance of a correspondence which passed between them on the subject of Werter. Hackman was refused the sight of this book by Miss R., who had a copy of the French translation, because, as she expresses herself, she saw too great a similarity between her lover and Werter, not only in point of situation, but in the impetuosity of their tempers. "The book you mention," says Miss R., "is just the only book you should never read. On my knees, I beg you never to read it! Perhaps you have read it; perhaps—I am distracted! Heaven only knows to whom I may be writing this letter." To this, Hackman, who was in Ireland, replies: "Nonsense! to say it will make me unhappy, or that I shall not be able to read it. Must I pistol myself because a thick-blooded German has been fool enough to set the example, or because a German novelist has feigned such a story." Werter was read, and the effect was most injurious on his mind. Whilst confined in Newgate, he wrote the following letter:—"Among my papers you will see, my friend, some lines I wrote on reading Goëthe's Werter, translated from German into French, which, whilst I was in Ireland, Miss R. refused to lend me. When I returned to England, I made her let me read it. But I never shewed her these lines, for fear they should make her uneasy. Unhappy Werter! still less pretence hadst thou for suicide than I. After finally seeing thy Charlotte married to another—marrying her thyself—hadst thou a right over thy existence, because she was not thy wife? Yet wast thou less barbarous than I; for thou didst not seek to die in her presence,—but neither didst thou doubt her love. We can neither of us hope for pardon!"

The lines were these, supposed to be found, after Werter's death, upon the ground by the pistol—

> "If chance some kindred spirit should relate
> To future times unhappy Werter's fate;
> Should in some pitying, almost pardoning age,
> Consign my sorrows to some weeping page;
> And should the affecting page be haply read
> By some new Charlotte—mine will then be dead.
> (Yes; she shall die—sole solace of my love!
> And we shall meet—for so she said—above.)
> O Charlotte! (Martha—by whatever name,
> Thy faithful Werter hands thee down to fame,)
> O be thou sure thy Werter never knows
> The fatal story of my kindred woes!
> O do not, fair one,—by my shocking end
> I charge thee!—do not let thy feeling friend
> Shed his sad sorrows o'er my tearful tale:
> Example, spite of precept, may prevail."

It may be mentioned, as a fact corroborating the opinion, that productions of an infidel character have a tendency to originate a disposition to suicide by weakening the moral principles; that when the celebrated and notorious Tom Paine's "Age of Reason" was first published, the papers of the day recorded many cases of self-murder committed by persons who avowed that the idea never entered their heads until they had become familiar with the works of the above-mentioned writer. An individual, zealous in the diffusion of Paine's principles, purchased several hundred copies of his work, which he most industriously circulated, gratuitously, in quarters where he knew the doctrines of Christianity had already obtained a footing. A copy of the "Age of Reason," elegantly bound, was received by a young lady who was acting in the capacity of a governess in the family of a gentleman of great respectability. The lady had no conception from whom the present came, and having heard of the book, she felt a curiosity to become acquainted with the doctrines which it inculcated. The circumstance of her having received the book was not mentioned to any member of the family with whom she resided; and in the evening, when she retired to her own room, she read it with great attention. The family noticed, in a few weeks, a perceptible alteration in the appearance of the young lady. She became extremely thoughtful and contemplative. Her health also appeared sensibly affected. The mother of the children whom she was instructing took advantage of the first opportunity of speaking to her on the subject. She expressed herself very unhappy in her mind, but refused to disclose the cause of her mental uneasiness. It was thought she had formed an attachment, and was suffering from the effects of disappointed affection. She was questioned on these points, but persisted in concealing the circumstances which had been operating so injuriously on her mind. The mental dejection increased, and the result was, an alarming attack of nervous fever, of which she was cured by an able physician with much difficulty. When convalescent, she was noticed one day busily employed in writing, and when interrupted, shewed great anxiety to secrete the piece of paper on which she had been transcribing her thoughts. In the course of the evening of the same day, a deep groan was heard to issue from her room. The servant immediately entered, when, to her great horror, she saw the governess on the floor with a terrible gash in her throat. Assistance was directly obtained, but, alas! not in time to save the life of the poor unfortunate girl. On searching her desk, a sheet of paper was discovered, on which she had disclosed her reasons for the rash act. She said, that from the moment she read the "Age of Reason," her mind became unsettled. Her previous religious impressions were undermined; in proportion as she was induced to imbibe the doctrines of Tom Paine, so she became miserable and wretched. From one error she fell into another, until she actually believed that death was annihilation; and although she appeared firmly rooted in this belief, she expressed herself horrified beyond all expression at the bare idea of dissolution. For some time prior to her illness, she had felt an impulse to sacrifice her life, but had not the courage to perform the act. After her recovery, she felt the impulse renewed with increased strength, until, with a hope of escaping from an accumulation of misery which was weighing her to the earth, she determined to commit suicide. She also, in the document referred to, asked her friends to forgive her, and to take warning from her fate.

That many rush into suicide in order to escape the just and legal punishment of their crimes cannot be a matter of doubt. Many under such circumstances are influenced by a fear of public exposure, and prefer death to the idea of being compelled to undergo the ordeal of a trial in a court of justice. The following case is but the type of many that could be related:—

A young man of family, the Hon. Mr. — —, staying at an inn in Portsmouth, previously to sailing for India, where he was going out as an aide-de-camp to General — —, with a party of friends, also officers, joined company at supper one evening with Mr. Bradbury, the clown of Covent Garden Theatre, a person of very gentlemanlike exterior and manners, and ambitious of the society of gentlemen. He was in the habit of using a very magnificent and curious snuff-box, and on this occasion it was much admired by the party, and handed round for inspection from one to the other. Mr. Bradbury soon after left the inn, and retired to his lodging, when he missed his box, and immediately returned to inquire for it. The gentlemen with whom he had spent the evening had all retired to bed; but he left word with the porter to mention to the officers early the next day that he had left the box, and to request them to restore it to him when found.

The next morning, Mr. Bradbury again hastened to the inn, anxious to recover his property, and met on his way the Hon. Mr. — —, and communicated his loss to him; when he was informed by that gentleman that a similar circumstance had occurred to himself, his bed-room having been robbed the night before of his gold watch, chain, and seals, &c., and that he was on his way to a Jew in the town to apprize him of the robbery, in order that if such articles should be offered for sale, he might stop them and detain the person who presented them. This was very extraordinary! Mr. Bradbury then met the other gentlemen of the party, and was told by them that their rooms had also been robbed, one of bank notes to a great amount, another of a gold watch, &c.

The Hon. Mr. — — was violently infuriated by his loss; and as he was bound to sail from Portsmouth when the ship was ready, he naturally dreaded being compelled to depart without his property. He hinted, too, that he had certain suspicions of certain people. An officer was sent for from London. This man came down promptly, to the great satisfaction of the Hon. Mr. — —; and after searching the house and their trunks, Rivett (the officer) addressed the gentlemen, observing, that there was yet a duty unperformed, and which was a painful one to him—he must search the *persons* of all present, and as the Hon. Mr. — — 's trunks had been the first to be inspected, perhaps he would allow him to examine him at once. To this he agreed; but the next moment he was observed to look very ill. Rivett was proceeding to search him, as a matter of course, when he requested that everybody would leave the room, except the officer and Mr. Bradbury, which request was immediately complied with. He then fell upon his knees, entreated for mercy, and placed Mr. Bradbury's box in his hand, begging him to forgive him and spare his life. Rivett upon this proceeded to search him, but he resisted; the object was effected by force, and the greater part of the property found that had been stolen in the house. The officer, conceiving that he had not got the whole of the bank notes, inquired of Mr. — — where the remainder was; when he pointed to a pocket-book which was under the foot of the bed; and while Rivett relaxed his hold of him, and was in the act of stooping to pick up the book, Mr. — — caught up a razor and cut his throat. Rivett and Mr. Bradbury seized an arm each, and forced the razor from him; but he was so determined on self-destruction, that he twisted his head about violently in different ways, in order to make the wound larger and more fatal. To prevent him from continuing this, he was braced up with linen round his neck so tightly that he could not move it. A surgeon of the town, with two assistants, came, and after seeing the wound, gave it as their opinion that it was possible for him to recover, and by the assistance of some powerful soldiers holding him, they dressed the wound. His clothes were then cut off, and he was carried down stairs into another room. During this operation he coughed violently; but whether naturally or by design, to make his wound worse, was not ascertained. It had, however, the effect of setting his wound bleeding again, and the dressing was obliged to be repeated.

The sequel of this distressing case was of an equally melancholy character.

Poor Mr. Bradbury was standing close to the unfortunate young man when he committed the sudden attempt upon his own life. The horror of the act, and the shocking appearance of his lacerated throat, the blood from which flowed out upon Mr. Bradbury, in short, this heart-rending result of the previous agitation and discovery, acted upon the sensibility of Mr. Bradbury to such an extent as to deprive him of reason. This fact was noticeable two days after the above scene, by his entering a church, and after the service was ended, going into the vestry, and requesting the clergyman to pray for him, as he intended to cut his throat! This distemper of mind was not too great at first to admit of partial control; but it daily increased, and ultimately caused him to be placed under restraint.[34]

A woman, about thirty-six years of age, who had been well educated, but whose conduct had not been exempt from some irregularities, in consequence of intemperance and manifold disappointments, became affected with madness. She was by turns furious and melancholic, and conceived she had murdered one of her children, for which she ought to suffer death. She detailed the manner in which she had destroyed the child, and the motives which actuated her, so circumstantially, and with so much plausibility and feeling, that if it had not been known that her child was living, the physician under whose care she was placed might have been deceived. By her own hands she had repeatedly endeavoured to terminate her existence, but was prevented by constant vigilance and due restraint. Her disposition to suicide was afterwards relinquished; but she still persisted that for the murder of the child she ought to suffer death, and requested to be sent to Newgate, in order to be tried, and undergo the sentence of the law; indeed, she appeared to derive consolation from the hope of becoming a public example, and expiating her supposed crime on the scaffold. While in this state, and with a hope of convincing her of its safety, the child was brought to visit her. When she beheld it, there was a temporary burst of maternal affection; she kissed it, and for a few moments appeared to be delighted: but a look of suspicion quickly succeeded, and this was shortly followed by a frown of indignation, which rendered the removal of the child a measure of wholesome necessity. Perhaps in no instance was the buoyancy of madness more conspicuous over reason, recollection, and feeling.

[34] Vide Mathews' Life, by his widow, vol. ii. p. 158.

She insisted they had attempted to impose on her a strange child, which bore a faint resemblance to her own; however, by such subterfuges she was not to be deceived; she had strangled the child until life had totally departed, and it was not in the order of nature that it should exist again. The effect of this interview was an exasperation of her disorder: she became more cunning and malignant, and her desire for an ignominious death was augmented. To render this more certain, and accelerate her projected happiness, she enticed into her apartment a young female patient to whom she appeared to be attached, and having previously platted some threads of her bed-quilt into a cord, she fixed it round the neck of the young woman, and proceeded to strangle her. Fortunately, some person entered the room and unloosed the cord in time to save her. When this unhappy maniac was questioned concerning the motive which induced her to attempt the destruction of a person for whom she had manifested kindness, she very calmly replied, that as the murder of her own child was disbelieved, she wished to exhibit a convincing proof of the ferocity of her nature, that she might instantly be conveyed to Newgate and hanged, which she desired as the greatest blessing. With considerable satisfaction, we may add, that in a few months, notwithstanding her derangement had been of three years' duration, this woman perfectly recovered, and for a considerable time performed the duties of an important and respectable office.[35]

The great increase of the crime of suicide has been referred by many able physicians of the present day to the political excitement to which the minds of the people have been exposed of late years. In despotic countries, suicide and insanity are seldom heard of: the passions are checked by the nature of the government; the imagination is not elevated to an unhealthy standard; every man is compelled to follow the calling in life to which he is born, and for which he has capacity; and on this account the evil and corrupt dispositions of the mind are, to a certain extent, kept in abeyance. In republican governments, the greatest latitude is allowed to the turbulent passions; all mankind are theoretically placed on an equality; the man whose "talk is of bullocks" considers himself as fit to carry on the complicated business of government as he whose education, associations, and experience tend to qualify him for the duties of a legislator.

In proportion as men are exposed to the influence of causes which excite the passions, so will they become predisposed to mental derangement in all its forms. The French and American revolutions increased considerably the crime of suicide. It has been said that during the "reign of terror" statistical evidence does not shew that self-murder was more common than at any other period. Perhaps the alleged unfrequency of suicide may be attributed to the circumstance of the French people having been so busy in killing others that they had no time to think of killing themselves. More than the average number of suicides may not have really occurred during the crisis of the Revolution, but it is an undisputed fact that, both before and after that political convulsion, self-destruction prevailed to an alarming extent. Disappointed hopes, wounded pride and vanity, blighted ambition, loss of property, death of friends, disgust of life, all came into active operation after the turbulence and bloodshed of the Revolution had somewhat subsided: these

[35] Dr. Haslam.

passions, working upon minds easily excited, and not under the benign influence of religion, it was almost natural to expect that great recklessness of life should be exhibited. Such facts demonstrate to us the folly of uselessly exciting the passions of the people, and raising in their minds exaggerated expectations from political changes.

The tendency of refined sensibility to become wound up in a paroxysm, terminating in suicidal attempts, is strikingly illustrated in a case reported by Dr. Burrows: —

"A gentleman of a family of rank, and distinguished for talent, married early in life the object of his most ardent affections. He possessed extreme sensibility, with a most highly cultivated and refined mind. It may be remarked, as a constitutional peculiarity, that his natural pulse did not exceed forty beats in a minute. When anything suddenly occurred to agitate him, it produced an attack of fever, and his pulse was accelerated in an astonishing degree. Though in ordinary affairs he was a man of firm resolution and great spirit, yet when this fit happened, he was seized with such a panic, or impulse, that he knew not what he did, and he was unnerved for days. His lady being well acquainted with the infirmities of his constitution, rendered him, by her good sense and soothing, a happier man than he had previously been. Most unfortunately, she died in the first year of her marriage. His grief at her loss was excessive; and even when time had abated its poignancy, he continued very miserable. His thoughts were always reverting to the virtues of her whom he had lost, and the comparative happiness he had enjoyed in her society. He tried everything to divert his melancholy; but these impulses would follow reflection; and then his ideas adverted to self-destruction. He reasoned with himself upon the subject till, he confessed, he had become an infidel in religion, and could no longer view the act as wicked. I had," said Dr. Burrows, "an opportunity of knowing the exact state of his mind during this struggle, from perusing some notes which he had written, describing it. He expressed himself with the utmost tenderness and affection with respect to his departed wife, and of his intention of soon joining her by a voluntary death; not, however, in heaven, but in Elysium. One night, after having been occupied in reading to some dear relations, and apparently much enjoying the subject, he retired to his chamber. He undressed, and dismissed his valet. His gloomy reflections recurred. One of these strange impulses came over him. He seized a pistol, and discharged it: it failed of effect. He fired another: he wounded himself severely, but not mortally; neither was the effusion of blood great. He then called for assistance. Little constitutional disturbance followed, and the wound readily healed. It was during the time he was confined from the effects of this wound that Dr. Burrows was consulted. He could not detect the slightest aberration of the mind, nor was there a trait in his countenance of a propensity to commit suicide. He freely conversed on his past and present situation and opinions; was perfectly ready to submit to any supervision Dr. Burrows might advise, or plan that might be suggested, to bring him into a better and happier state of mind. By degrees, he acquired more composure. He afterwards travelled for a year and a half on the Continent. Upon his return, he seemed much improved in general appearance. Nothing, however, conquered his constitutional susceptibility."

That the LOVE OF NOTORIETY often impels to suicide there cannot be a doubt. The man who was killed by attaching himself to a rocket, and he who threw himself into the crater of Mount Vesuvius, were, no doubt, stimulated by a desire for posthumous fame. Shortly after the suicide at the Monument, a boy made an unsuccessful endeavour to poison himself; and on being questioned as to his motives, he said, "I wished to be talked of, like the woman who killed herself at the Monument!" How strange and anomalous are the motives which influence human actions!

Many are induced to think of suicide from the circumstance of their being conscious that they labour under an hereditary disposition to insanity. We know the case of a lady whose mind has been dwelling upon the subject of suicide for some time, and she has told her friends repeatedly that she feels assured she shall commit some rash act. "The disposition to suicide and insanity is in the family, and how can I fight against my physical organization?" Such is the mode of reasoning she adopts whenever urgently persuaded to banish from her mind the horrid sensations which are embittering her life.

A gentleman, in full possession of his reasoning faculties, and a man of considerable powers of intellect, said to us one day, in a conversation we had with him on the subject of suicide, "You may probably smile when I tell you that, happy and contented as I appear to be in my mind at this moment, I feel assured I shall fall by my own hands." Upon our asking him why he thought so, he replied, that a relation of his had killed himself some years previously, and that he laboured under an hereditary predisposition which nothing would subdue.

A woman, thirty-five years of age, placed herself, in 1821, under the care of M. Falret, for symptoms of phthisis. When nineteen years old, the death of an uncle, by his own hands, made a deep impression on her mind. She heard that insanity was hereditary, and the idea pursued her that she should one day fall into this melancholy condition. She confessed her apprehensions only to the priests, who endeavoured to dissipate the mournful impression. In this state she continued for two years, when the death of her reputed father, also by suicide, riveted the conviction on her mind that her own doom was sealed. She was convinced that *her blood was corrupted*; and this idea appeared to be confirmed by other circumstances. Tortured by this notion, she resolved to drown herself. After leaving a letter in her chamber, apprising her friends of the manner of her meditated death, she plunged into the river; but being immediately taken out, she was restored to life. The night following this attempt, she was harassed with a pain in her head, and after a short sleep, awoke, incapable of recognising any of the friends about her. She was evidently delirious, but made no allusion to her former melancholy impressions. Although previously religious and well-behaved, she uttered nothing but obscenities. This delirious excitement continued three days, and was succeeded by melancholy and a disposition to suicide. Headache again came on, with nausea and bilious vomitings, which, however, soon subsided. She became considerably emaciated after this, and looked the picture of despair; in fact, she could not look into the glass at herself without terror. Once more she wished the aid of religion, which afforded her some consolation, but was insufficient to dissipate entirely her sufferings. Meanwhile, her mother revealed to her the secret that her real father was still alive; and, after considerable scepticism on the point, she consented to an interview with him. The physical resemblance was so striking, that all doubt was instantly removed from her mind. From that moment all idea of suicide vanished; her spirits and health became progressively re-established. Fourteen years, says Falret, have now elapsed since the attempt at self-destruction. She is the mother of three children, and, during her married state, has been reduced to the greatest penury and distress; but has never, since the period alluded to, entertained the remotest idea of suicide; on the contrary, she has proved an exemplary wife and affectionate parent, having the full possession of her intellectual faculties.[36]

Everything that tends to throw the mind off its healthy balance will, of course, predispose to suicide. Excessive devotion of the attention to any particular branch of study, or to business, often originates cerebral disease and suicidal mania. In alluding to the injurious effects of excessive study, Marcilius Ficinus, as quoted by Burton, justly observes—"Other men look to their tools: a painter will wash his pencils; a smith will look to his hammer, anvil, and forge; a husbandman will mend his plough-irons and grind his hatchet, if it be dull; a falconer or huntsman will have an especial care of his hawks, hounds, horses, and dogs; a musician will string and unstring his lute,—only scholars neglect that instrument (their *brain* and *spirit*, I mean) which they daily use, and by which they range over all the world, and which by much study is consumed."

The melancholy case of William Eyton Tooke, Esq., who committed suicide some years ago, will illustrate the operation of the cause referred to.

"This gentleman," says a relative, in a letter to the *Times* newspaper, explanatory of the causes of Mr. T.'s death, "from a very early period of life, devoted himself to the most abstruse inquiries into moral and political philosophy, and has thus fallen a victim to the absorbing and exclusive nature of the pursuit." One of the witnesses who was examined at the inquest stated, that the deceased was of an exceedingly studious turn, and had for many months past been directing his attention particularly to commercial subjects. This subject was his constant study, and the theme of his conversation. It seemed to engross the whole of his attention, and his health, both bodily and mentally, was evidently impaired by it. A short period before his death, he was heard frequently to say, placing his hand upon his head, "This subject is too much for me; my head is distracted!" It was under the influence of this over-excited state of brain that he committed suicide.

It has been observed, in another part of this work, that many commit suicide from the notion that death from natural causes is attended with considerable agony.[37] This is the generally received notion, but it is an erroneous one. Those who have often witnessed the act of dying allow that it is not a painful process.

[36] "Revue Médicale," Dec. 1821.

[37] Under the heathen mythology, it was believed that the struggles of death continued till Proserpine had cropped the hair on the crown of the head, as victims were treated at the altar. Virgil has preserved this opinion in the fourth book of the Æneid, where he gives so fine a picture of the dying agonies of Dido.

In some delicate and irritable persons, a kind of struggle is indeed sometimes excited when respiration becomes difficult; but more frequently the dying obviously suffer nothing, and express no uneasiness. Dr. Ferriar says, "In those who die of chronic diseases, the gradation is slow and distinct. Consumptive patients are sometimes in a dying state for several days; they appear at such times to suffer little, but to languish for complete dissolution; nay, I have known them express great uneasiness when they have been recalled from the commencement of insensibility, by the cries of their friends, or the efforts of the attendants to alleviate pain. In observing persons in this situation, I have always been impressed with an idea that the approach of natural death produces a sensation similar to that of falling asleep. The disturbance of respiration is the only apparent source of uneasiness to the dying; and sensibility seems to be impaired just in proportion to the decrease of that function. Besides, both the impressions of present objects and those recalled by memory are influenced by the extreme debility of the patient, whose wish is for absolute rest. I could never see the close of life under these circumstances without recollecting those beautiful lines of Spencer—

> "Sleep after toil, port after stormy seas,
> Ease after war, death after life, doth greatly please."

Professor Hufeland, on the subject of death, observes, "that many fear death less than the operation of dying." People, he continues, "form the most singular conceptions of the last struggle—the separation of the soul from the body, and the like; but this is all void of foundation. No man certainly ever felt what death is; and insensibly as we enter life, equally insensibly do we leave it. The beginning and the end are here united. My proofs are as follows:—First, man can have no sensation of dying; for to die means nothing more than to lose the vital powers; and it is the vital power which is the medium of communication between the soul and the body. In proportion as the vital power decreases, we lose the power of sensation and consciousness; and we cannot lose life without, at the same time, or rather before, losing our vital sensation, which requires the assistance of the tenderest organs. We are taught also by experience that all those who ever passed through the first stage of death, and were again brought to life, unanimously asserted that they felt nothing of dying, but sunk at once into a state of insensibility.[38]

---

[38] It is only by reasoning physiologically that we can conclude that the act of dying is not a painful process. In proportion as death seizes its victim, so must consciousness be suspended. What can be more painful to the beholder than to witness the convulsive struggles, and the foaming at the mouth, of a person in an epileptic fit, who, when restored to consciousness, has no recollection of what has occurred? He remembers the premonitory indications, and that is all. Death is but an epileptic struggle. A phenomenon attends the dying moment which we do not recollect to have seen noticed. A man who fell into the water, and who rose several times to the surface, had a consciousness of the hopelessness and awfulness of his situation; he felt that death was inevitable. With this conviction on his mind, he saw presented to him a picture of his past life; the minutest action in which he had been engaged was brought in a kind of tableau before him. Circumstances that had long been forgotten were conjured from his brain, and he had a bird's-eye view of his past career. Possibly, this may occur to every person at the moment of dying. The expressions of those placed under such circumstances would indicate as much.

"Let us not be led into a mistake by the convulsive throbs, the rattling in the throat, and the apparent pangs of death, which are exhibited by many persons when in a dying state. These symptoms are painful only to the spectators, and not to the dying, who are not sensible of them. The case here is the same as if one, from the dreadful contortions of a person in an epileptic fit, should form a conclusion respecting his internal feelings: from what affects us so much, he suffers nothing.

"Let one always consider life, as it really is, a mean state, which is not an object itself, but a medium for obtaining an object, as the multifarious imperfections of it sufficiently prove: as a period of trial and preparation, a fragment of existence, through which we are to be fitted for, and transmitted to, other periods. Can the idea, then, of really making this transition—of ascending to another from this mean state, this doubtful, problematical existence, which never affords complete satisfaction—ever excite terror? With courage and confidence we may, therefore, resign ourselves to the will of that Supreme Being who, without our consent, placed us in this sublunary theatre, and give up to his management the future direction of our fate.

"Remembrance of the past, of that circle of friends who were nearest, and always will be dearest to our hearts, and who, as it were, now smile upon us with a friendly look of invitation from that distant country beyond the grave, will also tend very much to allay the fear of death."

We recollect attending the case of a young lady labouring under a disease which produced extreme mental and physical suffering, who exhibited, a short period before her death, some singular phenomena. This lady had not been seen to smile, or to shew any indication of freedom from pain, for some weeks prior to dissolution. Two hours before she died, the symptoms became suddenly altered in character. Every sign of pain vanished; her limbs, from being subject to violent spasmodic contractions, became natural in their appearance; her face, which had been distorted, was calm and tranquil. All her friends supposed that the crisis of the disease had arrived, and that it had taken a favourable turn, and delight and joy were manifested by all who were allowed access to her chamber, and who were made acquainted with the change which had taken place. She conversed most freely, and smiled as if in a happy condition. We must confess that the case puzzled us, and that we were for a short time induced to entertain sanguine hopes of her ultimate recovery. But, alas! how fragile are all our best hopes! For two hours we sat by the bed, watching the patient's countenance with great anxiety. Every unfavourable indication had vanished; her face was illuminated by the sweetest smile that ever played on the human countenance. During the conversation we had with her, she gave a slight start, and said, in a tone of great earnestness, "Did you see that?" Her face became suddenly altered; an expression of deep anguish fixed itself upon her features, and her eyes became more than ordinarily brilliant. We replied, "What?" She answered, "Oh! you must have seen it. How terrible it looked as it glided over the bed. Again I see it," she vociferated, with an unearthly scream, "I am ready!" and, without a groan, her spirit took its flight!

Dr. Symonds recollects to have heard a young man, who had been but little conversant with any but civic scenes, discourse most eloquently, a short period before his death, of sylvan glen and bosky dells, purling streams and happy valleys, as if his spirit had been already luxuriating itself in the gardens of Elysium. Nothing more frequently prognosticates the approach of death than the appearance of a spectre at the bed-side of the patient. In some cases, the mind, when in a happy frame, dwells with delight on the contemplation of the last struggle, and has a foretaste of that heavenly joy which is the reward of a well-spent life. The spirits of good men and of angels are said to hover round the departing soul of the Christian, as if waiting to bear it to the mansions of bliss:—

> "Saw you not even now a blessed troop
> Invite me to a banquet, whose bright faces
> Cast thousand beams upon me, like the sun?
> They promised me eternal happiness;
> And brought me garlands, Griffith, which I feel
> I am not worthy yet to wear."

KING HENRY VIII.

Many have, under the notion that the fear of death is beneficial to the mind, done their best to keep the idea constantly before them.

> "If I must die, I'll snatch at anything
> That may but mind me of my latest breath;
> Death's-heads, graves, knells, blacks, tombs, all these shall bring
> Into my soul such useful thoughts of death,
> That this sable king of fears
> Shall not catch me unawares."

Young raised about him an artificial idea of death; he darkened his sepulchral study, placing a skull on his table by lamp-light. At the end of an avenue in his garden was placed on a seat an admirable chiaro-oscuro, which when approached presented only a painted surface, with an inscription, alluding to the deception of the things of this world.

Dr. J. Donne, the celebrated English divine and poet, is said to have longed for the hour of dissolution. Previous to his death, he gave instructions for a monument, which his friends had declared their intention to erect to his memory. A carver made him in wood the figure of an urn, and having secured the services of a painter, the Doctor ordered the urn to be brought into his chamber. Having taken off his clothes, he procured a white sheet, which was put on him, and tied with knots at his hands and feet. In this state he stood upon the urn, with his eyes closed, and a portion of the sheet turned aside in order to shew his lean, pale, and death-like face. In this posture, the painter sketched him; and when the monument was finished, it was placed by his bed-side, and was hourly the source of contemplation until his death.

The "lightening up before death," so often perceptible, is but the result of venous blood being sent to the brain. When respiration becomes imperfect, the blood does not undergo the proper chemical change in the lungs (arterialization), and its effect on the sentient organ is such as is occasionally witnessed prior to dissolution. Abernethy considers the sensations of the dying similar to those experienced by persons labouring under delirium. He relates the case of a man who appeared, during his delirious state, to meet with old acquaintances. The companions of his youthful days flocked once more around him—old associations were revived. "How are you, my dear fellow?" he exclaimed. "It is long since we met. Give us your fist, my hearty. Now, that is a good joke; I never heard a better. Ah! ah! ah!"

.   We had once the painful duty of watching the expiring struggles of a man whose life had been one long career of vice and debauchery. His death was truly appalling. It was evident, from the expressions which escaped him when dying, that his mind had a vivid conception of the scenes in which he had played so conspicuous a part. "Now for the dice!" he exclaimed, with the fury of a maniac. "That's mine! No! all, all is gone! More wine, d— — you; more wine! Oh! how they rattle! Fiends, fiends, assail me! I say, you cheat! the cards are marked! Now the chains rattle! O death! O death!" and with a terrific groan he breathed his last.

Among the causes which operate in producing the disposition to commit suicide, we must not omit to mention those connected with erroneous religious notions. M. Falret justly remarks, that the religious system of the Druids, Odin, and Mahomet, by inspiring a contempt for death, have made many suicides. The man who believes that death is an eternal sleep, scorns to hold up against calamity, and prefers annihilation. The sceptic also often frees himself by self-destruction from the agony of doubting. The maxim of the Stoics, that man should live only so long as he ought, not so long as he is able, is, we may observe, the very parent of suicide. The Brahmin, looking on death as the very entrance into life, and thinking a natural death dishonourable, is eager at all times to get rid of life. The Epicureans and Peripatetics ridiculed suicide, as being death caused by fear of death. M. Falret, however, goes perhaps too far when he asserts that the noble manner in which the gladiators died in public, not only familiarized the Romans with death, but rendered the thoughts of it rather agreeable than otherwise.

Misinterpretations of passages of scripture will sometimes lead those who are piously inclined to commit suicide. M. Gillet hung himself at the age of seventy-five, having left in his own handwriting the following apology:—"Jesus Christ has said, that when a tree is old and can no longer bear fruit, it is good that it should be destroyed." (He had more than once attempted his life before the fatal act.) Dr. Burrows attended a nobleman who, for fear of being poisoned, though he pretended it was in imitation of our Saviour's fast, took nothing but strawberries and water for three weeks, and these in very moderate quantities. He never voluntarily abandoned his resolution. He was at length compelled to take some nutriment, but not until inanition had gone too far; and he died completely attenuated. When sound religious principles produce a struggle in the mind which is beginning to aberrate, the contest generally ends in suicide.

Some murder themselves to get rid of the horrid thoughts of suicide; whilst others brood over them like Rousseau, for months and for years, and at length perpetrate the very action which they dread. A countryman of Rousseau's, who advocated suicide as a duty, and who spent the greater part of a long life in writing a large folio volume to prove the soundness of his doctrine, thought it his duty, after he had completed his work, to give a practical illustration of his principles, and, accordingly, at the age of seventy, threw himself into the Lake of Geneva, and was drowned.

It may appear strange that religion, the greatest blessing bestowed by Heaven on man, should ever prove a cause of one of his severest calamities. But perhaps it would be more accurate to impute such unhappy effects to fanaticism, or to the total want of religion.

Instances very frequently occur in practice in which patients have appeared, some suddenly, and others gradually, to be seized with a species of religious horror, despairing of salvation, asserting that they had committed sins which never could be forgiven, who had never previously appeared to be under religious impressions. Some of these have been visited by divines of various denominations, and been induced to hear sermons and read books well calculated to dispel gloomy apprehensions, and excite religious hope and confidence. With some this has succeeded, especially when conjoined with medical aid; but it has been observed, that in the cases of those who have recovered, the patients have *emerged* precisely as they *immerged*; for as they before were unconcerned about religious matters, so they remained after their recovery; thus the indisposition has been very erroneously imputed to religion when it has no kind of affinity to, or concern with it. Such cases almost invariably exhibit the same symptoms, which generally turn on these points—despair of temporal support, or despair of final salvation. But the medical practitioner, and not the divine, is the proper person to be consulted in such cases; and, however the mind may be affected in them, the patient is to be relieved by means of medicine. It may be added, that the agonies of mind under which some persons labour who are called fanatically mad arise from a sense of moral turpitude, independent of any peculiar religious tenets or opinions.

The true doctrines of Christianity, when properly inculcated, never excite a gloomy state of mind. "To be religious," says South, "it is not necessary to be dull." Cowper (perhaps, however, the most miserable and melancholy of men) beautifully says—

> "True piety is cheerful as the day,
> Will weep indeed, and heave a pitying groan,
> For others' woes, but smile upon her own."

CHAPTER V.

IMITATIVE, OR EPIDEMIC SUICIDE.

Persons who act from impulse liable to be influenced—Principle of imitation, a natural instinct—Cases related by Cabanis and Tissot—The suicidal barbers—Epidemic suicide at the Hôtel des Invalides—Sydenham's epidemic—The ladies of Miletus—Dr. Parrish's case—Are insanity and suicide contagious?

The most singular feature connected with the subject of suicide is, that the disposition to sacrifice life has, at different periods, been known to prevail epidemically, from a perversion, as it has been supposed, of the natural instinct of imitation. This is not only the case with reference to suicide, but is witnessed also in cases of murder. The atrocities of the French Revolution are, to a certain extent, to be traced to the influence of this imitative principle. Persons whose feelings are not thoroughly under their command, who act from impulse and not from reflection, are very prone to be operated upon by the cause referred to. Man has been defined an imitative animal; and in many instances we witness this propensity controlling almost irresistibly the actions of the individual. Tissot relates the case of a young woman in whom this faculty was so strongly developed that she could not avoid doing everything she saw others do. Cabanis gives the account of a man in whom the tendency to imitate was so strongly marked, and active, from disease, that "he experienced insupportable suffering" when he was prevented from yielding to its impulses. A woman, in the ward of an hospital, will be seized with an epileptic fit; in the course of a short period, other cases will occur in the same ward. A child was brought into one of our metropolitan hospitals, labouring under a violent attack of convulsions. She had not been in the house five minutes before three children who were present were seized with spasmodic convulsions of a similar character. The commission of a great and extraordinary crime produces not unfrequently the mania of imitation in the district in which it happened. A criminal was executed at Paris, not many years ago, for murder. A few weeks afterwards, another murder was perpetrated; and when the young man was asked to assign a reason for taking away the life of a fellow-creature, he replied, that he was not instigated by any feeling of malice, but, after having witnessed the execution, he felt a desire, over which he had no control, to commit a similar crime, and had no rest until he had gratified his feelings. It is only on the same principle that we can account for the following singular case of suicide. It is related by Sir Charles Bell, in his "Institutes of Surgery." The surgeon of the Middlesex Hospital who preceded Sir Charles Bell went into a barber's shop, in the neighbourhood of the institution, to be shaved.

As the barber was operating upon his chin, the conversation turned upon the case of a man who had been admitted the previous day into the hospital, and who had attempted, unsuccessfully, to kill himself, by cutting his throat. "He could easily have managed it," said the surgeon, in rather a jocular strain, "had he been acquainted with the situation of the carotid artery. He did not cut in the proper place." "Where should he have cut?" asked the barber, quietly. The surgeon, not suspecting what was passing through the barber's mind, gave a popular lecture on the anatomy of the neck—pointed out the exact position of the large vessels, and shewed where they could easily be wounded. After the conversation, the barber made some excuse for leaving the room; and, not returning as soon as was expected, the surgeon went to look for him, when he was discovered in the yard, behind the house, with his head nearly severed from his body!

The following case is, perhaps, more strange and inexplicable than the one just related. The brother of a hairdresser and barber had killed himself by blowing out his brains. The circumstance appeared to affect seriously the mind of his relative. He left his business for a few days; and then returned, apparently more tranquil in his mind. In the morning, several persons came in to be shaved; and, all at once, he felt a strong, and almost overwhelming, inclination to cut some one's throat. He fought manfully, however, against this horrid desire. During the whole of the earlier part of the day, he had been able to resist the gratification of the feeling. Every time he placed the razor in contact with the throat, he fancied he heard a voice within him exclaim, "Kill him! kill him!" In the afternoon, an elderly gentleman came into the shop to be shaved; and when the barber had nearly concluded the operation, he was again seized with the desire; and, before he could summon courage enough to suppress it, he gave the man's throat a tremendous gash; fortunately, however, the wound was not fatal.

Gall informs us of a man who, on reading in the newspapers the particulars of a case of murder, perpetrated under circumstances of peculiar atrocity, was instantly seized with a desire to murder his servant, and would have done so, had he not given his intended victim timely warning to escape.

Some years ago, a man hung himself on the threshold of one of the doors of the corridor at the *Hôtel des Invalides*. No suicide had occurred in the establishment for two years previously; but in the succeeding fortnight, five invalids hung themselves on the same cross bar, and the governor was obliged to shut up the passage.

Sydenham informs us that, at Mansfield, in a particular year, in the month of June, suicide prevailed to an alarming degree, from a cause wholly unaccountable. The same thing happened at Rouen, in 1806; at Stuttgard, in the summer of 1811; and at a village of St. Pierre Montjean, in the Valais, in the year 1813. One of the most remarkable epidemics of the kind was that which prevailed at Versailles in the year 1793. The number of suicides within the year was 1300—a number out of all proportion to the population of the town.

In the olden time, the ladies of Miletus, in a fit of melancholy for the absence of their husbands and lovers, resolved to hang themselves, and vied with each other in the alacrity with which they did the deed. In the time of the Ptolemies, a stoic philosopher pleaded so eloquently, one day, to an Alexandrian audience on the advantages of suicide, that he inspired his hearers with his principles, and a great number voluntarily sacrificed their lives.

A clergyman, master of a very large and popular school, the locality of which, for obvious reasons, it would not do to specify, recently informed one of his friends that he had discovered a new pupil in the act of practising a disgraceful vice. "Send him home to his parents, and say nothing about it," was the friend's judicious recommendation. The schoolmaster, however, placed great confidence in his own eloquence and the corrective powers of the birch. He assembled his boys, made an excellent harangue on the guilt of the delinquent, and gave him a sound flogging. The example of crime proved more influential than the example of punishment, and the vice spread so rapidly that the whole school was broken up in consequence.[39]

The particulars of the following case are recorded in the "American Journal of the Medical Sciences," by Dr. Parrish. He says, "I was called to visit a child in the family of J. S., a respectable gentleman residing in my neighbourhood. On my arrival, at 3 P. M., I found, on going into the chamber of my patient, that death had occurred. The patient was a girl in her fifteenth year, who had been carefully brought up by a family with whom she had lived between seven and eight years. She had generally enjoyed good health, with the exception of occasional attacks of sickness of the stomach, and headache. She had just passed the age of puberty, and possessed a docile disposition. Her situation in life, as far as could be ascertained, was in every respect agreeable, and congenial to her wishes.

"On the morning of the day of her death, she was engaged as usual in the domestic concerns of the family until eight o'clock, when she was observed in the yard vomiting. Upon inquiring into the history of the case, I found that early in the morning on which the patient died, she had held a conversation with a little girl residing in the next house, in which she mentioned having lately read in a news-paper of a man who had been unfortunate in his business, and had taken arsenic to destroy himself; she also spoke of an apothecary's shop near by, and said she frequently went there.

"The narration of this conversation afforded strong suspicion to my mind that she had committed suicide; a suspicion which was strengthened by the fact, that a few months previous I had been called upon to visit a person residing in the same house, who had suffered for some years under mental derangement, and had recently been discharged from the insane hospital near Frankford; he had taken lau-danum, with the intent of destroying himself.

"This circumstance would naturally produce a strong impression upon the mind of the child, which was increased, no doubt, by the reading of the case detailed in the newspaper. In this way the desire to commit a similar act was kindled up in the mind of the deluded girl, and thus, by that inexplicable connexion which, in some instances at least, appears to exist between the knowledge of such a horrible act and the desire to perform it, she was almost irresistibly impelled to the

---

[39] Foreign Quarterly Review, vol. xvi.

deed.

"This case is stated as affording strong testimony in favour of a principle which is now beginning to attract the attention of medical men—viz., that the publicity which is given to cases of suicide, in the newspapers and by other means, forms one of the strongest incentives to the commission of the act, in those who have a secret disposition to destroy themselves.

"If this be the fact, a high responsibility rests upon physicians, so to influence public opinion, and more especially editors, as to prevent the narration of the circumstances connected with the death of this unfortunate class. No good can certainly arise (to the public) from the exposure of facts which ought to remain concealed in the bosom of distressed families; while there is reason to believe the list of victims to suicide is annually very much swelled from the course which is now so generally pursued."[40]

It has been noticed that certain atmospherical phenomena have attended or preceded the suicidal epidemics that have prevailed at various periods. Whether these electrical conditions of the air are in any way connected with this peculiar form of contagious malady is a point not easily to be decided. A certain degree of atmospherical moisture appears to favour the spread of the suicidal disposition; but this may result from the well known influence of moist air on the disposition of the mind, and may operate by causing a degree of mental despondency and lassitude, very favourable to the development of the suicidal mania, particularly after the occurrence of any very remarkable case of self-destruction. It is notorious that nothing is so likely to unsettle the mind, especially if an hereditary disposition be present, than constantly associating with lunatics, and allowing the mind to dwell for any length of time on the subject of insanity. If actual mental derangement does not result from an exposure to the causes referred to, a certain degree of eccentricity bordering on the confines of aberration is generally perceptible. With our present amount of knowledge of the subtle principle of contagion, it is difficult to say whether an effluvium may not be generated in such cases which, under certain conditions of the system, may communicate disease. We cannot possibly say that this is not the case. If we are justified, which we by no means are willing to admit, in the opinion that the disposition to suicide and insanity may be propagated by contagion, using this term in its usual acceptation, it is a great consolation to the mind to think that only occasionally does the disease exhibit the slightest approach to virulence, and that, unlike many of the admitted contagious maladies, we may approach the patient without much fear or apprehension.

---

[40] Vol. xxi. for 1837.

CHAPTER VI.

SUICIDE FROM FASCINATION.

Singular motives for committing suicide—A man who delighted in torturing himself—A dangerous experiment—Pleasures of carnage—Disposition to leap from precipices—Lord Byron's allusion to the influence of fascination—Miss Moyes and the Monument—A man who could not trust himself with a razor—Esquirol's opinion of such cases—Danger of ascending elevated places.

How strange, extraordinary, and inexplicable are the motives which often lead to the commission of suicide! Many have been induced to rush into the arms of death in order to avoid the pain which they fancy accompanies dissolution. "*Hic, rogo, non furor est, ne moriare mori?*" Others have been apparently led to the perpetration of the crime by a desire to ascertain what sensations attended the act of dying; whilst some have been influenced by a feeling of fascination, and have stated that they experienced ecstatic delight at the idea of self-immolation.

The case of a man is recorded who felt the most exquisite delight in torturing himself. He had often expressed a wish to be hanged, from the notion that this Newgate mode of terminating life must give rise to sensations of great pleasure. The idea occurred to him one day of trying the experiment. He procured a piece of cord, attached it to the ceiling, and suspended himself from it; fortunately for the poor infatuated man, the servant entered the room a few minutes afterwards, and cut him down. Life was not extinct. The man expressed that he felt, during the few moments that he was hanging, a thrilling delight, which no language that he could use could convey anything like an adequate expression of. There was no doubt that this man laboured under an abnormal condition of the mind, which, if not amounting to insanity, certainly approached very nearly the confines of that disease.[41]

---

[41] It is related by Lord Bacon, in his "Historia Vitæ et Mortis," that a friend of his, who was particularly anxious to ascertain whether criminals suffered much pain in undergoing the sentence of the law, on one occasion suspended himself by the neck, having for that purpose thrown himself off a stool, on which he supposed he could readily remount, when he had carried his experiment sufficiently far to satisfy his curiosity. The report goes on to state, that the loss of consciousness which followed would have led to a fatal termination of the experiment, had not a friend accidentally entered the apartment in time to save the life of the adventurous experimentalist. Foderé relates a similar incident of one of his fellow-students. This young man, after an argument respecting the cause of death in hang-

A woman was admitted some years back into one of our metropolitan hospitals who had a propensity to cut her person with every sharp instrument that she could procure. It was not her intention to kill herself; and when reasoned with on the folly of her actions, she observed that she was impelled by no other motive than the fascinating pleasure she experienced whenever she succeeded in drawing blood.

A lady, a passenger on board of a ship bound for the East Indies, was frequently heard to express a wish to know what feeling a person experienced in the act of being drowned. She fancied the sensations must be of a pleasurable character. Her fellow-passengers laughed at her whenever she alluded to the matter. Having introduced the subject again during dinner, she observed, "Well, I intend to try the experiment to-morrow morning." The threat only excited the merriment of those who heard it. In the morning, whilst the passengers were on deck, the lady plunged into the sea, to the astonishment of everybody. Luckily for her, the ship was becalmed, and her life was saved.

An extraordinary young man, who lived at Paris, and who was passionately fond of mechanics, shut himself up one evening in his apartment, and bound not only his chest and stomach, but also his arms, legs, and thighs, with ropes full of knots, the ends of which he fastened to hooks in the wall. After having passed a considerable part of the night in this situation, he wished to disengage himself, but attempted it in vain. Some neighbouring females, who were up, heard his cries, and, calling for assistance, they forced open the door of his room, when they found him swinging in the air, with only one arm extricated. He was immediately carried to the lieutenant-general of the police for examination, when he declared that he had often put similar trials into execution, as he experienced *indescribable pleasure in them*. He confessed that at first he felt pain, but that after the cords became tight to a certain degree, he was soon rewarded by the most exquisite sensations of pleasure.[42]

"As the chill dews of evening were surrounding our bivouac," says the author of the "Recollections of the Peninsula," "a staff officer, with a courier, came galloping into it, and alighted at the quarters of our general. It was soon known amongst us that a severe and sanguinary action had been fought by our brother soldiers at Talavera. Disjointed rumours spoke of a dear-bought field, a heavy loss, and a subsequent retreat. I well remember how we all gathered round our fires to listen, to conjecture, and to talk about this glorious, but bloody event. We regretted that we had borne no share in the honours of such a day; and *we talked with an*

ing, resolved personally to gratify his curiosity, by passing a ligature round his neck, and attaching it to a hook behind the door. To accomplish this, he had raised himself on tip-toe, and now gradually brought his heels to the ground. He soon lost all consciousness, but was cut down by a companion, who discovered him, in a state of insensibility, very soon after the commencement of the experiment, and by the prompt application of remedial measures he was finally recovered. From cases of this description we learn that the first effect experienced in hanging is the appearance of a dazzling light before the eyes, accompanied by tingling in the ears. These sensations are, however, momentary, for insensibility and death rapidly close the scene.

[42] Gazette Litteraire.

undefined pleasure about the carnage. Yes! strange as it may appear, soldiers, and not they alone, talk of the danger of battle fields with a sensation which partakes of pleasure."

A watchmaker of Aberdeen, who had been looking over the precipices of Loch-na-Gair, suddenly felt a desire to precipitate himself from the height, and having first taken a step or two back for the purpose, he flung himself off.

A gentleman travelling through Switzerland, with his wife, came to an eminence commanding an extensive and beautiful view of the surrounding country. He went, accompanied by his wife, to the edge of a mountainous cliff, and, turning round to his lady, he observed—"I have lived long enough!" and in a moment threw himself down the precipice.

It was a notion of this kind which induced Lord Byron to observe that he believed no man ever took a razor into his hand who did not at the same time think how easily he might sever the silver cord of life. The noble poet evidently alludes, in the following stanzas, to the strange and unaccountable influence of fascination in exciting the mind to commit suicide:—

> "A sleep without dreams, after a rough day
> Of toil, is what we covet most, and yet
> How clay shrinks back from more quiescent clay!
> The very suicide that pays his debts
> At once, without instalments, (an old way
> Of paying debts, which creditors regret,)
> Lets out impatiently his rushing breath,
> Less from disgust of life than dread of death.
>
> 'Tis round him, near him, there, everywhere;
> And there's a courage which grows out of fear,
> Perhaps of all most desperate, which will dare
> The *worst* to know it:—when the mountains rear
> Their peaks beneath your human foot, and there
> You look down o'er the precipice, and drear
> The gulf of rock yawns,—you can't gaze a minute
> Without an awful wish to plunge within it!
>
> 'Tis true, you don't—but, pale and struck with terror,
> Retire: but look into your past impression!
> And you will find, though shuddering at the mirror
> Of your own thoughts, in all their self-confession,
> The lurking bias, be it truth or error,
> To the *unknown*; a secret prepossession,
> To plunge with all your fears—but where? You know not,
> And that's the reason why you do—or do not."

A gentleman with whom we are acquainted, informed us that, a few days after Miss Moyes had thrown herself from the Monument, a friend of his had the curiosity to visit the spot, and on looking down the awful height from which this poor unfortunate girl had precipitated herself, he felt suddenly an attack of giddiness, which was succeeded in a moment by one of the most pleasurable sensations he had ever experienced, accompanied with a desire to jump off. He was not influenced, apparently, by any other motive than that of a wish to gratify a feeling of ecstasy which for a minute suspended all the operations of the mind. A gentleman who was by him asked him a question with reference to the height of the Monument, and this circumstance recalling him to the exercise of his reasoning faculties, he immediately left the spot, shuddering at the recollection of the idea which had momentarily flashed across his mind.

The case is related of a man who had this feeling so strongly manifested that he never dared trust himself with a razor. He was not devoid of religious feeling, and was most happy in his domestic relations. On occasions which required the exercise of moral resolution, he was never found wanting. He declared his life would not be safe for a day if he were permitted to shave himself. Such instances are by no means uncommon, and require much ingenuity to account satisfactorily for them, unless they be referred to the effect of fascination.

Andral observes, "that there are many men perfectly rational, and completely undisturbed by care or pain, who, singular to state, have been suddenly seized by a headlong, groundless inclination to destroy themselves. There are hundreds who cannot approach the brink of a cliff, or ascend a lofty tower, without experiencing an almost invincible desire to precipitate themselves to the bottom, from which fate they only save themselves by an instantaneous effort to retire from the temptation. I knew a gentleman who, while shaving himself one day, alone, was three times so vehemently urged to plunge the razor into his throat, that he was at length compelled to throw the instrument from him, in absolute horror and dismay. In rational men, however, these trying and dangerous moments are but of very short duration."

A sailor informed us that he had often, when at the top of the mast, felt disposed to precipitate himself from the giddy eminence, influenced by no other motive than that of pleasure.

In such cases, what course is the medical man to pursue? It is difficult to give any instructions for the treatment of such cases of mental idiosyncrasy. Persons who are subject to feelings of this character should be advised to avoid ascending elevated places.

CHAPTER VII.

OF THE ENTHUSIASM AND MENTAL IRRITABILITY WHICH, IF ENCOURAGED, WOULD LEAD TO SUICIDE.

Connexion between genius and insanity—Authors of fiction often feel what they write—Metastasio in tears—The enthusiasm of Pope, Alfieri, Dryden—Effects of the first reading of Telemachus and Tasso on Madame Roland's mind—Raffaelle and his celebrated picture of the Transfiguration—The convulsions of Malbranche—Beattie's Essay on Truth—Influence of intense study on Boerrhave's mind—The demon of Spinello and Luther—Bourdaloue and his violin—Byron's sensitiveness—Men do not always practise what they preach—Cases of Smollett, La Fontaine, Sir Thomas More, Zimmerman—Tasso's spectre—Johnson's superstition—Concluding remarks.

It has been observed that the act of suicide may often originate in a feeling analogous to the enthusiasm exhibited by men of great genius and sensibility. This mental idiosyncrasy, which borders so closely on the confines of insanity, has been compared to the narrow bridge of Al Sirat, which leads the followers of Mahomet from earth to heaven, but by so narrow a path that the passenger is in momentary danger of falling into the dismal gulf which yawns beneath him. This abnormal condition of the nervous system is, to a certain extent, dependent on natural organic structure, aided materially by an unhealthy exercise of the imaginative faculty. Fielding spoke but the history of his own sensations when he declared that he "had no doubt but the most pathetic scenes had been writ with tears." Metastasio was found weeping over his Olympiad. He says: "When I apply with attention, the nerves of my sensorium are put into a violent tumult; I grow as red as a drunkard, and am obliged to quit my work." Pope could not proceed with certain passages of his translation of Homer without shedding tears. Alfieri declares that he frequently penned the most tender passages in his plays "under a paroxysm of enthusiasm, and whilst shedding tears." Dryden was seized with violent tremors during the composition of his celebrated ode. Rousseau, in conceiving the first idea of his Essay on the Arts, became almost delirious with enthusiasm.

Madame Roland has thus powerfully described the ideal presence in her first readings of Telemachus and Tasso:—"My respiration rose, I felt a rapid fire colouring my face, and my voice changing had betrayed my agitation. I was Eucharis for

Telemachus, and Emenia for Tancred. Having my reason during this perfect transformation, I did not yet think that I myself was anything for any one: the whole had no connexion with myself. I sought for nothing around me; I was they; I saw only the objects which existed for them; it was a dream without being awakened."

Raffaelle says, alluding to his celebrated picture, the Transfiguration—"When I have stood looking at that picture, from figure to figure, the eagerness, the spirit, the close unaffected attention of each figure to the principal action, my thoughts have carried me away, that I have forgot myself, and for that time might be looked upon as an enthusiastic madman; for I could really fancy the whole action was passing before my eyes."

Malbranche was seized with violent palpitations of the heart when reading Descartes's Treatise on Man:—

> "With curious art, the brain too finely wrought
> Preys on itself, and is destroyed by thought;
> Constant attention wears the active mind,
> Blots out her powers, and leaves a blank behind."

Intense occupation of mind to any particular branch of study, often brings the mind on the verge of madness. "Since the 'Essay on Truth' was printed in quarto," says Dr. Beattie, "I have never *dared* to read it over. I durst not even read the sheets to see whether there were any errors in the print, and was obliged to get a friend to do that office for me. These studies came, in time, to have dreadful effects upon my nervous system; and I cannot read what I then wrote without some degree of horror, because it recalls to my mind the horrors that I have sometimes felt after passing a long evening in these severe studies."

Boerrhave has related of himself that, having imprudently indulged in intense thought on a particular subject, he did not close his eyes for six weeks afterwards.

Spinello, having painted the fall of the rebellious angels, had so strongly imagined the illusion, and more particularly the terrible features of Lucifer, that he was himself struck with such horror as to have been long afflicted with the presence of the demon to which his genius had given birth. Swedenburg saw a terrestrial heaven in the glittering streets of his New Jerusalem.

Malbranche declared he heard the voice of God distinctly within him. Pascal often was seen to rush suddenly from his chair at the appearance of a fiery gulf by his side. Luther maintained that during his confinement the devil used to visit him.

Hudibras says—

> "Did not the devil appear to Martin
> Luther, in Germany, for certain?"

He declares that he had many a contest with his satanic majesty, and that he had always the best of the argument. At one time, the devil so enraged Luther that he threw the ink-stand at him, an action which the German commentators greatly applaud, from a conviction that there is nothing which the devil abhors more than ink.

Descartes, after long confinement, was followed by an invisible person, calling upon him to pursue the search of truth.

Mozart's sensibility to music was connected with so susceptible a nervous system that, in his childhood, the sound of a trumpet would turn him pale, and almost induce convulsions. Dr. Conolly relates an amusing anecdote of the celebrated Bourdaloue. It is said that the composition of his eloquent sermons so excited his mind that he was unable to deliver them until he discovered some mode of allaying his excitement. "His attendants one day were both scandalized and alarmed, on proceeding to his apartment, for the purpose of accompanying him to the cathedral, by hearing the sound of a fiddle, on which was played a very lively tune. After their first consternation, they ventured to look through the keyhole, and were still more shocked to behold the great divine dancing about, without his gown and canonicals, to his own inspiring music. Of course, they concluded him to be mad. But, when they knocked, the music ceased; and after a short and anxious interval, he met them with a composed dress and manner; and, observing some signs of astonishment in the party, explained to them that without his music and his exercise he should have been unable to undertake the duties of the day."

In the character of Lord Byron we have an apt illustration of the kind of mental irritability and morbid sensitiveness of feeling that so often incites to acts of desperation. It has been said that the noble poet was the child of passion, born in bitterness and "nurtured in convulsion." The true state of his mind can best be divined from the delineation of his own sensations as given in Childe Harold:—

> "I have thought
> Too long and darkly, till my brain became
> In its own eddy boiling, and orwrought
> A whirling gulf of phantasy and flame:
> And thus untaught in youth my heart to tame,
> My springs of life were poisoned."

Byron was subject to attacks of epilepsy; and perhaps this fact may account for much of the spleen and irritability which he manifested through life, and which made him so many enemies. It also teaches us an important lesson. We are too apt to form our estimate of character without taking into consideration all those circumstances which are known materially to influence human thought and actions. The state of the organization and the health ought to be maturely weighed before we pronounce authoritatively as to the motives of individuals, or denounce them for not acting or thinking according to what our preconceived opinions have taught us to consider as orthodox. Byron's mind was morbidly alive to impressions. The most trifling circumstance would cause him to swoon. At Bologna, in 1819, he describes one of his convulsive attacks:—"Last night I went to the representation of Alfieri's Myrrha, the last two acts of which threw me into convulsions; I don't mean by that word lady's hysterics, but an agony of reluctant tears, and the choking shudder which I do not often undergo for fiction." He was seized in a similar manner at seeing Kean in Sir Giles Overreach; he was carried out of the theatre in convulsions. From early life, Byron exhibited this abnormal excitability. There can be no doubt that it was but the natural effect of a peculiar condition of nervous function; but, instead of endeavouring to subdue the feeling, he did his best to encourage it, and to fan the fire into a flame. He appears to have been tortured by horrid dreams. He says in his Journal—"I awoke from a dream: well, have not others dreamed? Such a dream! But she did not overtake me! I wish the dead would rest for ever. Ugh! how my blood is chilled! I do not like this dream; I hate its foregone conclusion."

The "Bride of Abydos" was written to distract the poet's mind from his dreams. He was in such a nervous state at this period, that he says if he had not done something, he must have gone mad, or have eat his own heart.

Stendhal, alluding to Byron's apparent remorse, asks, "Is it not possible that Byron might have had some guilty stain on his conscience, similar to that which wrecked Othello's fame? Can it be, have we sometimes exclaimed, that, in a frenzy of pride or jealousy, he had shortened the days of some fair Grecian slave, faithless to her vows?"[43]

It is not just to form our opinions of the character of men by their writings or actions. In the mass, we are ready to admit that we have no other criteria by which to be guided; but we may charitably consider that Byron was not himself the "dark original he drew."

> "O memory! torture me no more:
> The present's all o'ercast—
> My hopes of future bliss are o'er;
> In mercy, veil the past."

Such were his feelings at the age of seventeen.

La Fontaine penned tales fertile in intrigues, and yet he was never known, says D'Israeli, to have been engaged in a single amour. Smollett was anything but what his writings would lead us to expect. Cowley boasted of his mistresses, and wanted the courage to address one. Burton declaimed against melancholy, and yet he was the most miserable of men. Sir Thomas More preached in favour of toleration, yet in practice was a fierce persecutor. Zimmerman, whilst he was inculcating beautiful lessons of benevolence, was by his tyranny driving his son into madness, and leaving his daughter an outcast from home. Goëthe says, "Zimmerman's harshness towards his children was the effect of hypochondria, a sort of madness or moral assassination, to which he himself fell a victim after sacrificing his offspring."

Byron occasionally fancied he was visited by a spectre, which he confesses was but the effect of an overstimulated brain.

Tasso, whose fine imagination the passions of hopeless love, and of grief occasioned by ill treatment, disordered, was in daily communication with a spirit. This circumstance is alluded to in the following anecdote of him, prefixed to Hoole's translation of his *La Gierusalemme Liberata.*"

"In this place (at Bisaccio, near Naples) Manso had an opportunity of examining the singular effects of Tasso's melancholy, and often disputed with him con-

[43] Foreign Literary Gazette.

cerning a familiar spirit, with which he pretended to converse. Manso endeavoured in vain to persuade his friend that the whole was the illusion of a disturbed imagination; but the latter was strenuous in maintaining the reality of what he asserted; and to convince Manso, desired him to be present at one of these mysterious conversations. Manso had the complaisance to meet him next day; and while they were engaged in discourse, on a sudden he observed that Tasso kept his eyes fixed upon a window, and remained in a manner immovable. He called him by his name several times, but received no answer. At last Tasso cried out, 'There is the friendly spirit, who is come to converse with me. Look, and you will be convinced of the truth of all that I have said.' Manso heard him with surprise; he looked, but saw nothing except the sunbeams darting through the window: he cast his eyes all over the room, but could perceive nothing, and was just going to ask where the pretended spirit was, when he heard Tasso speak with great earnestness, sometimes putting questions to the spirit, and sometimes giving answers, delivering the whole in such a pleasing manner, and with such elevated expressions, that he listened with admiration, and had not the least inclination to interrupt him. At last the uncommon conversation ended with the departure of the spirit, as appeared by Tasso's words, who, turning to Manso, asked him if his doubts were removed? Manso was more amazed than ever; he scarce knew what to think of his friend's situation, and waved any further conversation on the subject."

Boswell says, Dr. Johnson mentioned a thing as not unfrequent, of which he (Boswell) had never heard before,—being called, that is, hearing one's name pronounced, by the voice of a known person at a great distance, far beyond the possibility of being reached by any sound, uttered by human organs. An acquaintance, on whose veracity Boswell says he could place every dependence, told him that, walking home one evening to Kilmarnock, he heard himself called from a wood, by the voice of a brother who had gone to America, and the next packet brought the account of that brother's death. Macbean asserted that this inexplicable *calling* was a thing very well known. Dr. Johnson said, that one day at Oxford, as he was turning the key of his chambers, he heard distinctly his mother call *Sam!* She was then at Lichfield; but nothing ensued.

Sir Joshua Reynolds gives an amusing instance of Dr. Johnson's eccentricity. He says, "When he and I took a journey into the west, we visited the late Mr. Banks, of Dorsetshire. The conversation turning upon pictures, which Johnson could not well see, he retired to a corner of the room, stretching out his right leg as far as he could reach before him, then bringing up his left leg, and stretching his right still further on. The old gentleman observing him, went up to him, and in a very courteous manner assured him that, though it was not a new house, the flooring was perfectly safe. The Doctor started from his reverie, like a person waked out of a sleep, but spoke not a word."

Dr. Johnson had one peculiarity, says Boswell, of which none of his friends dared to ask an explanation. This was an anxious care to go out or in at a door or passage by a certain number of steps from a certain point, so that either his right or left foot should constantly make the first actual movement. Thus, upon innumerable occasions, Boswell has seen him suddenly stop, and then seem to count his steps with deep earnestness; and when he had neglected, or gone wrong in this sort of magical movement, he has been noticed to go back again, put himself in a proper posture to recommence the ceremony, and having gone through it, break from his abstraction, briskly walk on, and join his companions.

An inordinate cultivation of any one faculty of the mind, but more particularly the imagination, will tend to produce the peculiarities which have been illustrated in this chapter. A person who accustoms himself to live in a world created by his own fancy—who surrounds himself with flimsy idealities—will, in the course of time, cease to sympathize with the gross realities of life. The imaginary intelligences which his own morbid mind has called into existence will exercise a terrific influence over him. A German poet commenced writing a poem on the Deity. He allowed his mind to dwell so intensely on the subject, that he fancied he was commanded to "flee from a world of sin and iniquity;" to effect which, he cut his throat, and was found dead in bed, with the razor in one hand and a portion of his poem in the other. The apparitions which the monomaniac fancies to haunt him are as real and sensible existences to him, as objects are to persons who have a healthy use of the media through which ideas obtain access to the mind. Mr. Calcraft, the late member of parliament, committed suicide. He imagined that a strange unearthly-looking being sat night and day perched at the top of his bed, watching with earnestness his every movement. This, which to all around him was an hallucination, to him *was* a reality. It is possible for a person of vivid imagination to conjure into apparent existence the most grotesque images of the fancy, by allowing the mind to dwell with intenseness on a particular train of thought, and by perfectly abstracting the attention from all materiality.

CHAPTER VIII.

PHYSICAL CAUSES OF SUICIDE.

Influence of climate—The foggy climate of England does not increase the number of suicides—Average number of suicides in each month, from 1817 to 1826—Influence of seasons—Suicides at Rouen—The English not a suicidal people—Philip Mordaunt's singular reasons for self-destruction—Causes of French suicides—Influence of physical pain—Unnatural vices—Suicide the effect of intoxication—Influence of hepatic disease on the mind—Melancholy and hypochondriasis, Burton's account of—Cowper's case of suicide—Particulars of his extreme depression of spirits—Byron and Burns's melancholy from stomach and liver derangement—Influence of bodily disease on the mind—Importance of paying attention to it—A case of insanity from gastric irritation—Dr. Johnson's hypochondria—Hereditary suicide, illustrated by cases—Suicide from blows on the head, and from moral shocks communicated to the brain—Dr. G. Mantell's valuable observations and cases demonstrative of the point—Concluding remarks.

THE following are the physical causes which are commonly found to operate in producing the suicidal disposition—viz., climate, seasons, hereditary predisposition, cerebral injuries, physical suffering, disease of the stomach and liver complicated with melancholia and hypochondriasis, insanity, suppressed secretions, intoxication, unnatural vices, and derangement of the *primæ viæ*. These causes can only act by influencing sympathetically the brain and nervous system, and in that way interfering with the healthy operations of the mind. Much will, of course, depend upon the physical conformation of the individual exposed to such agents. Should he labour under an hereditary predisposition to insanity, or to suicidal delirium, a very trifling corporeal derangement may call into existence the self-destructive propensity, and *vice versa*. It will be our object to consider *seriatim* all the physical agents just enumerated.

Among the causes of suicide, the foggy climate of England has been brought prominently forward. The specious and inaccurate conclusions of Montesquieu on this point have misled the public mind. The climate of Holland is much more gloomy than that of England, and yet in that country suicide is by no means common. The reader will perceive from the following tabular statement that the popular notion of the month of November being the "suicide's month" is founded on erroneous *data.*

The average number of suicides in each month, from 1817 to 1826, was as follows:—

January	213
February	218
March	275
April	374
May	328
June	336
July	301
August	296
September	246
October	198
November	131
December	217
	— —
	3133

It has been clearly established that in all the European capitals, when anything approaching to correct statistical evidence can be procured, the *maximum* of suicide is in the months of June and July; the *minimum* in October and November. Temperature appears to exercise a much more decided influence than the circumstances of moisture and dryness, storms or serenity. M. Villeneuve has observed a warm, humid, and cloudy atmosphere to produce a marked bad effect at Paris; and that so long as the barometer indicated stormy weather, this effect continued.[44] Contrary, however, to the opinion of Villeneuve, it appears that by far the fewer number of suicides occur in the autumn and winter at Paris, than in the spring and summer.

Number of suicides for seven years.

In Spring	997
In Summer	933
In Autumn	627
In Winter	648

When the thermometer of Fahrenheit ranges from 80° to 90° suicide is most prevalent.

[44] In 1806, upwards of sixty voluntary deaths took place at Rouen, during June and July, the air being at that time remarkably humid and warm; and in July and August of the same year, more than three hundred were committed at Copenhagen, the constitution of the atmosphere presenting the same characteristics as it did at Rouen. The year 1793, presented in the town of Versailles alone the horrible spectacle of thirteen hundred suicides.

The English have been accused by foreigners of being the *beau-ideal* of a suicidal people. The charge is almost too ridiculous to merit serious refutation. It has clearly been established that where there is one suicide in London, there are five in Paris. In the year 1810, the number of suicides committed in London amounted to 188; the population of Paris being near 400,000 less than that of London. From the year 1827 to 1830, no less than 6900 suicides occurred; that is, an average of nearly 1800 per annum. Out of 120,000 persons who ensured their lives in the London Equitable Insurance Company, the number of suicides in twenty years was only fifteen; so much for the English being *par excellence* disposed to suicide.

The causes which frequently lead to self-destruction in France are, defective religious education, *ennui*, and loss at dice or cards. In considering the circumstances which produce this disparity in the number of voluntary deaths in the two countries, we must bear in mind the moral and religious habits of the people. When Christianity is not acknowledged as a matter of vital importance in the affairs of man; when morality is considered only as a conventional term, conveying no definite idea to the mind, it is natural that there should exist, co-relative with this tone of feeling, a marked recklessness of human life. Some notion may be formed of the state of religious feeling in Paris, when our readers are informed of the existence in the French metropolis of a "society for the mutual encouragement of suicide," all the members of which, on joining it, swear to terminate their existence by their own hands, when life becomes insupportable.

Dr. Schlegel dwells at much length on the abandoned state of Paris, and after giving us some important statistical evidence, he alludes to the gross immorality of the people, and denounces the French capital as "a suffocating boiling cauldron, in which, as in the stew of Macbeth's witches, there simmer, with a modicum of virtue, all kinds of passions, vices, and crimes."

Alluding to the peculiarities of the French people, particularly their indifference to human life, an eminent writer observes, speaking of their notions of suicide, that a Frenchman asks you to see him "go off," as if death were a place in the *malle poste*. "Will you dine with me to-day?" said a Frenchman to a friend. "With the greatest pleasure;—yet, now I think of it, I am particularly engaged to shoot myself; one cannot get off *such* an engagement." This is not the suicide *à la mode* with us. We ape at no such extra civilization and refinement. We can be romantic without blowing out our brains. English lovers do not, when "the course of true love" does not run smooth, retire to some sequestered spot, and rush into the next world by a brace of pistols tied with cherry-coloured ribbons. When we do shoot ourselves, it is done with true English gravity. It is no joke with us. We have no inherent predilection for the act; no "hereditary imperfection of the nervous juices," as Montesquieu, with all the impudence and gravity of a philosopher, asserts, forcing us to commit suicide. "Life," said a man who had exhausted all his external sources of enjoyment, and had no internal ones to fly to, "has given me a headache; and I want a good sleep in the churchyard to set me to rights," to procure which, he deliberately shot himself.[45]

____

[45] This was Philip Mordaunt, cousin-german to the celebrated Earl of Peterborough, so well known to all European courts, and who boasted of having seen more postillions and

A late French writer thus attempts to account for the prevalence of suicide in France:—"The external circumstances which tend to suggest the idea of suicide are very numerous, at the present day, in France; but more particularly so in the capital. The high development of civilization and refinement which prevails here—the clash of interests—the repeated political changes—all contribute to keep the moral feelings in a perpetual state of tension. Life does not roll on among us in a peaceful and steady current; it rushes forward with the force and precipitation of a torrent. In the terrible *mêlée*, it often happens that the little minority, which has obtained a footing high above the multitude for a time, falls down as suddenly as they have risen. The struggles of life are full of miscalculations, disappointments, despair, and disgust. Hence the general source of our frequent suicides. But there are other causes in operation; and not the least, the strange turn that plays and spectacles have lately taken. The public taste has undergone a complete revolution in this respect. Nothing is more patronized now at the theatre than the display of crime unpunished, human misery unconsoled, and a low literature, impregnated by a spurious philosophy, declaiming against society, against domestic life, against virtue itself; applauding the vengeance of the assassin, and recognising genius only as it is seen in company with spleen, poison, and pistols. We appeal to all who read the novels of the present day, and who visit the theatres, whether what we say is not the fact."

It has been questioned whether physical suffering often originates the desire for suicide. Too many lamentable cases are on record to prevent us from coming to an opposite conclusion. Esquirol has justly observed, that "He who has no intervals of ease from corporeal pain; who sees no prospects of relief from his cruel malady, fails at length in resignation, and destroys his life in order to put a period to his sufferings. He calculates that the pain of dying is but momentary, and commits the act in a cool and meditated despair. It is the same in respect to *moral* condition, that drives the hypochondriac to suicide, who is firmly persuaded that his sufferings are beyond imagining; that they are irremediable, either from some fatal peculiarity in his own constitution, or the ignorance of his physicians. It is a remarkable feature in hypochondriasis, and in no other disease, that there is such a fear of death and a desire to die combined. Both fears proceed from the same pusillanimity. Finally, it may be remarked that the hypochondriac talks most of death; often wishes his attendants to perform the friendly office; even makes attempts on his own life, but rarely accomplishes the act. The most trifling motive, the most frivolous pretext, is a sufficient excuse for procrastinating, from day to day, the threatened catastrophe."

The following case occurred in a provincial mad-house, in France. An apothecary who was confined there was haunted with *ennui*, and was always begging his companions to put him to death. At length, an insane patient was admitted,

kings than any other man. Mordaunt was young, handsome, of noble blood, highly educated, and beloved by those who knew him. He resolved to die. Preparatory to his doing so, he wrote to his friends, paid his debts, and even made some verses on the occasion. He said his soul was tired of his body, and when we are dissatisfied with our abode, it is our duty to quit it. He put a pistol to his head and blew out his brains. An uninterrupted course of good fortune was the only motive that could be assigned for this suicide.

who instantly complied with the apothecary's request. They both watched an opportunity, got out of a window in the back yard, and from thence into the kitchen. They pitched upon the cook's chopper, and the apothecary laying his head on a block, his companion deliberately and effectually severed it from his body. He was seized, and examined before a tribunal, where he candidly confessed the whole transaction, and observed that he would again perform the same friendly office for any unhappy wretch who was tired of his existence![46]

Lucinius Cæcinius, the prætor, subdued by the pain and *ennui* of a tedious disease, swallowed opium. Dr. Haslam relates the case of a gentleman who destroyed himself to avoid the tortures of the gout. It is recorded that the pain of the same disease drove Servius the grammarian to take poison. Pliny informs us that one of his friends, Corellius Rufus, having in vain sought relief from the pangs of a disease under which he was labouring, starved himself to death at the age of sixty-seven. It is related of Pomponius Atticus and the philosopher Cleanthes, that they both starved themselves to death in order to get rid of physical pain. In the course of these attempts, the corporeal sufferings were removed — probably in consequence of the great exhaustion and attenuation; but both individuals persevered till death took place, observing that as this final ordeal must one day be undergone, they would not now retrace their steps or give up the undertaking.

Few, perhaps, are aware how frequently suicide results from the habit of indulging, in early youth, in a certain secret vice which, we are afraid, is practised to an enormous extent in our public schools. A feeling of false delicacy has operated with medical men in inducing them to refrain from dwelling upon the destructive consequences of this habit, both to the moral and physical constitution, as openly and honestly as the importance of the subject imperatively demands.

Medical men are, in the most enlarged acceptation of the term, guardians of the public health; and no fastidious desire to avoid saying what might possibly offend the taste of some, ought to keep them from discharging what may be termed a sacred duty. The physical disease, particularly that connected with the nervous system, engendered by the pernicious practice alluded to, frequently leads to the act of self-destruction. We have before us the cases of many suicides in whom the disposition may clearly be traced to this cause. This habit most seriously affects the brain and nervous system; and insanity, hypochondriasis, and melancholia, in their worst forms, are frequently the baneful consequences.

If disease, structural or functional, of the abdominal viscera gives rise to the disposition to commit suicide, it will not require much ingenuity to establish the fact that the habitual indulgence in intoxicating liquors may originate a similar feeling.

It has been already established by statistical evidence, that, in a very large proportion of the cases of insanity admitted into the asylums and hospitals devoted to the reception of this unhappy class of patients, the mental impairment can clearly be traced to habits of intemperance.

The brain and nervous system become materially affected in those who in-

---

[46] M. Falret.

dulge frequently in "potations pottle deep." Delirium tremens, softening of the cerebral substance, palsy, epilepsy, extreme hypochondriasis, are daily witnessed as the melancholy effects of intoxication.

M. Falret knew the case of a man who always felt disposed to cut his throat when under the influence of spirits. No reasoning could induce him to abstain from his favourite draught. The inevitable consequences were pointed out to him; he was reasoned with, and threatened with confinement in a mad-house; but nothing had the desired effect. One Sunday evening, after having drunk several glasses of spirits, although not sufficient to produce complete inebriation, he stabbed himself to the heart, and died in a few minutes.

Incurable indigestion and organic disease of the liver are very commonly met with in habitual drunkards. In such persons, the constitution of the mind appears to undergo a complete change. At first it may not be perceptible, and the patient may not be conscious of it himself, but the mental disease will, sooner or later, unequivocally evince itself.

In such cases, the medical man has fearful odds to contend against.

A young man, who had become insane in consequence of long continued intoxication, made violent efforts to maim himself, and especially to pull out his right eye, which appeared to give him great offence. Rest, temperance, seclusion, the application of half a dozen leeches to the temple, and a few doses of opening medicine, restored him, in about a fortnight, to the full possession of his faculties.

Many cases of suicide, in those who have a natural predisposition to it, arise from the brain sympathizing with the liver; nor can this be a matter of surprise to any one who has felt the depression of spirits incident to disease of that organ. So many cases have occurred from this cause, that some writers, from not finding, on subsequent dissection, any organic lesion of the brain, have referred it to diseased viscera only. But as we find that the insanity ceases when the liver is restored to health, there is no reason for supposing that the mental alienation is, in these instances, any other than the effect of disease of the brain.

J. C., about fifty years of age, was insane for two years. He was formerly in respectable circumstances, and employed in the situation of writer in an office. He made several attempts on his life. He had been in the habit of drinking spirits very freely, and had a disease of the liver which appeared of some standing. At the time of his admission into Hanwell asylum, under the care of Sir W. Ellis, he was in a most emaciated state; his legs scarcely able to support him. His face and body also were covered with an eruption; tongue furred; his stools very dark: he was much depressed, and always moaning most piteously; complained of heat and numbness in his head, and pain in all his limbs. Leeches and cold lotions were applied to his head, his bowels opened by calomel and colocynth, and he went into the warm bath every other day. He was much relieved by these means. He still continued, however, to moan as before. His tongue remained furred, and stools unhealthy. He took five grains of blue pill every alternate night for some time. These were then left off awhile; no improvement taking place, he began the pills again, and continued them for two months, with evident advantage. His tongue was clean;

he was less depressed; became strong, and gained flesh; the biliary secretions were much improved. He is now occupied in the office; and every day, as the action of the liver seems to improve, his mind makes a corresponding advance.

There is no more frequent cause of suicide than visceral derangement, leading to melancholia and hypochondriasis. It has been a matter of dispute with medical men whether hypochondriacal affections have their origin in the mental or physical portion of the economy. Many maintain that the mind is the seat of the disease; others, that the liver and stomach are primarily affected, and the brain only secondarily. In this disputed point, as in most others, truth will generally be found to lie between the two extremities. That cases of hypochondria and melancholia can clearly be traced to purely mental irritation cannot for one moment be disputed; and that there are many instances in which the derangement appears to have commenced in one of the gastric organs, is as equally self-evident. Whatever may be the origin of these affections, there can be no doubt of their producing most disastrous consequences. Burton's account of the horrors of hypochondria is truly graphic. "As the rain," says Austin, "penetrates the stone, so does this passion of melancholy penetrate the mind. It commonly accompanies men to their graves. Physicians may ease, but they cannot cure it; it may lie hid for a time, but it will return again, as violent as ever, on slight occasions, as well as on casual excesses. Its humour is like Mercury's weather-beaten statue, which had once been gilt; the surface was clean and uniform, but in the chinks there was still a remnant of gold: and in the purest bodies, if once tainted by hypochondria, there will be some relics of melancholy still left, not so easily to be rooted out. Seldom does this disease produce death, except (which is the most grievous calamity of all) when these patients make away with themselves—a thing familiar enough amongst them, when they are driven to do violence to themselves to escape from present insufferable pain. They can take no rest in the night, or, if they slumber, fearful dreams astonish them. Their soul abhorreth all meat, and they are brought to death's door, being bound in misery and in iron. Like Job, they curse their stars, for Job was melancholy to despair, and almost to madness. They are weary of the sun, and yet afraid to die, *vivere nolunt et mori nesciunt*. And then, like Æsop's fishes, they leap from the frying pan into the fire, when they hope to be cured by means of physic—a miserable end to the disease; when ultimately left to their fate by a jury of physicians, are furiously disposed; and there remains no more to such persons, if that heavenly physician, by his grace and mercy, (whose aid alone avails,) do not heal and help them. One day of such grief as theirs is as a hundred years: it is a plague of the sense, a convulsion of the soul, an epitome of hell; and if there be a hell upon earth, it is to be found in a melancholy man's heart. No bodily torture is like unto it; all other griefs are swallowed up in this great Euripus. I say the melancholy man then is the cream and quintessence of human adversity. All other diseases are trifles to hypochondria; it is the pith and marrow of them all! A melancholy man is the true Prometheus, bound to Caucasus; the true Tityrus, whose bowels are still devoured by a vulture."

"Dull melancholy— —
She'll make you start at ev'ry noise you hear,

> And visions strange shall to your eyes appear.
> Her voice is low, and gives a hollow sound;
> She hates the light, and is in darkness found;
> Or sits by blinking lamps, or taper small,
> Which various shadows make against the wall.
> She loves nought else but noise which discord makes,
> As croaking frogs whose dwelling is in lakes;
> The raven hoarse, the mandrake's hollow groan,
> And shrieking owls, that fly i'th' night alone;
> The tolling bell, which for the dead rings out,
> A mill, where rushing waters run about.
> She loves to walk in the still moonshine light,
> And in a thick dark grove she takes delight;
> In hollow caves, thatch'd houses, and low cells,
> She loves to live, and there alone she dwells."

"There are individuals who, from various physical or moral causes," says Esquirol, "fall into a state of corporeal torpor and mental depression. They complain of want of appetite, dull pain in the head, sense of heat in the stomach and viscera, borborygmi, and constipation of the bowels; while they exhibit little or no indication of disease. In the female sex, the natural secretions become suspended. As the complaint advances, the features alter, and the countenance exhibits anxiety; the complexion becomes pale or sallow; there is a sense of tightness, or even pain, in the epigastrium; a kind of compression in the head, which prevents them from fixing their attention, or arranging their thoughts; a general torpor or lassitude, which keeps them inactive. They dislike to move out, and love to loll about on a sofa; they are irritated if you advise them to take exercise; they abandon their ordinary avocations, neglect their domestic concerns, become indifferent to their nearest connexions; in short, they will neither converse, nor study, nor read, nor write, shunning society, and being impatient of the inquiries and importunities of friends. In this state they become filled with gloomy ideas (*idées noires*), despair of ever being better, desire or even invoke death, and sometimes destroy themselves, from a conviction that they are no longer capable of fulfilling their duties in society. These people are perfectly sane on all subjects of conversation; their impulse to suicide being strong in proportion to the activity of their former avocations, and the importance of their former duties. I have seen their disease (for it is a disease) continue for months, and even years. I have seen it alternate with mania and with perfect health. I have seen patients who would be six months of the year maniacal or in sound health, and the other six months tormented with these gloomy ideas and impulses to suicide."

In confirmation of this view of Esquirol's, the following cases are related:[47]—A gentleman of apparently sound constitution, aged 32, was married to a woman whom he affectionately loved. His affairs became deranged a few years after his marriage, which greatly discouraged him, and rendered him inactive, but without apparently affecting his health. He now embarked in a speculation which

---

[47] Dict. des Sciences Med., vol. liii.

promised much advantage, and at first applied himself to business with unremitting assiduity. In the course of a month he encountered some difficulties, which depressed him beyond measure. He considered himself ruined, refused to quit his bed, and would not superintend his workmen, from a conviction that he was no longer capable of directing their operations. He complained of headache, heat in his stomach, &c. His affection for his wife and children, his pecuniary interests, all failed to rouse him from this moral and physical prostration. He reasoned sanely on the critical state of his affairs, and yet made no effort to rescue himself from his difficulties. Eight days passed in this way, when all at once he sprung from his bed in perfect integrity of mind and body. He resumed instantaneously all his activity for business, all his affection for his family. The same state, however, recurred ten or twelve times since, at irregular intervals, caused in general by trifling contrarieties of business, which, under other circumstances, would be considered as nothing. During several of these paroxysms he had impulses to suicide; but this dreaded catastrophe has not yet taken place.

A female was admitted into the Salpetriere on the 23d of September, 1819, in the 34th year of her age, and fourteen years after marriage. At the age of 21 she had a child, after which she was affected with an ulcer in the foot, which was healed in six months. From this time she was troubled with cardialgia, at first slight, but afterwards with intense pain and vomiting of her food. At the age of 33 she became irresolute in her ideas and actions. She expressed an aversion for those things which she had been previously pleased with, and was occasionally incoherent. After suffering from other derangements of her general health, she abandoned her household affairs, became quite despondent, and tried more than once to commit suicide. In this state she was admitted into the hospital, and was put upon diluents, low diet, &c. As she shewed indications of having recovered, she was allowed to return to her family; but in a short period she was harassed with gloomy ideas, despaired of recovery, and expressed a desire to quit life, the duties of which she said she was no longer able to fulfil.

In the case of Cowper, we have a melancholy instance of hypochondriasis leading to suicidal mental derangement. That the poet's mind was unsound when he attempted to kill himself, must be evident to those who are conversant with the history of his life. He never appears to have been free from hypochondriacal disorder. In a letter to Lady Hesketh, he says, "Could I be translated to paradise, unless I could leave my body behind me, my melancholy would cleave to me there." A friend procured him the situation of reading clerk to the House of Lords, forgetting that the nervous shyness which made a public exhibition of himself "mortal poison," would render it impossible for him ever to discharge the duties of his office. This difficulty presented itself to the mind of the poet, and gloom instantly enveloped his faculties. At his request, his situation was changed to that of clerk of the journals; but even before he could be installed into office he was threatened with a public examination before the House. This made him completely wretched; he had not resolution to decline what he had not strength to do: the interest of his friend, and his own reputation and want of support, pressed him forward to an attempt which he knew from the first could never succeed. In this miserable state, like Goldsmith's traveller,

> "To stop too fearful, and too faint to go,"

he attended every day for six months at the office where he was to examine the journals in preparation for his trust. His feelings were like those of a man at the place of execution, every time he entered the office door; and he only gazed mechanically at the books, without drawing from them the least portion of information he wanted. As the time of his examination approached, his agony became more and more intense; he hoped and believed that madness would come to relieve him; he attempted also to make up his mind to suicide, though his conscience bore stern testimony against it; he could not by any argument persuade himself that it was right; but his desperation prevailed, and he procured from an apothecary the means of self-destruction. On the day before his public appearance was to be made, he happened to notice a letter in the newspaper, which to his disordered mind seemed like a malignant libel on himself. He immediately threw down the paper, and rushed into the fields, determined to die in a ditch; but the thought struck him that he might escape from the country. With the same violence he proceeded to make hasty preparations for his flight; but while he was engaged in packing his portmanteau his mind changed, and he threw himself into a coach, ordering the man to drive to the Tower wharf, intending to throw himself into the river, and not reflecting that it would be impossible to accomplish his purpose, in that public spot, unobserved. On approaching the water, he found a porter seated upon some goods; he then returned to the coach, and drove home to his lodgings in the Temple. On the way, he attempted to drink the laudanum, but as often as he raised it, a convulsive agitation of his frame prevented its reaching his lips; and thus, regretting the loss of the opportunity, but unable to avail himself of it, he arrived half dead with anguish at his apartments. He then closed the door and threw himself on the bed, with the laudanum near him, trying to lash himself up to the deed; but a voice within seemed constantly to forbid it; and as often as he extended his hand to the poison, his fingers were contracted, and held back by spasms. At this time some of the inmates of the place came in, but he concealed his agitation; and as soon as he was left alone, a change came over him, and so detestable did the deed appear, that he threw away the laudanum, and dashed the phial to pieces. The rest of the day was spent in heavy insensibility, and at night he slept as usual; but on waking at three in the morning, *he took his penknife and laid with his weight upon it, the point being directed towards his heart.* It was broken, and would not penetrate. At day-break he rose, and passing a strong garter round his neck, fastened it to the frame of his bed. This gave way with his weight; but on securing it to the door, he was more successful, and remained suspended until he had lost all consciousness of existence. After a time, the garter broke, and he fell to the floor, so that his life was saved; but the conflict had been greater than his reason could endure. He felt a contempt for himself not to be expressed or imagined. Whenever he went into the street, it seemed as if every eye flashed upon him with indignation and scorn. He felt as if he had offended God so deeply that his guilt could never be forgiven, and his whole heart was filled with pangs of tumultuous despair.[48]

---

[48] Previous to Cowper's attempt at suicide, he had fallen into the company of two

When Cowper had once admitted the thought of self-destruction, he could not go into the street without meeting with something to tempt or drive him to the act. It seemed to him as if the whole world had conspired to make death by his own hand inevitable. When he ventured into the streets, after the failure of all his efforts, a ghastly shame and alarmed suspicion were his torments; and perhaps nothing in Cowper's autobiography goes deeper into the heart than the following description of his sufferings.

"I never went into the street but I thought the people stood and laughed at me, and held me in contempt; and could hardly persuade myself but that the voice of conscience was loud enough for any one to hear it. They who knew me, appeared to avoid me, and if they spoke to me, seemed to do it in scorn. I bought a ballad of one who was singing it in the street, because I thought it was written on me. I dined alone, either at a tavern, where I went in the dark, or at the chop-house, where I always took care to hide myself in the darkest corner of the room. I slept generally an hour in the evening, but it was only to be terrified in dreams; and when I awoke, it was some time before I could steadily walk through the passage into the dining-room. I reeled and staggered like a drunken man. The eyes of man I did not fear; but when I thought that the eyes of God were upon me, (which I felt assured of,) it gave me the most intolerable anguish. If, for a moment, a book or a companion stole away my attention from myself, a flash from hell seemed to be thrown into my mind immediately; and I said within myself, 'What are these things to me, who am damned?'"

Cowper is not the only instance, however, of a man of exquisite taste and genius whose life has been rendered miserable by hypochondria. We have alluded elsewhere to Byron's morbid sensitiveness, and the reader's attention is now called to the influence of hypochondriasis on the poet's mind. He says in his journal, "What can be the reason I awake every morning in actual despair and despondency?" He had a great apprehension of insanity. In order to overcome his melancholy, considering that his diet had much to do with it, he put himself under a strict regimen, avoiding most scrupulously all animal food. He states that his diet for a week consisted of tea and six dry biscuits per diem. After having indulged in an ordinary dinner, he writes, "I wish to God I had not dined now; it kills me with heaviness; and yet it was but a pint of bucellas, and fish. Oh, my head! how it aches!—the horrors of indigestion!" Again he says, "This head was given me to ache with." After a severe fit of indigestion, he writes, "I've no more charity than a vinegar cruet. Would that I were an ostrich, and dieted on fire-irons! O fool! I shall go mad!"

Burns suffered much from indigestion, producing hypochondria. Writing to his friend, Mr. Cunningham, he says, "Canst thou not minister to a mind diseased? Canst thou speak peace and rest to a soul tost on a sea of troubles, without one friendly star to guide her course, and dreading that the next surge may overwhelm

---

sophists, who both advanced claims to the right of self-destruction, and whose fallacious arguments won him to their pernicious views, which were, besides, aided by his recollection of a certain book containing similar reasoning, which, however weak in itself, now seemed to his disordered mind irrefragable.

her? Canst thou give to a frame tremblingly alive to the tortures of suspense the stability and hardihood of a rock that braves the blast? If thou canst not do the least of these, why wouldst thou disturb me in my miseries with thy inquiries after me?" From early life, the poet was subject to a disordered stomach, a disposition to headache, and irregular action of the heart.

He describes, in one of his letters, the horrors of his complaint:—"I have been for some time pining under secret wretchedness. The pang of disappointment, the sting of pride, and some wandering stabs of remorse, settle on my life like vultures, when my attention is not called away by the claims of society, or the vagaries of the muse. Even in the hour of social mirth my gaiety is the madness of an intoxicated criminal under the hands of an executioner. My constitution was blasted *ab origine* with a deep incurable taint of melancholy that poisoned my existence."

Nothing can be more interesting to a physician who is endowed with only a moderate share of the spirit of observation than to watch the progress of hypochondriasis in a number of patients, especially in regard to its effect on the mind. They always struggle, more or less in the beginning, with the lowness and dejection which affect them; and it is not until many a severe contest has taken place between their natural good sense and the involuntary suggestions which arise from the obscure and painful feelings of the diseased nerves, that a firm belief in the reality of such thoughts gains a full conquest over their judgment. A firm belief in any one perception never takes place until it has acquired a certain degree of force; and as all impressions which arise from the viscera of the abdomen are naturally obscure, we see the reason why these must continue for a great length of time, or be often repeated, before they can withdraw a person's attention from the ordinary impression of external objects, which are clear and distinct, and before they acquire such a degree of vividness as to destroy the operations of reason.

We meet every day with hypochondriacs in whom the disease is just beginning to be formed, and who, being possessed of a good understanding, seem unwilling to tell, even to their medical friends, the singular, and often melancholy, thoughts with which they are tormented. They acknowledge them to be unreasonable, and yet insist that they cannot help believing in them. A very curious display of this kind of struggle between the habitudes of reason and the approach of delirium is to be found in the diary of an hypochondriac, from which we make the following extract:—

"On the 14th of November, the idea that some person intended to kill me sprung up suddenly and involuntarily in my mind, and yet, I must confess, there was no reason why I should have harboured this thought, for I am convinced that no one ever formed such a cruel design against me. People who had a stick in their hands I looked on as murderers. As I was walking out of town, a countryman happened to follow me, and I was instantly filled with the greatest apprehension, and stood still to let him pass. I asked the fellow in a threatening voice, and with a view of intimidating him from his purpose, what was the name of the town before us. The man answered my question and walked on, and I found great relief, because he was no longer behind me.

"In the evening, I observed some water in the glass out of which I commonly drink, and I instantly believed it was poisoned. I therefore washed it carefully out, and yet I knew, at the same time, that I myself had left the water in it.

"18th November.—At particular periods I believe all mankind have conspired to murder me. I think I am deprived of my office; that I am doomed to die of hunger; and, to add to all this, I am tormented with horrid doubts concerning futurity, and these thoughts persecute me like furies. Those whom I used to love most, I now hate. I avoid my best friends, and my dear wife appears to me a much worse kind of woman than she really is.

"I cannot describe the exertion it requires to conquer in society the aversion I feel to my fellow-creatures, and to prevent my ill-humour from breaking out against the most innocent people. When it really does so, I spare no one. I am sorry for it afterwards, but then I am too proud to acknowledge my error.

"I find myself so enraged on seeing a stupid, vacant countenance, that I have almost an irresistible inclination to box the person's ears to whom it belongs: the refraining from it is a severe effort.

"20th November.—A boy with a face like a satyr met me, and occasioned me the greatest uneasiness. Although he did nothing to displease me, I was forced to go to him, and tell him that I was sure he would die on the gallows.

"23rd November.—My sensibility is often extreme, and then my best friends become insupportable to me. To their expressions of regard I am either purposely cold or else I answer by rude and offensive speeches. I can seldom explain to myself the reason of this too great sensibility. If two people whisper to each other in my presence, I grow uneasy, and lose all command of mind, because I think they are speaking ill of me; and I often assume a satirical manner in company, in order to frighten them. Anxiety, dreadful anxiety, seizes me, if a person overlooks my hand at cards, or if a person sits down beside me when I am playing the harpsichord."

"From numerous facts which have come within my own observation," says a distinguished living medical authority,[49] "I am convinced that many strange antipathies, disgusts, caprices of temper, and eccentricities which are considered solely as obliquities of intellect, have their source in corporeal disorder.

"The great majority of these complaints, which are considered as purely mental, such as irascibility, melancholy, timidity, and irresolution, might be greatly remedied, if not entirely removed, by a proper system of temperance, and with very little medicine. There is no accounting for the magic-like spell which annihilates for a time the whole energy of the mind, and renders the victim of dyspepsia afraid of his own shadow, or of things, if possible, more unsubstantial than shadows.

"It is not likely that the great men of the earth should be exempt from these visitations any more than the little; and if so, we may reasonably conclude, that there are other things beside 'conscience' which 'make cowards of us all,' and that,

---

[49] Dr. J. Johnson.

by a temporary gastric irritation, many an 'enterprise of vast pith and moment' has had 'its current turned away,' and 'lost the name of action.'

"The philosopher and the metaphysician, who know but little of these reciprocities of mind and matter, have drawn many a false conclusion from, and erected many a baseless hypothesis on, the actions of men. Many a happy thought has sprung from an empty stomach; many a terrible and merciless edict has gone forth in consequence of an irritated gastric nerve. Thus health may make the same man a hero in the field whom dyspepsia may render imbecile in the cabinet."

The following case will shew how powerfully indigestion may affect the mind's operations:—

A young lady, after eating some heavy paste, was attacked by a sensation of burning heat at the pit of the stomach, which increased till the whole of the upper part of the body, both externally and internally, appeared to her to be all in flames. She rose up suddenly, left the dinner table, and ran into the street, from which she was immediately brought back. She soon came to herself, and thus described her horrible ideas. She declared that she had been very wicked, and had been dragged into the flames of hell. She continued in a precarious situation for some time. Whenever she experienced the burning sensation of which she first complained, the same dreadful thoughts occurred to her mind. She seized hold of whatever was nearest to prevent her from being forced away; and such was her alarm that she dreaded to be alone. This lady had long been distressed by family concerns, and harassed by restless and sleepless nights, which greatly affected her health.

Dr. Johnson used to declare that he inherited "a vile melancholy" from his father, which made him "mad all his life, or, at least, not sober." Insanity was his constant terror. Boswell says that, at the period when this great philosopher was giving to the world proofs of no ordinary vigour of understanding, he actually fancied himself insane, or in a state as nearly as possible approaching to it.

Murphy says, "For many years before Johnson's death, so terrible was the prospect of final dissolution that when he was not disposed to enter into the conversation which was going forward, he sat in his chair, repeating the well-known lines of Shakspeare—

"To die, and go we know not where."

Like Metastasio, he would not, if he could help it, permit the word death to be pronounced in his presence. Boswell once introduced the topic in the course of conversation, which made Johnson highly indignant. He observed, that he never had a moment in which it was not terrible to him.

Three or four days before he died, he declared that he would give one of his legs for a year more of life. The ruling passion was exhibited strong in death. At Dr. Johnson's own suggestion, the surgeon was making slight punctures in the legs, with the hope of relieving his dropsical affection, when he cried out, "Deeper! deeper! *I want length of life,* and you are afraid of giving me pain, which I do not value." If we had not a thorough conviction that this fear of death was but the result of physical disease, which no moral and religious principles could subdue, Dr.

Johnson's conduct towards the end of his life would excite a feeling in our mind towards him very opposite to that of respect.

With reference to suicide, there is no fact that has been more clearly established than that of its hereditary character. Of all diseases to which the various organs are subject, there are none more generally transmitted from one generation to another than affections of the brain. It is not necessary that the disposition to suicide should manifest itself in every generation; it often passes over one, and appears in the next, like insanity unattended with this propensity. But if the members of the family so predisposed are carefully examined, it will be found that the various shades and gradations of the malady will be easily perceptible. Some are distinguished for their flightiness of manner, others for their strange eccentricity, likings and dislikings, irregularity of their passions, capricious and excitable temperament, hypochondriasis and melancholia. These are often but the minute shades and variations of an hereditary disposition to suicidal madness. A gentleman suddenly, and without any apparent reason, cut his throat. The father had always been a man of strong passions, easily roused, and when so, was extremely violent. The brother was a man of impulse; he always acted by fits and starts, and therefore never could be depended upon. The sister had a strange, unnatural, and superstitious horror of particular colours and odours. A yellow dress caused a feeling approaching to syncope, and the smell of hay produced great nervous excitement. The grandfather had been convicted of homicide, and had been confined for two years in a mad-house.

Andral relates the case of a father who died from the effects of disease of the brain; the mother died sane. They had six children, three boys and three girls. Of the boys, the eldest was a man of original mind; the second was very extravagant in his habits, and was ultimately confined in a mad-house; the third was extremely violent in his temper. Of the girls, one had fits of apoplexy, and became insane; the other died at her accouchement, with symptoms of derangement; the third died of cholera, not, however, until she exhibited indications of mental aberration.

A case more singular than the last is recorded. All the members of a particular family, being hereditarily disposed, exhibited, when they arrived at a certain age, a desire to commit self-destruction. It required no exciting cause to develope the fatal disposition. No wish was expressed, or attempt made, to overpower the suicidal inclination, and the greatest industry and ingenuity were exercised by the parties in order to effect their purpose. In two cases, the propensity was subdued by proper medical and moral treatment; but, just in proportion to its being suppressed, did the idea of suicide appear to fix itself resolutely in the mind. The desire came upon the individuals like the attacks of intermittent fever.

A. K., a man aged 57, was twice married. He was a shoe-maker by trade; but not having received any education, his wife was compelled to attend to all his accounts. He had experienced, when young, a blow on the head, which occasionally gave him pain. He became very intemperate in his habits, and at particular intervals he exhibited an uncontrollable temper, quarrelled with everybody, neglected his business, abused his wife, and became extravagant and melancholy. During the paroxysm he would exclaim—"*Oh, my unlucky head! I am again a lost man!*"

When the attack subsided, he returned to his business, was affectionate to his wife and family, most humbly begged her pardon for having ill-treated her, and expressed the greatest contrition for his conduct. These attacks came on at regular intervals. He procured a piece of rope for the purpose of hanging himself, and for some months carried it about with him in his pocket for that purpose. During one of his fits he effected his object. His grandfather had strangled himself, and his brother and sister had attempted suicide.

Dr. Gall knew several families in which the suicidal propensity prevailed through several generations. Among the cases he mentions is the following very remarkable one: — "The Sieur Ganthier, the owner of various houses built without the barriers of Paris, to be used as *entrepôts* of goods, left seven children, and a fortune of about two millions of francs to be divided among them. All remained at Paris, or in the neighbourhood, and preserved their patrimony; some even increased it by commercial speculations. None of them met with any real misfortunes, but all enjoyed good health, a competency, and general esteem. All, however, were possessed with a rage for suicide, and all seven succumbed to it within the space of thirty or forty years. Some hanged, some drowned themselves, and others blew out their brains. One of the first two had invited sixteen persons to dine with him one Sunday. The company collected, the dinner was served, and the guests were at the table. The master of the house was called, but did not answer; he was found hanging in the garret. Scarcely an hour before, he was quietly giving orders to the servants, and chattering with his friends. The last, the owner of a house in the Rue de Richelieu, having raised his house two stories, became frightened at the expense, imagined himself ruined, and was anxious to kill himself. Thrice they prevented him; but soon after, he was found dead, having shot himself. The estate, after all the debts were paid, amounted to three hundred thousand francs, and he might have been forty-five years old at the time of his death."

Falret, whose researches have thrown much light on this affection, believes that it is more disposed to be hereditary than any other kind of insanity. He saw a mother and her daughter attacked with suicidal melancholy, and the grandmother of the latter was at Charenton for the same cause. An individual, he says, committed suicide in Paris. His brother, who came to attend the funeral, cried out on seeing the body — "What fatality! My father and uncle both destroyed themselves; my brother has imitated their example; and twenty times during my journey hither I thought of throwing myself into the Seine!"

Gall also relates the case of a dyer, of a very taciturn humour, who had five sons and a daughter. The eldest son, after being settled in a prosperous business with a family around him, succeeded, after many attempts, in killing himself by jumping from the third story of his house. The second son, who was rather taciturn, had some domestic troubles, lost part of his fortune at play, and strangled himself at the age of thirty-five. The third threw himself from the window into his garden, but did not hurt himself; he pretended he was trying to fly. The fourth tried one day to fire a pistol down his throat, but was prevented. The fifth was of a bilious, melancholic temperament, quiet, and devoted to business; he and his sister shewed no signs of being affected with their brothers' malady. One of their cousins committed suicide.

Among the physical causes of self-destruction, insidious affections of the brain must stand prominently forward. It is not often that the physician is permitted to examine after death the state of this organ; but there can be no doubt that, in the great majority of instances, the brain will be found to have undergone a serious structural alteration. "During the last twenty-five years," says Dr. G. Mantell, "many cases of suicide have come under my notice in which the mental hallucination which led to self-destruction has depended on lesions of the brain, occasioned by slight or neglected injuries of the head, to which neither the patient nor his friends attached any importance. In several instances of self-destruction, without any assignable moral cause, and in which no previous signs of fatuity or insanity were manifested, I have found, upon a post mortem examination, either circumscribed induration or softening of the brain, or thickening and adhesions of some portions of its membranes. The conviction was forced upon my mind that very many of the *so called* nervous or hypochondriacal affections, which are generally considered as imaginary and dependent on mental emotions, are ascribable to physical causes, and frequently originate from slight lesions of the brain."

The learned doctor relates the following cases in illustration of his views:—

"A respectable tradesman, between fifty and sixty years of age, of temperate habits, was knocked down during an electioneering contest, and struck his head on the ground. He was stunned for a few minutes by the shock, and slightly bruised above the right temple, but experienced no further inconvenience, and the circumstance was considered of no consequence.

"About six months after the event, he was seized, one evening, with rigors and a pain over the right brow; a smart reaction took place, which terminated in perspiration, and the following morning, the symptoms disappeared. A similar paroxysm came on daily for five or six days; the attack was considered intermittent, and, I believe, bark was freely administered. At the end of a week, the patient was well. After this period, he was subject to occasional pain over the right brow, accompanied with great mental despondency, the prevailing apprehension being that of eternal damnation. This state would continue for an uncertain time, the duration varying from a few days to three weeks; and by slow degrees he would lose all trace of disease, regain his accustomed cheerfulness, and be able to transact the affairs of an extensive business.

"About two years from the occurrence of the accident, I saw him, at the request of his friends, while he was labouring under great despondency, which his relations assured me arose from some religious opinions he had imbibed; and I found that the medical treatment had been in accordance with such a notion. My inquiries led to the detection of the injury he had received two years previously, but neither the patient nor his friends would allow that there was any connexion between the blow and the symptoms under which he now suffered. Both general and local bleeding appeared to me necessary; a strict regimen was adopted, and he regained his usual flow of spirits, and expressed himself much better than he had been for years. The occasional use of leeches, and a rigid abstinence from fermented liquors, spirits, and stimuli of all kinds, maintained this favourable condition for a considerable time; but his occupation led him to occasional excess in diet, and a moderate quantity of wine or beer invariably brought on despondency and its accompanying hallucination; in other words, when the system was kept in a tranquil state, the cerebral functions were not impaired; but when excited, the morbid manifestations of the mind were produced.

"During one of these attacks he cut his throat, and expired in the course of a few hours. A short time previous to his death, when greatly exhausted by the loss of blood from his wound, his intellect was unclouded, and he expressed to me his astonishment at what he had done, and assured me he had no reason for acting thus; but it was an impulse which he could not resist.

"The only abnormal appearance upon inspecting the body after death was, a circumscribed adhesion of the dura mater to the pia mater, to the extent of about two inches in diameter, over the upper and anterior portion of the right hemisphere of the brain, opposite to the spot where the blow of the head had been inflicted some years previously.

"I will not presume to offer any comment on a case which I am well aware presents nothing unusual, my only object being that of calling particular attention to those slight injuries of the head which, although unmarked by any striking symptoms at the moment of their occurrence, may give rise to the most distressing results years after their infliction, and when the original cause of disordered action is forgotten, and can no longer be detected; and of pointing out the possibility that many cases of suicide, apparently referrible to moral causes only, may be found to result solely from physical derangement of the organ through which the manifestations of the mind must be displayed. It is under circumstances of this kind that the medical philosopher, in his painful duty of exploring the relics of mortality, may have the high gratification of protecting the memory of an unfortunate individual from the censure of a world but too apt to judge harshly, and thus afford a lasting consolation to those by whom that memory will be cherished and revered."

No complaints can be more insidious than those connected with the brain. An apparently slight blow on the head in early life has been known, if not to give rise at the time to actual disease of the sentient organ, to predispose the person to attacks of cerebral derangement when exposed to the influence of causes so trivial as to be incapable, under any other circumstances, of producing any effect. The following case will demonstrate that moral irritation may derange the structure of the brain as effectually as any physical injury: —

A gentleman in early life was exposed for a few weeks to an amount of mental excitement almost sufficient to bring on a severe maniacal attack. He complained for some time of a sensation in his head as if some person was hammering on his brain. In the course of a few years he apparently recovered. During a tour through Italy, he had a renewal of his old sensation, and became liable to head-aches, giddiness, and severe attacks of indigestion. He placed himself under the care of an Italian physician of eminence, who did his best to restore him to health. Instead of improving, the symptoms of his disease became more apparent; and one morning he was found dead on the floor of his dressing-room, having with a penknife effectually divided the carotid artery. On examining the brain, extensive *ramollissement* was discovered. In this case the structural disease originated in a *moral shock*, the effects of which remained suspended for some years, and then gave rise to the train of symptoms that drove the unfortunate man to terminate his life. It is one of the most important facts connected with this subject, that mental excitement may produce as extensive and serious organic disease as that which so commonly follows the receipt of physical injury. With a knowledge of this fact, how cautious we ought to be in pronouncing an opinion as to the absence of disease of the brain in cases of suicide resulting from an apparently trifling departure from mental quietude, without being intimate with the previous history of the individual.

"The English," says Montesquieu, "frequently destroy themselves without any apparent cause to determine them to such an act, and even in the midst of prosperity. Among the Romans, suicide was the effect of education; it depended upon their customs and manner of thinking: with the English, it is the effect of disease, and depending upon the physical condition of the system." A young man, twenty-two years of age, was intended by his parents for the church. He disliked the profession exceedingly, and absolutely refused to take orders. For this act, at once of integrity and disobedience, he was forced to quit his father's house, and to exert his inexperienced energies for a precarious subsistence. He turned his thoughts to several different employments; and, at length, he went to reside with a family, where he was treated with great kindness, and where he appeared to enjoy a degree of tranquillity. His enjoyment, however, was not of long continuance, for his imagination was assailed by gloomy and distressing reflections. His life became more and more burdensome to him, and he considered by what method he should put an end to it. He one day formed the resolution of precipitating himself from the top of the house, but his courage failed him, and the execution of the project was postponed. Some days after, he took up a pistol with the same design of self-destruction. His perplexities and terrors returned. A friend of this unhappy youth called upon Pinel one day to inform him of the projected tragedy. Every means of prevention were adopted that prudence could suggest, but the most pressing solicitations and friendly remonstrances were in vain. The propensity to suicide unceasingly haunted him, and he precipitately quitted the family from whom he had experienced so many proofs of friendship and attachment. Financial considerations prohibited the suggestion of a distant voyage or a change of climate. He was therefore advised, as the best substitute, some constant and laborious employment. The young melancholic, sensibly alive to the horror of his situation, entered fully into Pinel's views, and procured an engagement at Bled Harbour, where he mingled with the other labourers with a full determination to deserve his stipulated wages. But, completely fatigued and exhausted by the exertion of the first two days of his engagement, he was obliged to have recourse to some other expedient. He entered into the employment of a master-mason, in the neighbourhood of Paris, to whom his services were peculiarly acceptable, as he devoted his leisure hours to the instruction of an only son. No situation, apparently, could have been more suitable to his case than one of this kind, admitting of alternate mental and bodily exercise. Wholesome food, comfortable lodgings, and every attention due to misfortune, seemed rather to aggravate than to divert his gloomy propensities. After the expiration of a fortnight, he returned to his friend, and, with tears in his eyes, acquainted him with the internal struggles which he felt, and the insuperable disgust of life, which bore him irresistibly to self-destruction. The reproaches of his friend affected him exceedingly, and, in a state of the utmost anxiety and despair, he silently withdrew, probably to terminate a hated existence by throwing himself into the Seine.

When laying down rules for the physical treatment of suicide, we have developed our view as to the influence of derangement of the *primæ viæ*, suppressed secretions, &c., on the healthy state of the mind; and we have only to refer the reader to that portion of the work for information on these points. In discussing the important question whether suicide invariably results from mental derangement, numerous instances have been brought forward that may be undoubtedly traced to that cause, therefore it will not be necessary to recapitulate in this chapter what has been there advanced.

CHAPTER IX.

MORAL TREATMENT OF SUICIDAL MANIA.

Diseases of the brain not dissimilar to affections of other organs—
Early symptoms of insanity—The good effects of having plenty
to do—Occupation—Dr. Johnson's opinion on the subject—The
pleasure derived from cultivating a taste for the beauties of nature—Effect of volition on diseases of the mind—Silent grief injurious to mental health—Treatment of *ennui*—The time of danger,
not the time of disease—The Walcheren expedition—The retreat
of the ten thousand Greeks under Xenophon—Influence of music
on the mind in the cure of disease—Cure of epidemic suicide—
Buonaparte's remedy—How the women of Myletus were cured
of the disposition to suicide, and other illustrations—Cases shewing how easily the disposition to suicide may be diverted—On the
cure of insanity by stratagems—On the importance of removing
the suicidal patient from his own home—On the regulation of the
passions.

In treating this most important class of affections, we must dismiss from our
minds all those pre-conceived notions which we have been led to form of what
constitutes mental derangement. We must view the subject as medical philosophers in the most liberal acceptation of the term, and not as *nisi prius* barristers;
we must consider ourselves at the bed-side of a suffering patient, demanding from
our skill that relief which he is led to believe we have in our power to afford, and
not as in a court of justice, undergoing an examination at the hands of a lawyer
anxious to establish his case; and, above all, we must apply to the disease of the
brain and its disordered manifestations those pathological principles which guide
us in the elucidation of the affections of other organs. If we consider insanity not
as a specific disease invariably exhibiting the same phenomena, but as it really is,
the effect of a disordered condition of the sentient organ, having an incipient, as
well as an advanced stage, we may, by a judicious application of the principles of
therapeutics, succeed in many cases in crushing the disposition to suicide before
it has taken a formidable hold of the constitution. In the great majority of cases
the premonitory indications are well marked and unequivocal. The experienced
physician and accurate observer will be able to detect, before the mental alienation
becomes apparent to others, the early dawnings of derangement. He knows that
it is frequently manifested by some change in the person's usual healthy habits
of thinking and acting,—by the exhibition of odd fancies and whims. Although

surrounded by everything calculated to contribute to his happiness, he is the most miserable of human beings. Trifles annoy and irritate him; he sees in his dearest friends his deadliest enemies; talks of conspiracies, of plots, and stratagems; becomes suspicious of everything and everybody; his former objects of pleasure afford him no delight; he avoids society, and is occasionally heard muttering strange things to himself. In the majority of cases these are the early dawnings of cerebral disease leading to unequivocal insanity, and yet so tied down are we to definitions, arbitrary standards and poetical tests, that we will not admit derangement of mind to be present until the symptoms are so self evident and glaring that the condition of the mind becomes apparent to the most superficial observer. When this view of insanity is recognised as orthodox, and moral treatment adopted in the early stages of the disease, much good may be expected to result.

How often do we see in society, and during the intercourse of private friendship, individuals complaining of the severest mental sufferings, the effect of morbid alterations of feeling almost in every respect similar to insanity, dependent upon the same causes, manifesting the same symptoms, and removed by the same remedial agents. How are these mental ailments treated? The poor sufferer is perhaps smiled at; he is considered to be fanciful, and no regard is paid to the cerebral affection. The disease is allowed to advance until other faculties of the mind are implicated, and then the mental alienation exhibits itself so unequivocally that no one doubts its existence.

The success of the mental treatment of suicide will be mainly dependent on our paying strict attention to those apparently trifling alterations of temper and disposition, those deviations from the usual mode of thinking and acting, which so often predicate the presence of the incipient stage of insanity. An invincible love of solitude exhibited in a patient considered as labouring under an hypochondriacal affection, and who, when induced to converse, complains of being constantly pestered with one or two trains of ideas from which he cannot for a moment escape, although his efforts are great and unremitting, let his friends beware. These changes are, however, but rarely noticed, until some alarming event causes every friend to lament the want of timely attention.

Occupation is an infallible specific for many of the imaginary and real ills of life. In cases where the mind is sinking under the influence of its own weight, and the fancy is allowed to dwell uninterruptedly on the ideas of its own creation, until the individual believes himself to stand apart from all the world, the very personification of human misery and wretchedness, the physician can recommend no better remedy than constant and steady occupation for the mind and body. Burton concludes his able work on Melancholy with this valuable piece of advice:—"Be not solitary; be not idle." Dr. Reid recommended a patient, labouring under great mental depression, to engage in the composition of a novel, which, during the time he was occupied in the task, effected much good. By interesting himself in the distresses of fictitious beings, he diverted his attention from sufferings which were no less the offspring of the imagination.

It has been suggested with great truth that the habit of gaming, prevalent as it is among persons in the upper ranks of life, is not to be attributed exclusively to a feeling of avarice. The man who is surrounded by everything to make his condition in life happy, as far as wealth is concerned, does not fly to dice for the purpose of aggrandisement, but he does so to seek refuge from the miseries of indolence and vacuity; from the gnawings of his own mind; from an eager desire to expose himself to that mental agitation which nature tells him is so necessary to make life supportable. "A woman is happier than a man," says Dr. Johnson, "because she can hem a pocket-handkerchief."

Our faculties, like the vulture of Prometheus, devour our souls, if they have no action beyond ourselves. "Real lassitude is always mingled with grief," says an eminent female genius; and Madame de Staël considers the observation a profound one.

"The man in the Spectator who hanged himself to avoid the intolerable annoyance of having to tie his garters every day of his life, is but a satire on the misery of many who, having no useful occupation, find the flight of time marked only by the swift repetition of petty troubles.

"The restlessness of Rousseau, his discontented and morbidly irritable disposition, was closely allied to insanity; and the painful struggles of Lord Byron, when 'came the fit again,' are detailed in words which shew too plainly how they disturbed and threatened the integrity of his judgment. In such natures, every strong emotion, or the occurrence of disease, may destroy the delicate balance, and make a ruin of a mind which even in ruins continues to excite a mournful admiration. The diversion of social intercourse, which to other men is necessary to prevent mental torpor, becomes to them a source of irritation by impeding the workings of their imagination: they find that, when alone, all the nobler aspirations of the soul are free, and images of beauty, and virtue, and wisdom, occupy the mind. Society transforms them into a being they despise, deprives them of all their high and valued thoughts, and it enables them to feel what slight circumstances, acting on the man without, may affect the man within. But the pleasures of solitude are transient; their train is followed by baseless fancies, by fears undefined, by griefs unexpressed, and black despondency, from which society can alone relieve. We learn, from observing such effects, arising from such causes, the advantage of mixed and varied occupations, suited to a being not made solely for contemplation or for action; and we may gather rules from these observations, the application of which to minds in a morbid state is very direct."[50]

With no less beauty than truth has the author of Rasselas depicted the insanity of the astronomer as gradually declining under the sanative influence of society and mental gratification. The sage confesses, that since he has mixed in the gay scenes of life, and divided his hours by a succession of amusements, he found the notion of his influence over the skies gradually fade away, and began to trust less to an opinion which he could never prove to others, and which he now found subject to variations from causes in which reason had no part. "If," says he, "I am accidentally left alone for a few hours, my inveterate persuasion rushes upon my soul, and my thoughts are chained down by an uncontrollable violence; but they are soon disentangled by the prince's conversation, and are instantaneously released

[50] Vide Dr. Conolly.

by the entrance of Pekuah. I am like a man habitually afraid of spectres, who is set at ease by a lamp, and wonders at the dread which harassed him in the dark."

It is difficult to lay down general rules for the treatment of particular cases of melancholia with a tendency to suicide. Travelling, agreeable society, works of light literature, should be had recourse to, in order to dispel all gloomy apprehensions from the mind.

In persons predisposed to insanity, or who manifest some slight indication of disease, how important it is to endeavour to call into exercise the higher faculties of the mind,—the judgment and reasoning powers,—and thus preserve the intellectual faculties in a healthy state of equilibrium. There is much wisdom in Lord Bacon's advice, that "if a man's wits be wandering, he should study the mathematics." The patient should be taught to derive a pleasure from the contemplation of those objects that afford variety, and that are always within his reach. A beneficent Creator has wisely placed around us endless sources of the purest and most elevating enjoyments. In a ratio to our intellectual attainments, so are we enabled to derive pleasure from circumstances that appear trifling and foolish to others. Mungo Park could, in the solitude of an African desert, when exposed to the most distressing circumstances, derive a most exquisite pleasure from the sight of a small flower. How fully can we enter into the feelings of the man who, after being prostrated to the earth by an accumulation of worldly disappointments, yet spoke in a tone of noble triumph at his having retained, amidst the wreck of all his hopes, a perception of the beauties of nature!

> "I care not, Fortune, what you me deny;—
> You cannot rob me of free Nature's grace;
> You cannot shut the windows of the sky,
> Through which Aurora shews her bright'ning face;
> You cannot bar my constant feet to trace
> The woods and lawns by living stream at eve:
> Let health my nerves and finer fibres brace,
> And I these toys to the great children leave:
> Of fancy, reason, virtue, nought can me bereave."

A devotion to the common pleasures of sense is better than a state of absolute indifference; for even if these give no kind of pleasure, whilst all higher pursuits are neglected, there is danger lest a man become of the same opinion as Dr. Darwin's patient, "that all which life affords is a ride out in the morning, and a warm parlour and a pack of cards in the afternoon;" and, like him, finding these pleasures not inexhaustible, should shoot himself because he has nothing better to do!

The miserable man should endeavour to make himself practically acquainted with the distresses of others. However desperate the circumstances of a person may be, he may still have it in his power to whisper a word of consolation to one whose situation may be more humiliating than his own.

Human nature is accused of much more selfishness than it has any just claim to; a thousand kindly emotions break in upon and redeem our daily and interested life.

> "The poorest poor
> Long for a moment in a weary life
> When they can know and feel that they have been
> Themselves the fathers and the dealers out
> Of some small blessings; have been kind to such
> As needed kindness; for this single cause,
> That we have all one human heart."[51]

How few have anything like a proper conception of the power which the will can be made to exercise over the physical and mental ailments.[52] The stimuli which we all more or less have at command, if properly directed, will often subdue the early dawnings of disease, which, if permitted to take its own course, would have assumed a most formidable character. It is our duty to combat with the first menace of disordered feeling. Once the enemy is allowed to take up a favourable position, it will be fruitless to enter single-handed into the contest. "I will be good," says the child, when he sees the rod ready to direct the will into the way of goodness; and "I will be cheerful," ought the dull and dyspeptic to say, who observes a cloud of hypochondriacal fancies ready to burst upon his head. It may be said it is useless to struggle against the natural tendencies of the mind and body, or to declare war with habits which have become firmly rooted in the constitution. In reply to this we would say, let not the patient yield to the influence of those causes which have formed the habit; let him not hug to his bosom the viper which is preying upon his mind; let him not exclaim to gloom, "Henceforth be thou my god."

The hypochondriac may say, when advised to rouse himself from his state of mental despondency, and to exhibit the attributes of a free agent—

> "Go, you may call it madness, folly;
> You shall not chase my gloom away:
> There's such a charm in melancholy,
> I would not, if I could, be gay."

But it is exercising a *conscientious duty* to resist the encroachments of those ideal pleasures which sap the foundation of our moral constitution.

I am inclined to concur in the opinion expressed by the late Dr. Uwins, that when melancholy is stripped of all its ornamental and poetical accompaniments, it will be found to be based in a great measure upon pride, selfishness, and indolence. This benevolent physician observes—"I cannot conceive a more delightful spectacle than that of an individual, whose constitutional cast is melancholy, warring against his temperament, and determining to enter with hilarity into the scenes and circumstances of social life."

Dr. Haindorft, in his German translation of Dr. Reid's "Essay on Hypochondriasis," in alluding to the possibility of the patient labouring under hypochondria being able, by an exercise of the power of volition, to control his morbid sensa-

---

[51] Wordsworth.

[52] The *possunt quia posse videuntur* feeling is not sufficiently encouraged by medical philosophers in treating mental affections.

tions, justly observes—"We should have fewer disorders of the mind if we could acquire more power of volition, and endeavour, by our own energy, to disperse the clouds which occasionally arise within our own horizon; if we *resolutely tore the first threads of the net* which gloom and ill-humour may cast around us, and made an effort to drive away the melancholy images of a morbid imagination by incessant occupation. How beneficial would it be to mankind if this truth were universally acknowledged and acted upon—viz., that our state of health, mental as well as bodily, principally depends upon ourselves!"

"By *seeming gay*, we grow to what we seem."

It was the remark of a man of great observation and knowledge of the world—"Only wear a mask for a fortnight, and you will not know it from your real face."

"I am determined to believe myself a happy man," said a poor fellow, sunk in the lowest stage of melancholy, to Esquirol; and he did endeavour to triumph over his gloomy apprehensions, and for a short period he enjoyed the sunny aspect of life; but not having sufficient resolution to continue this effort of volition, he again gave way to despair.

A thousand years before the Christian era, there were, at the two extremities of Egypt, temples devoted to Saturn, to which those labouring under hypochondriasis resorted in quest of relief. Some cunning priests, profiting by the credulity of these patients, associated with the pretended miracles of their powerless divinities and barren mysteries, natural means by which they always solaced their patients, and succeeded often in effecting cures by amusing the mind, and withdrawing the attention from the contemplation of physical suffering. The patients were religiously subjected to a variety of diversions and recreative exercises. Voluptuous paintings and seducing images were exposed to their view; agreeable songs and melodious sounds perpetually charmed their ears; gardens of flowers and ornamental groves furnished delightful walks and delicious perfumes. Every moment was consecrated to some diverting scene and amusement, which had a most beneficial result on the diseased mind, interrupted the train of melancholy thought, dissipated sorrow, and wrought the most salutary changes on the body through the agency of the mind. The Egyptian physicians recommended their patients to repair to these famous temples, as the faculty of the present day suggest a trip to a fashionable spa.

That many suicides result from an indulgence in long-continued and corroding grief must be apparent to all who have given this subject any consideration. The medical man will find it difficult to manage such patients. Everything should be done to rouse the person from his state of mental abstraction. The immortal poet had a just conception of the baneful influence of silent grief on the mind and body; he makes Malcolm say, imploringly, to Macbeth,

> "Give sorrow words; the grief that does not speak
> Whispers the o'er-wrought heart, and bids it break."

An eminent London physician communicated to me the particulars of the following case:—A young lady, connected with a family of rank, and possessing great accomplishments, had formed, unknown to her parents, a secret attachment to a gentleman who often visited the house. When it was discovered, he was requested to abandon all notions of the lady, as it was the determination of her relations to refuse their consent to an alliance with him. Both parties took it much to heart. The lady suffered from a severe attack of nervous disorder, which terminated in suicidal mania. She endeavoured several times to jump out of the window, and would have done so had she not been most carefully watched. Her symptoms were most distressing. The mind appeared to be weighed down to the earth by an accumulation of misery and wretchedness, which she was unable to shake off. "Oh! could I but be happy!" she would exclaim. "Will no one come to my relief? What can I do?" She would walk about the room, occasionally giving utterance to expressions similar to those just quoted. More than once she observed, that, could she cry, she felt assured her mind would be relieved; but not a tear could she shed. After a fearful struggle for some time, one evening, as she was retiring to rest, she burst into a flood of tears. The effect was most beneficial; from that moment she began to recover. The copious lachrymal secretion had the effect of relieving the cerebral congestion, and in this way the brain was restored to the performance of its healthy functions.

It is difficult to lay down any particular instructions for the treatment of *ennui*. How is it possible to restore enjoyment to a man who has quite exhausted it? In such cases the advice which Fénélon gives to Dionysius the tyrant, by the mouth of Diogenes, will naturally apply, — "To restore his appetite, he must be made to feel hunger; and to make his splendid palace tolerable to him, he must be put into my tub, which is at present empty."

A lady became insane in consequence of a sudden and unexpected acquisition of wealth. In a few months she was reduced, by the failure of the house in which all her property was embarked, to complete indigence. Being compelled to work for her daily bread, her reason was soon restored. The great preservative from *tedium vitæ* is, in keeping the mind and body in a state of healthy activity. How true it is —

> "That many ills o'er which man grieves,
> And still more woman, spring from not employing
> Some hours to make the remnant worth enjoying."

Byron.

In the army, it is proverbial that the time of fatigue and danger is not the time of disease; it is during the inactive and listless months of a campaign that crowds of patients pass to the hospitals. In both these cases it is the active exercise of the mind giving strength to the brain, and through it, healthy vigour to the body, which produces the effect. Shakspeare has not been unobservant of the consequences of excitement of mind on the bodily functions. In King Henry IV., when Northumberland is told of the fatal tidings from Shrewsbury, and is informed of the death of his son Percy, he breaks out, —

> "For this I shall have time enough to mourn.
> In poison there is physic; and these news
> That would, had I been well, have made me sick,

Being sick, have in some measure made me well:
And as a wretch whose fever-weakened joints,
Like strengthless hinges, buckle under life,
Impatient of his fit, breaks like a fire
Out of his keeper's arms; *even so my limbs*,
Weakened with grief, being now enraged with grief,
Are thrice themselves."

In illustration of the same principle, we have only to refer our readers to the ever-memorable Walcheren expedition. It has been stated that while our troops and seamen were actively engaged in the siege and bombardment of Flushing, exposed to intense heat, heavy rains, and poisonous exhalations from the malarious soil, inundated by the turbid waters of the Scheldt, scarcely a man was on the sick list; the excitement of warfare, the prospects of victory, and the expectation of booty, completely fortifying the body against all the potent causes of disease that environed the camp and the fleet.

In the celebrated retreat of the "Ten thousand Greeks" under Xenophon, the troops were subjected to great mental despondency. They had to cross rapid rivers, penetrate gloomy forests, drag their weary way over vast and burning deserts, scale the summits of rugged mountains, and wade through deep snows and pestilent morasses, in continual fear of death or capture. It was a sense of the despondency which misfortune was producing among the troops that induced Xenophon, in his address to his companions on the fearful night which preceded the murder of Clearchus, to say, "The soldiers have at present nothing before their eyes but misfortune. If any one can persuade them to turn *their thoughts into action* it would greatly encourage them." It was to effect this purpose that the consummate general ordered everything in the camp, except the sword, to be abandoned. He inspired the hopes of his soldiers, roused their minds into activity, and thus prevented the development of serious disease among the troops.

Lord Anson says, in speaking of the ravages which the scurvy made under his command, that "whatever discouraged the seamen, or damped their hopes, never failed to add new vigour to the distemper; for it usually killed those who were in the last stages of it, and confined those to their hammocks who before were capable of some kind of duty."

In certain diseases of the nervous system, particularly when associated with morbid conditions of the mind leading to suicide, the influence of music may be had recourse to with great advantage to the patient. The ancients, who paid more attention to the moral treatment of disease than the moderns have done, had a just appreciation of the beneficial effect of music on the nervous system. The learned Dr. Bianchini has collected all the passages found in ancient authors relative to the medical application of music; and from these it appears that it was used as a remedy by the Egyptians, Hebrews, Greeks, and Romans, not only in chronic, but in acute cases of disease.

M. Burette, in his able and scientific work on music, allows it to be possible, and even probable, that music, by the impressions it makes upon the nerves, may be of use in the cure of certain maladies; yet he by no means supposes the music of the ancients possessed this power in a greater degree than that of the moderns. Homer attributes the cessation of the plague among the Greeks, at the siege of Troy, to music:—

> "With hymns divine the joyous banquet ends,
> The pæans lengthened till the sun descends:
> The Greeks, restored, the grateful rites prolong;
> Apollo listens and approves the song."
>
> POPE.

In the Memoirs of the French Academy of Sciences, for 1707 and 1708, there are many accounts of cases of disease which, after having long resisted and baffled the most efficacious remedies, had yielded under the influence of the soft impressions of harmony; and M. de Mairan, in the same records, published in 1735, has entered very fully into the consideration of the *modus operandi* of music on the body in health and disease.

The effect of music on the system is explained in two different ways. The monotony of the sound is supposed to have a soothing influence over the mind, similar to what is known to result from the gurgle of a mimic cataract of some mountain rill, or to a distant waterfall. How often has the music caused by the waves gently dashing upon the beach excited sleep, when all our narcotics have failed in producing a similar effect. This soporific effect of the repetition or monotony of sound is beautifully alluded to by Mackenzie, in his Man of Feeling. When his hero, Mr. Harley, arrives in London, he finds that the noise and varied excitement of the metropolis increase his nervous state of habit, and prevent him from sleeping. Ordinary narcotics produce no effect upon him, and he must have continued to suffer from watchfulness if he had not happily touched his shoe-buckle, which lay upon the table, when the vibration produced a monotonous sound so closely resembling the voice of his good aunt, who nightly read him asleep in the country, that from that time he regularly applied to the same narcotic, and always slept soundly. Music acts, secondly, by causing an association of agreeable ideas. A lady who was confined in an asylum in the vicinity of London, and who had been separated for some months from her home, and from all she held dear, was pronounced partially convalescent. She was, however, still melancholy; and it was suggested by her father that a piece, of which she was passionately fond, and which was associated with the happiest period of her life, should be played within her hearing. This wish was complied with; the effect produced was highly gratifying. For the first few minutes, no notice was taken of the music; in a short period, however, a smile was seen to play upon a countenance where all had been dark and gloomy for months. As the music proceeded, the effect became more sensible and powerful; ideas of a most pleasurable kind appeared to rush upon a mind which had previously been a blank; a chord had been touched which thrilled through her, until she appeared absorbed in the pleasing associations which the favourite air had conjured to her recollection. The past was no longer forgotten, and she for the first time gave evidence of being conscious of the situation in which she was in. A fatal blow had been given to the disease, and in a short period she was considered sufficiently recovered to be allowed to return home to the bosom of her family.

The disease of Saul was alleviated by David's harp. Aristotle maintains that actual madness in horses may be cured by the melody of lutes. "Experience has proved," says Gibbon, "that the mechanical operation of sounds, by quickening the circulation of the blood and spirits, will act on the human machine more forcibly than the eloquence of reason and honour." In illustration of the above observation the following fact may be adduced: — At the battle of Quebec, in April, 1760, while the troops were retreating in great confusion, the general complained to a field-officer of Fraser's regiment of the bad behaviour of his corps. "Sir," he answered, in great warmth, "you did very wrong in forbidding the bagpipes to play this morning; nothing encourages Highlanders so much in the day of action, — nay, even now the pipes would be of use." "Let them blow, then, like the devil," replied the General, "if it will bring back the men." The bagpipes were ordered to play a favourite martial air. The Highlanders, the moment they heard the music, returned and formed with alacrity, and fought like infuriated lions.

The influence of music over animals is known to be very great. Burney says that an officer, being shut up in the Bastille, had his lute allowed him; upon which, after a trial or two, the mice came issuing from their holes, and the spiders, suspending themselves from their threads, assembled round him to enjoy the melody.[53]

Falret alludes particularly to the benefit which often accrues from music in peculiar disorders of the nervous system attended with a disposition to suicide. So exalted an idea had M. Appert of its effects on the mind, that he has observed, alluding to criminals, *that the man sensible to the influence of harmony is not irretrievably lost.* A young lady passionately fond of music manifested an inclination to kill herself; she was sent by her family to an hospital, where she was carefully watched. The idea of suicide was not, however, removed until she was allowed the use of her favourite instrument, the harp. The good effect was soon perceptible; her melancholy gradually subsided, and with it the suicidal disposition. She expressed to her friends how grateful she felt that she was allowed to indulge in her favourite amusement, and was conscious of the benefits which she had derived from it.

The progress of epidemic suicide has been stayed by having recourse to measures which have powerfully affected the imagination.

The young women of Marseilles, at one period, were seized with a propensity to commit suicide. In order to prevent the contagion from spreading, a law was passed to the effect that the body of every female who was guilty of self-murder should be publicly exposed after death. The beneficial result of this law became immediately apparent; the epidemic was stopped; the sense of shame prevailed over the recklessness of human life.

In the French army, during the reign of Napoleon Buonaparte, a grenadier killed himself. This suicide was followed by another case, and it was feared that

[53] History of Music.

the disposition would assume an epidemic character. Buonaparte saw the necessity of prompt and decisive measures, and with a view of striking terror in the minds of the soldiers, and putting a stop at once to the spread of what appeared to be a contagious malady, he issued the following "order of the day," dated *St. Cloud, 22 Floreal, an* X.:—

"The grenadier Groblin has committed suicide, from a disappointment in love. He was, in other respects, a worthy man. This is the second event of the kind that has happened in this corps within a month. The First Consul directs that it shall be notified in the order of the day of the guard, that a soldier ought to know how to overcome the grief and melancholy of his passions; that there is as much true courage in bearing mental affliction manfully as in remaining unmoved under the fire of a battery. To abandon oneself to grief without resisting, and to kill oneself in order to escape from it, is like abandoning the field of battle before being conquered.

"Signed,
"Napoleon, "Bessieres."

The effect of this masterly appeal to the courage of the French soldiery was truly magical. The disposition was completely quelled, and no case of suicide occurred for a considerable time afterwards. The course which Napoleon adopted shewed his great knowledge of human nature, as well as the thorough insight he had obtained into the character of the people over whose minds he exercised so tremendous an influence.

An account of the punishment inflicted on the women of Miletus, a city of Ionia, who were seized with an epidemic suicide, is transmitted to us in the writings of Plutarch. He says, "The Milesian virgins were at one time possessed with an uncommon rage for suicide. All desire of life seemed suddenly to leave them, and they rushed on death (by the help of the halter) with an impetuous fury. The tears and entreaties of parents and friends were of no avail; and if they were prevented by force for awhile, they evaded all the attention and vigilance of their observers, and found means to perpetrate the horrid deed. Some ascribed this extraordinary species of desperation and frenzy to certain occult and maddening qualities of the air at that season, somehow or other peculiarly injurious to the female frame and texture, both of body and mind, (since the men were not visibly affected by it;) while the superstitious considered it as a calamity sent from the gods, and therefore beyond the power of human remedy. But whatever was the cause, the effect was visible and important, and could not be suffered to rage long without manifest injury to the state. While speculative men, therefore, were attempting to account for the phenomena, the active magistrate was endeavouring to arrest the progress of the contagion, for which purpose the following decree was issued;—"That the body of every young woman who hanged herself should be dragged naked through the streets by the same rope with which she committed the deed." This wise edict had in a short time the desired effect. Plutarch adds—"The fear of shame and ignominy is an argument of a good and virtuous mind; and they who regarded not pain and death, which are usually esteemed the most dreadful of evils, could not, however, endure the thoughts of having their dead bodies exposed to indignity and shame."

In the Magdalen Asylum, at Edinburgh, a girl was seized with typhus fever, at the time that it was raging in the city, and though she was instantly removed, as well as all her bed-clothes &c., two more were seized next day, and an alarm or panic was soon spread over the whole house. Next day, no fewer than sixteen were in the sick-room, and in the course of four days, out of a community of less than fifty individuals, twenty-two were apparently labouring under decided fever. It now struck Dr. Hamilton that there was mad delusion in all this, and that the disease arose as much from panic and irritation as from any other causes. Acting on this belief, he went to the sick-room, and told the girls that such a rapid spread of the disease was entirely unprecedented; that they were under the delusion of yielding to their fears, and of imitating others who were now undergoing all the tortures of bleeding, blistering, and purging, in Queensbury Hospital. He assured them that the fumigation and other precautions must have destroyed the contagion, and that if they would only keep a good heart and dismiss their fears, he would pledge himself the fever would soon disappear. The effect of the Doctor's speech was magical. All apprehension was instantly banished from the mind, the cheering influence of hope was inspired, moral courage was developed, and the progress of the pestilence stopped. Not one case of fever occurred afterwards, and those who had the fever at the time perfectly recovered.[54]

It is only on the same principle that we can account for the success which Dr. A. T. Thompson met with in the treatment of the following case of whooping-cough, which had been kept up by habit. The patient, a young boy, was threatened with the application of a large blister; although it was not applied, but merely placed within his view, yet the dread of it completely removed the cough. Boerrhave cured epilepsy in a whole school, by marching into it at the moment of the expected attack with a red-hot poker, which he threatened to thrust down the throats of those who should have a fit.

A remarkable instance of epidemic suicide occurred as far back as the reign of Tarquinius Priscus, which as it required, so it received, an effectual check by the spirited introduction of an extraordinary mode of punishment. After this king had employed the Roman people in successful wars abroad, he filled up their leisure at home in works of less apparent honour, though of greater utility. These were to cut drains and common sewers of immense size and durability. When the soldiers disdained these servile offices, and saw no end to their labours, many of them committed suicide by throwing themselves off the Capitoline Hill. Others followed their example, until the contagion spread through the whole of the men. The king, in order to strike terror into the minds of those who might contemplate self-destruction, issued an order commanding the bodies of those who should commit suicide to be nailed on crosses, and then exposed as spectacles to the rest of the citizens, and left a prey to the fowls of the air. The feeling of shame and horror had the effect of checking the disposition to sacrifice life, and thus the king's purpose was effected.

Whether any measures of a similar character could be adopted in cases where the disposition to suicide has a tendency to assume an epidemic form is a matter

---

[54] Edinburgh Medical Trans.

of considerable doubt.

Experience has established the effect of some simple remedies in preventing the return of paroxysms of melancholia with a propensity to suicide. But it has likewise, and not unfrequently, evinced their insufficiency, and at the same time the influence of a strong and deeply impressed emotion in producing a solid and durable change. A man who worked at a sedentary trade consulted Pinel, about the end of October, 1783, for dyspepsia and great depression of spirits. He knew of no cause to which he could ascribe his indisposition. His unhappiness at length increased to such a pitch that he felt an invincible propensity to throw himself into the Seine. Unequivocal symptoms of a disordered stomach induced Pinel to pre-scribe some opening medicines, and for some days occasional draughts of whey. His bowels were effectually opened, and he suffered but little from his propensi-ty to self-destruction during the remainder of the winter. Fine weather appeared to restore him completely, and his cure was considered as perfect. Towards the decline of autumn, however, his melancholia returned. Nature assumed to him a dark and dismal aspect, and his propensity to throw himself into the Seine re-turned with redoubled force. The only circumstance that in any degree restrained the horrid impulse was, the idea of leaving unprotected a wife and child, whom he tenderly loved. This struggle between the feelings of nature and his delirious frenzy was not permitted to continue long; for the most unequivocal proofs soon after appeared of his having executed his fatal project.

A literary gentleman, devoted to the pleasures of the table, and who had lately recovered from a fever, experienced in the autumnal season all the horrors of the propensity to suicide. He weighed with shocking calmness the choice of various methods to accomplish the deed of death. A visit which he paid to London appears to have developed, with a new degree of energy, his profound melancholy, and his immovable resolution to abridge his term of life. He chose an advanced hour of the night, and went towards one of the bridges of that capital for the purpose of pre-cipitating himself into the Thames; but at the moment of his arrival at the destined spot, he was attacked by some robbers. Though he had little or no money about him, he felt extremely indignant at this treatment, and used every effort to make his escape, which, however, he did not accomplish before he had been exceedingly terrified. Left by his assailants, he returned to his lodgings, having forgot the orig-inal object of his sally. This rencontre seems to have caused a thorough revolution in the state of his mind. His cure was complete.

A watchmaker was for a long time harassed by the propensity to suicide. He once so far gave way to the horrid impulse, that he withdrew to his house in the country, where he expected to meet no obstacle to the execution of his project. Here he took a pistol, and retired to an adjoining wood, with the full intent of per-petrating the fatal deed; but missing his aim, the contents of the piece entered his cheek. Violent hæmorrhage ensued. He was discovered, and conveyed to his own house. During the healing of the wound, which was long protracted, an important change took place in the state of his mind. Whether from the agitation produced by the above tragic attempt, from the enormous loss of blood which it occasioned, or from any other cause, he never afterwards shewed the least inclination to put an end to his existence. This case, though by no means an example for imitation, is well calculated to shew that sudden terror, or any other lively or deep impression, may divert, and even destroy, the fatal propensity to suicide.

A few years ago, an officer went into Hyde Park with an intention of shooting himself. He applied a pistol to his forehead; the priming flashed, but no discharge followed. A man of poor appearance, whom the officer had not observed, or perhaps thought unworthy of his notice, instantly ran up, and wrested the pistol from his hands. The other drew his sword, and was about to stab his deliverer, who, with much spirit, replied, "Stab me, Sir, if you think proper; I fear death as little as you, but I have more courage. More than twenty years I have lived in affliction and penury, and I yet trust in God for comfort and support." The officer was struck with these spirited words, continued speechless and motionless for a short time, and then, bursting into tears, gave his purse to the honest man. He then inquired into his story, and became his private friend and benefactor; but he made the poor man swear that he would never make inquiries concerning himself, or seem to know him, if chance should ever bring them in sight of each other.

A female patient, who had often threatened to destroy herself, one day assured M. Esquirol that she was about to do it. "Very well," he answered; "it is nothing to me; and your husband will be delivered of a great torment." She instantly ceased the preparations she was making to accomplish the act, and never spoke of committing it again.

How easily lunatics may be diverted from their purpose by presence of mind, an intimacy with their character, and the tact to employ the destructive feeling by which they are actuated as the means of protection, is well exemplified in an anecdote related by Dr. Fox. He had accompanied a suicidal and furious maniac, who was at the time calm, to the upper story of his asylum to enjoy the prospect beyond the walls. In returning, the spiral staircase struck the eye of the patient; the opportunity roused the half-slumbering propensity, and a fit of frenzy ensued. His eyes glared, his teeth ground against each other; he panted like a bloodhound for his prey, and seizing the Doctor by the collar, howled into his ears, "You jump down, and I will jump after you." The Doctor for the moment was petrified with horror; he was alone with a powerful man, frenzied by insanity; to escape was out of the question; to attempt to overcome him by force was still more futile: in a moment he hit upon a stratagem. Turning to the infuriated madman, he exclaimed, with a look of coolness and collectedness, "Bah! my child could jump from this place; it requires no nouse to do that; the thing is to jump up—that is the difficulty." The madman listened with attention to what the Doctor said, and then observed, "But you cannot do so, can you?" The Doctor replied, he could, and they both hurried down to put the boast to the proof, and the sanguinary threat was forgotten before they reached the lobby.

Physicians not practically acquainted with the treatment of insanity are too much inclined to believe that it is fruitless to attempt to reason a madman out of his morbid delusion, and that to have recourse to a trick in order to dispel the mental illusion is a species of practice unbecoming the dignity of a professional gentleman. Numerous cases are recorded in which patients have been cured of monomania by a well-contrived artifice; and in many cases of suicidal insanity, when other treatment fails, the medical man may have recourse to this mode of cure without any danger of sinking himself in public or professional estimation. The following cases are illustrations of the foregoing remark:—

A celebrated watchmaker, at Paris, was infatuated with the chimera of perpetual motion, and to effect this discovery he set to work with indefatigable ardour. From unremitting attention to the object of his enthusiasm coinciding with the influence of revolutionary disturbances, his imagination was greatly heated, his sleep was interrupted, and, at length, a complete derangement of the understanding took place. His case was marked by a most whimsical illusion of the imagination. He fancied that he had lost his head on the scaffold; that it had been thrown promiscuously among the heads of many other victims; that the judges, having repented of their cruel sentence, had ordered them to be restored to their owners, and placed upon their respective shoulders; but that, in consequence of an unfortunate mistake, the gentleman who had the management of the business had placed upon his shoulders the head of one of his unhappy companions. The idea of this whimsical exchange occupied his thoughts night and day, on account of which his relations sent him to the Hôtel Dieu; and from thence he was transferred to the Asylum de Bicêtre. Nothing could equal the extravagant overflowings of his heated brain. He sung, cried, or danced incessantly; and as there appeared no propensity in him to commit acts of violence or disturbance, he was allowed to go about the hospital without control, in order to expend, by evaporation, the effervescent excess of his spirits. "Look at these teeth," he constantly cried; "mine were exceedingly handsome; these are rotten and decayed. My mouth was sound and healthy; this is foul and diseased. What a difference between this hair and that of my own head!" To this state of delirious gaiety, however, succeeded that of furious madness. He broke to pieces, or otherwise destroyed, whatever was within the reach or power of his mischievous propensity. Close confinement became indispensable. Towards the approach of winter, his violence abated; and, although he continued to be extravagant in his ideas, he was never afterwards dangerous. He was therefore permitted, whenever he felt disposed, to go to the inner court. The idea of perpetual motion frequently recurred to him in the midst of his wanderings; and he chalked on all the walls and doors as he passed the various designs by which his wondrous piece of mechanism was to be constructed. The method best calculated to cure so whimsical an illusion appeared to be that of encouraging his prosecution of it to satiety. His friends were accordingly requested to send him his tools, with materials to work upon, and other requisites, such as plates of copper and steel, watch-wheels, &c. The governor permitted him to fix up a work-bench in his apartment. His zeal was now redoubled; his whole attention was rivetted upon his favourite pursuit. He forgot his meals. After about a month's labour, which he sustained with a constancy that deserved better success, our artist began to think that he had followed a false route. He broke into a thousand fragments the piece of machinery which he had fabricated at so much expense of time, thought, and labour; entered on the construction of another upon a new plan, and laboured with equal pertinacity for an additional fortnight. The various parts being completed, he brought them together, and fancied that he saw a perfect harmony amongst them. The whole was now finally adjusted; his anxiety was indescribable; motion succeeded; it continued for some time, and he supposed it capable of continuing for ever. He was elevated to the highest pitch of enjoyment and triumph, and ran as quick as lightning into the interior of the hospital, crying out, like another Archimedes, "At length I have solved this famous problem, which has puzzled so many men celebrated for their wisdom and talents." But, grievous to say, he was disconcerted in the midst of his triumph. The wheels stopped; the perpetual motion ceased! His intoxication of joy was succeeded by disappointment and confusion. But to avoid a humiliating and mortifying confession, he declared that he could easily remove the impediment; but tired of that kind of employment, he was determined for the future to devote his whole time and attention to his business. There still remained another maniacal impression to be counteracted, — that of the imaginary exchange of his head, which unceasingly recurred to him. A keen and an unanswerable stroke of pleasantry seemed best adapted to correct this fantastic whim. Another convalescent, of a gay and facetious humour, instructed in the part he should play in this comedy, adroitly turned the conversation to the subject of the famous miracle of Saint Denis. Our mechanician strongly maintained the possibility of the fact, and sought to confirm it by an application of it to his own case. The other set up a loud laugh, and replied, with a tone of the keenest ridicule, "Madman as thou art, how could Saint Denis kiss his own head? Was it with his heels?" This equally unexpected and unanswerable retort forcibly struck the maniac. He retired confused, amidst the peals of laughter which were provoked at his expense, and never afterwards mentioned the exchange of his head. Close attention to his trade for some months completed the restoration of his intellect. He was sent to his family in perfect health, and has now for more than five years pursued his business without a return of his complaint.

Mr. Cox recollects a singular instance of a deranged idea in a maniac being corrected by a very simple stratagem. The patient asserted that he was the Holy Ghost; a gentleman present immediately exclaimed, "You the Holy Ghost! What proof have you to produce?" "I know that I am," was his answer. The gentleman said, "How is this possible? There is but one Holy Ghost, is there? How then can you be the Holy Ghost, and I be so too?" He appeared surprised and puzzled, and, after a short pause, said, "But are *you* the Holy Ghost?" When the other observed, "Did you not know that I was?" his answer was, "I did not know it before. Why, then, I cannot be the Holy Ghost."

A Portuguese nobleman became melancholy, and fancied that God would never forgive his sins. Various means were tried to subdue this morbid impression, but in vain, until the following artifice was adopted, which proved successful in restoring the lunatic to reason. During midnight, a person dressed as an angel was made to enter his bed-room, having a drawn sword in its right hand, and a lighted torch in the other. The imaginary angelic being addressed the monomaniac by name, who, rising from his bed, spoke to the supposed angel, beseeching it to tell him whether his sins would ever be forgiven; upon which the angel replied, "Be comforted, your sins are forgiven." The poor man's delight knew no bounds. He rose from his bed, summoned every one in the house to his presence, and explained to them all that had passed. From that moment the man rapidly recovered in bodily health, and his delusion has completely vanished.

A man fancied he was dead, refused to eat, and importuned his parents to bury him. By the advice of his physician, he was wrapped in a winding-sheet, laid upon a bier, and in this way he was carried on the shoulders of four men to the churchyard. On their way, two or three pleasant fellows (appointed for that purpose) meeting the hearse, demanded in a commanding tone of voice to know whose body they had in the coffin. They replied it was a young man's, and mentioned his name. "Surely," said one of them, "the world is well rid of him; for he was a man who led a bad and vicious life, and his friends have good reasons to rejoice that he has thus ended his days, otherwise he would have died an ignominious death on the scaffold." The young man overheard this observation, at which he felt extremely indignant; but feeling that it was not consistent with propriety or the laws of nature for a dead man on his way to his last home to exhibit any indications of passion, he satisfied himself by coolly replying, "That they were wicked men to do him that wrong, and that if he had been alive he would teach them to speak better of the dead." "It is well," said one of the men in reply, "that you are no more; both for yourself and family. You were a mean, pitiful scoundrel, guilty of every abomination, and the world is rejoiced that you no longer live." This was too much for the patience of the dead man to endure, and feeling that he could no longer suffer such unjust aspersions to be cast on his character, he leaped from the coffin, procured the first stick he could lay hands on, and commenced belabouring his vile accusers. As it may be supposed, they gave him plenty to do, and by the time he had gratified his indignation, and well chastised his calumniators, he had become completely exhausted. In this state he was taken home, and in a few days he was completely cured of the morbid idea which had taken possession of his imagination.

Menecrates, as we learn from Ælian,[55] become so mad, as seriously to believe himself the son of Jupiter, and to request of Philip of Macedon that he might be treated as a god. But it is not always that the man thus deranged falls into such good hands as those of the Macedonian monarch; for Philip humorously determining to make the madman's disease work its own cure, gave orders immediately that his request should be complied with, and invited him to a grand entertainment, at which was a separate table for the new divinity, served with the most costly perfumes and incense, but with nothing else. Menecrates was at first highly delighted, and received the worship that was paid to him with the greatest complacency; but growing hungry by degrees over the empty viands that were offered him, while every other guest was indulged with substantial dainties, he at length keenly felt himself to be a man, and stole away from the court in his right senses.

Many cases of suicidal insanity have been cured by removing the persons so unhappily afflicted from their own homes, friends, and relations. In these cases the physician has no little difficulty in persuading the friends of the invalid that a separation from old associations is absolutely indispensable; that without it, a return to sanity cannot be reasonably expected. When Dr. Willis undertook the cure

[55] Lib. xii. cap. 51.

of George III., he insisted, in the first instance, in dismissing all the old servants, changing the furniture, and removing everything from the king's sight that might tend to awaken in his mind ideas of the past. The success that attended his treatment is said mainly to have depended on this circumstance.

Mr. — —, forty-seven years old, of a neuro-sanguineous temperament, was happy in his domestic circle, and his business had prospered until the year, 1830, from which period he was much harassed in the management of his affairs. In December, 1831, after a very trifling loss, he grew sorrowful and melancholy; his face was flushed, his eyes became blood-shot, his breathing was difficult, and he shed tears, incessantly repeating that he was lost. On the next and following days, he made several attempts to commit suicide, so that they were obliged to cover his apartment with wadding. He wished to strangle himself, tried to swallow his tongue, filled his mouth with his fist in hopes of suffocating himself, and then refused all nourishment. At the expiration of six days, the patient was brought to Paris, and entrusted to Esquirol's care. From the moment of his arrival all desire to commit suicide vanished, and the patient appeared restored to reason. "The impression that I received," said he, "on finding myself transported to a strange house cured me." In fact, sleep, appetite, and a return of connected, and sometimes lively conversation, induced the belief that a cure was effected. Three weeks seemed enough for convalescence, when his wife and son came to fetch him. They passed two days at Paris to finish some business there, and then returned to the country. Scarcely had he arrived at his home when he felt himself impelled by the same desires, in consequence of which, he returned to Paris, transacted some business whilst he remained there, and appeared perfectly well. On returning to his home again, he made fresh attempts to commit suicide, struck his son, and those who waited upon him, and endangered the life of his wife. Neither the grief of his family, the watch placed over him, nor the pretended authority of those about him, could overcome these feelings. The patient passed several days without food; he tore up his linen to make a cord to hang himself, tied it round his neck, and got upon his bed in order to throw himself upon the floor; and at last, deceiving the watchfulness of his relations, escaped to throw himself into the river. He was immediately put into a carriage, and accompanied by his wife; but, notwithstanding the strait-waistcoat, he left no means untried to kill himself. On arriving at Paris, and being again confined, he became perfectly reasonable, and made no attempt to destroy himself during the six weeks that his second confinement lasted. There was reason to believe his cure complete. If he was asked why he did not overcome his terrible impressions at his own house as he did at Paris, he answered in an evasive manner, affirming that this time the trial had been long enough, that he was cured, and that he insisted upon returning home. "Deprived of my wife and son," said he, "I am the most unhappy of men, and I cannot live." "But if you are so unhappy here," said Esquirol to him one day, "why do you not try to destroy yourself, as it is very easy to do so?" "I know not," he replied; "but I am cured, and I wish to live." This patient enjoyed the greatest liberty, and although no apparent precaution was taken to prevent his destroying himself, he never made the least attempt. He afterwards ceased to talk unreasonably; but Esquirol was never able to obtain an avowal of the motives which induced him to commit suicide at his own house, whilst he thought no more of it as soon as he came amongst strangers. On returning to his home for the fourth time, although he was able to transact important business, the same phenomena returned with equal violence.

M. — —, twenty-seven years old, after experiencing some reverses of fortune, became maniacal, with a tendency to commit suicide. The elevated situation of the room which he inhabited, the position of the staircase, the reiterated visits of his friends, "who came to contemplate his misfortunes," and the despair of his wife, were so many circumstances which induced him to terminate his existence; and although he avowed that he had no motive for so doing, and that he was ashamed, and considered himself criminal for having attempted it, he left no means untried for more than a month to effect that end. When he was taken away from his home, and lodged in a ground-floor which led into a garden, the idea no longer harassed him. "It would be of no use," he said; "I could never kill myself here; every precaution is taken to prevent me."

A baker's wife, of a lymphatic temperament, experienced a violent fit of jealousy, which caused her much distress, and induced her to watch her husband's steps, who vented his discontent in threats and reproaches. At last, this unhappy woman, being unable to bear the feeling any longer, threw herself out of the window. Her husband ran to pick her up, and bestowed marks of the most attentive kindness upon her. "It is useless," she said; "you have a wife no longer." She refused every kind of nourishment, and neither the solicitations, tears, prayers of her relations, and those of her husband, who never quitted her room, were able to overcome her resolution. After seven days of total abstinence, Esquirol was called in. They hid from him the cause of the disease, but he observed that every time her husband approached the bed, her face became convulsed. The patient was told that she was about to be sent into the country, but that it was necessary for her to take a little nourishment in order to support the journey. A little broth which was offered her was accepted; but notwithstanding her attempts, she could only swallow a few drops. She tried again the following morning, but she expired in the course of the day. "Had this woman," says Esquirol, "been removed from her home immediately after the accident, there is little doubt but she would have been restored. How could she desire to live, her distress being continually aggravated by the presence of her husband?"

The chief means of controlling the passions, and of keeping them within just bounds, is to form a proper estimate of the things of this life, of the relation of our present to a future state of existence, and of the influence which our actions in this world will have upon our happiness hereafter. Such a right estimate every rational man will labour to attain. He will endeavour, by correcting error, and acquiring such habits as are consistent with just sentiments, to withdraw the nourishment from the very root of passion, rather than be for ever fruitlessly occupied in merely pruning the luxuriance of some of its branches.

It may be useful to impress strongly upon the minds of those who have not sufficient command over their feelings, the persuasion that the indulgence of any passion to excess, and especially of the selfish and malevolent ones, is likely to be injurious to health, will certainly be destructive of serenity and comfort; and of course, by diminishing happiness, will frustrate its own aim and intention, and may, by repetition, acquire accumulated force and facility of excitement, become at length unconquerable and habitual, and according to its nature, violence, and frequency, will, in a greater or less degree, be subversive of happiness, and leave them more or less open to the attacks of insanity.

Such persons will therefore see it highly expedient, while under the influence of these impressions, to do all in their power to avoid them; to compare their urgent and apparent importance when they occur, with the probable diminution of the comfort and health of body and mind which they might induce; and to lay it down as a rule never to indulge any passion whatever, till, independently of moral considerations, and the notions of duty and obligation, they have deliberately reflected, whether the importance of the cause will be a sufficient counterbalance to the certain pain inflicted and the injury which may be thence derived to their health of body and ease and soundness of mind. A habit of such deliberation once acquired,—and it may be acquired by diligence and resolution,—will entirely put an end to exorbitant excitement, since by checking the very beginnings of emotion, its growth and progress will be altogether prevented.

And as every one has some weak point on which he is more open to a successful attack, some constitutional or habitual feeling, the approaches of which he cannot easily withstand, all persons who are convinced of the expediency and necessity of subduing their passions, if they would consult their own ease, will be aware of the importance of keeping a diligent watch, and placing a strong guard, upon the one that most easily and successfully besets them.

And whoever would secure a reasonable portion of present happiness will be sensible of the necessity of learning the art of contentment, which, difficult as it may seem to those who have not used themselves to check the wanderings of imagination, and to keep their desires within prudent bounds, not only appears indispensable, but easy, to the man who feels a lively and practical conviction of its wonderful tendency to multiply the sum of actual enjoyment.

With the same view of promoting and securing their own present felicity, such persons will see the propriety of acquiring habits of good nature, and of cultivating the emotions of benevolence. And as virtue seldom fails to bring her own dowry, contentedness and benevolence will infallibly introduce habits of cheerfulness, which, while they improve our happiness, act as powerful preservatives against disease, and as determined enemies of insanity.

CHAPTER X.

PHYSICAL TREATMENT OF THE SUICIDAL DISPO-SITION.

On the dependence of irritability of temper on physical disease—Voltaire and an Englishman agree to commit suicide—The reasons that induced Voltaire to change his mind—The ferocity of Robespierre accounted for—The state of his body after death—The petulance of Pope dependent on physical causes—Suicide from cerebral congestion, treatment of—Advantages of bloodletting, with cases—Damien insane—Cold applied to the head, of benefit—Good effects of purgation—Suicide caused by a tape-worm—Early indications of the disposition to suicide—The suicidal eye—Of the importance of carefully watching persons disposed to suicide—Cunning of such patients—Numerous illustrations—The fondness for a particular mode of death—Dr. Burrows' extraordinary case—Dr. Conolly on the treatment of suicide—Cases shewing the advantage of confinement.

MEDICAL men have not considered with that degree of attention commensurate with its importance the relationship between physical derangement and those apparently trifling mental ailments which so often, if not subdued, lead to the commission of suicide. The origin of self-destruction is more frequently dependent upon derangement of the *primæ viæ* than is generally imagined. Every one must, in his own person, be aware of the influence of indigestion, and what is termed bilious disorder, upon the spirits. An inactive condition of the bowels is a common cause of mental disquietude. Voltaire, who was a man of great observation, appears to have paid considerable attention to this connexion. He advises a person who intends to ask a favour of a prime minister, or a minister's secretary, or a secretary's mistress, to be careful to approach them after they have had a comfortable evacuation from the bowels. Dryden invariably dosed himself before sitting down to compose. He says—"If you wish to have fairy flights of fancy, you must purge the belly." Carneades, the celebrated disputant of antiquity, was in the habit of taking white helebore, (a purgative,) preparatory to his refuting the dogmas of the Stoics. Lord Byron says, in one of his letters, "I am suffering from what my physician terms 'gastric irritation,' and my spirits are sadly depressed. I have taken a brisk cathartic, and to-morrow 'Richard will be himself again.'" The following anecdote is recorded of Voltaire:—"An English gentleman of fortune had been sitting many hours with this great wit and censurer of human character. Their discourse related chiefly to the depravity of human nature, tyranny and oppression of kings, poverty, wretchedness, and misfortune, the pain of disease, particularly the gravel, gout, and stone. They worked themselves up to such a pitch of imaginary evils that they proposed next morning to commit suicide together. The Englishman, firm to his resolution, rose, and expected Voltaire to perform his promise, to whom the genius replied, *"Ah! monsieur, pardonnez moi, j'ai bien dormi, mon lavement a bien operé, et le soleil est tout-à-fait clair aujourd'hui."*

We knew a gentleman whose temper was not controllable if he allowed himself to pass a day without his accustomed evacuation from the bowels. Pinel records the particulars of the case of a man who had fits of mental derangement whenever the action of the bowels became irregular.

The blood-thirsty miscreant Robespierre is said to have been of a *"costive habit, and to have been much subjected to derangement of the liver."* After death, it is said that "his bowels were found one adherent mass." It is indeed interesting to consider, both morally and medically, how far these morbid ailments influenced this monster in the bloody career in which he was engaged.

There can be no question but that the morbid irritability which many of our men of genius have manifested was but the effect of a derangement of the physical frame acting upon a mind naturally sensitive to such impressions.

Much of the petulance, personality, and malignity of Pope was dependent upon causes over which he had no control—viz., disease of the stomach and liver, producing hypochondriasis. It has been well observed by Madden, "Who knows under what paroxysms of mental irritation caused by that disease (indigestion), which more than any other domineers over the feelings of the sufferer, he might have written those bitter sarcasms which he levelled against his literary opponents? Who knows in what moment of bodily pain his irascibility might have taken the form of unjustifiable satire, or his morbid sensibility assumed the sickly shape of petulance and peevishness? Who knows how the strength of the strong mind might have been cast down by his sufferings, when 'he descended to the artifice' of imposing on a bookseller, and of 'writing those letters for effect which he published by subterfuge?' Who that has observed how the vacillating conduct of the dyspeptic invalid imitates the vagaries of this proteiform malady can wonder at his capriciousness, or be surprised at the anomaly of bitterness on the tongue, and benevolence in the heart, of the same individual?"[56]

That Pope was a severe sufferer from bodily disease will appear evident from the following account given by Dr. Johnson of the poet. He says, "Pope's constitution, which was originally feeble, became so debilitated that he stood in perpetual need of female attendance; and so great was his sensibility of cold that he wore a fur doublet under a shirt of very coarse warm linen. When he rose, he invested himself in a bodice made of stiff canvass, being scarcely able to hold himself erect till it was laced; and he then put on a flannel waistcoat. His legs were so slender

---

[56] When Pope was on his death-bed, Bolingbroke observed to the weeping attendants, "I have known Pope these thirty years; he was the kindest-hearted man in the world."

that he enlarged their bulk with three pairs of stockings, which were drawn off and on by the maid, for he was not able to dress or undress himself, and he neither went to bed nor rose without help."

His frequent attacks of indigestion made him at times a perfect picture of misery and wretchedness. It clothed everything with a gloomy aspect, made him quarrel with his friends and domestics, and he has been known to say that he sighed for death as a reprieve from mental and bodily agony. Sir Samuel Garth was frequently consulted when he had these attacks; and it was only by exacting a strict attention to diet and exhibiting medicine that he was enabled to restore the mind of the poet to a healthy tone.

This physical ailment, as it often does when long continued, ultimately affected the cerebral functions. At times he had symptoms of pressure on the brain, or at least of an unequal and imperfect distribution of blood to that organ. Spence says, he frequently complained of seeing everything in the room as through a curtain, and on other occasions, of seeing false colours on certain objects. At another period, on a sick-bed, he asked Dodsley what arm it was that had the appearance of coming out from the wall.

When the disposition to suicide is present, the physician should carefully ascertain whether the patient is not labouring under cerebral congestion, or a determination of blood to the head. The loss of a small quantity of blood has frequently been known to remove the propensity to self-destruction. A case is referred to by Schlegel of a woman who was liable to periodical fits of suicidal mania whenever she allowed a redundancy of blood to accumulate in the system. On two occasions she attempted suicide. On the first indications of a return of her delirium, she was generally bled, and relief was instantaneously afforded.

A gentleman who had received, during the peninsular campaign, a sabre cut in the head, felt for some years, whenever he was exposed to great mental excitement, or allowed himself to over-indulge in the use of spirits, a kind of suicidal delirium. Twice he was detected in the act of attempting to commit suicide, and was fortunately prevented from doing so. The local abstraction of blood from the neighbourhood of the head was the only remedy which appeared to subdue the disposition.

The cases which are related in another chapter of individuals who were insane at the moment when the act of self-destruction was attempted, but who recovered the use of their reasoning after having inflicted a wound attended with loss of blood, fully testify the importance of general and local depletion in certain cases of cerebral disease attended by this unfortunate propensity.

A blow on the head has been known to develope this feeling. The affection of the sentient organ may remain latent for many years, and then suddenly manifest itself. A man had received, when young, a kick from a horse, which produced at the time no very urgent symptoms. Six years after the accident, he, without giving any indications of previous derangement of mind, cut his throat. Upon examining the brain, it was found extensively diseased.

A man, feeling the suicidal disposition, bled himself from the arm, and recovered.

It will not be proper in all cases to abstract blood; for the destructive propensity has been known to exist where there has been a deficiency of blood in the brain. The practitioner should examine the condition of the patient thoroughly before he recommends active depletion. Sixty per cent. of the cases of suicide will, however, be found with cerebral disease either of a primary or secondary nature; and to that organ the medical man's attention should be particularly directed.

The following case happily illustrates the benefits which are sometimes derived from the local abstraction of blood in certain cases of temporary insanity, accompanied with a disposition to commit suicide. "A gentleman," says Dr. Burrows, "of a very irascible and impetuous disposition, with whom I was intimate, experienced in a public meeting a rebuke which exceedingly mortified him, and made so deep an impression upon his mind, that he was quite miserable. At night, instead of going to bed, he roamed abroad; and at length, early in the morning, without knowing whither he went, he found himself near a sheet of water. The view of it at once determined him to drown himself, and he accordingly plunged in. The action was perceived, and he was rescued from the water, insensible, and immediately conveyed to a place where means of resuscitation were adopted. As his address was found in his pocket, a communication was directly made to his family, and Dr. Burrows was called in to see the patient. He found him in a state of insensibility. As soon as consciousness returned, he was dressed, put into a coach, and Dr. B. accompanied him to his residence. As yet, he had not spoken, neither did he appear to observe anything. The motion of the carriage on the stones seemed to rouse him, and he looked about. He took no notice of those who were in the carriage with him. He soon became violent; his eyes were wild, and rolled in their sockets; his face became flushed; the vessels of the forehead were excessively distended, and all the symptoms of genuine delirium came on.[57] Dr. Burrows ascribed the symptoms to a violent reaction in the vascular system from the state of collapse it had sustained, and ordered the oppressed vessels of the head to be relieved by the application of cupping glasses, and the abstraction of sixteen ounces of blood; the head to be kept cool, and enemata to be administered until the bowels were well cleansed out. After these operations, he soon became passive and disposed to sleep. He slept six hours, and awoke tolerably composed, but not quite coherent. He took light nourishment, and at night awoke perfectly collected, but exceedingly low. The next day he was well, but languid. An explanation was given him, which removed the impression that the offensive part of the speech had given him, and he by degrees recovered his usual state of mind."

We are inclined to believe, with D'Israeli, "that there are crimes for which men are hanged, but of which they might easily have been cured by physical means." Damien, who attempted the assassination of Louis XV., and who in consequence was subjected to the most refined tortures, persisted to the last in declaring that if he had been bled, as he wished and implored to be, the morning previously, he never would have endeavoured to take the life of the king.

---

[57] Prior to the more urgent symptoms developing themselves, he appeared to be endeavouring to recollect Dr. B., and addressed him as Dr. Death.

Gaubius relates the case of a lady of a too inflammable constitution, whom her husband had reduced to a model of decorum by phlebotomy.

In the month of April, M. Delormel was called to Madame Chatelain, at the Chateau de Armanvillers, who, according to the statement of the physician in attendance, was "melancholic, hypochondriacal, and insane." She had made several attempts to commit suicide, and was carefully guarded. She had been bled, purged, and well dosed with anti-spasmodics, but to no purpose. M. Delormel examined the patient very carefully, and came to a conclusion respecting her case very different from that which had been formed by the other physicians who had seen her. The lady was thirty-seven years of age, of a very neuro-sanguineous temperament, active in body, and most amiable in disposition. For more than two years she had complained of burning heat in her stomach and bowels; digestion was painful, and constipation habitual. The catameniæ were irregular; she was much emaciated, and the symptoms of melancholia and hypochondriasis were well marked.

Madame C. could not bear to see her husband and children, to whom she had, when in good health, been affectionately attached. Her chief desire was solitude, and the predominant idea was the conviction of approaching death. From an attentive examination of the case, it was pronounced one of chronic gastro-enteritis. Eighty leeches were applied to the abdomen, proper medicines were administered, her diet regulated, and in less than a month she was completely restored to health of body and mind.

When it is evident that the patient is suffering from cerebral congestion, and yet general bleeding is inadmissible, the application of cold to the head by means of a shower bath has often been productive of much good. A young lady who laboured under the disposition to suicide consulted an eminent living physician, communicating to him the particulars of her malady, bitterly lamenting the unfortunate feeling that was undermining her health. After trying various remedies without effecting much relief, a cold shower bath was recommended every morning. In the course of ten days, the desire to commit self-destruction was entirely removed, and never afterwards returned.

A timely-administered purge has been known to dispel the desire of self-destruction. Esquirol knew a man who was decidedly insane whenever he allowed his bowels to be in an inactive condition.

A patient of Falret had well-marked suicidal delirium. So urgent were the symptoms, that he was placed under restraint and carefully watched. Active cathartics were administered, and Falret states that the largest tape-worm he ever saw was evacuated. The idea of suicide soon vanished, and the man was restored in perfect health to his friends and family.[58]

[58] A medical student, twenty years of age, was seized with mania, arising from the presence of worms in the intestines. He felt the most acute pains in the different regions of his body, appearing to him as if persons were driving arrows into him, more particularly in the palms of his hands and soles of his feet. This caused him to utter most distressing cries, to seek to be alone, and prevented him from walking. The intolerable pains and madness left him as soon as the worms were expelled.

Foderé examined the bodies of three persons in one family who fell by their own hands, and in the three cases considerable disease was discovered in the intestinal canal, which had been irritating the brain and disturbing its manifestations.

In the instances just referred to, the indication of physical disease of the *primæ viæ* were but trifling during life.

Disease of the stomach and liver frequently incite to suicide; hepatic affections notoriously disturb the equilibrium of the mind. Many a case exhibiting an inclination to suicide has been cured by a few doses of blue pill. The physician should direct his attention to the condition of the uterine function and the state of the skin. During the puerperal state, a tendency to suicide is often manifested.

A lady, shortly after her accouchement, expressed, with great determination, her intention to kill herself. Her bowels had not been properly attended to, and a brisk cathartic was given. This entirely removed the suicidal disposition.

Any irregularity in the action of the uterine organ may give rise to the same inclination. Under such circumstances, emmenagogues will do much good.

German writers dwell much upon the connexion between suicide and derangement of the cutaneous secretion. That this function should also be attended to there cannot be a doubt, although we cannot call to mind any cases of suicide which could be directly traced to suppressed perspiration.

In some cases, a blister applied and kept open in the neighbourhood of the head has effected much good. In other instances, issues have been beneficial, particularly in persons subject to cerebral congestion. There is, however, a condition of brain accompanying the suicidal disposition which may be denominated a state of *cerebral irritation*, in which bleeding or depletion would be injurious. In such cases, friction on the spine, and the administration of anti-spasmodics, gentle aperients, and alteratives, will be serviceable.

Sufficient attention is not paid to those precursory symptoms which indicate the existence of a disposition to suicide. In two-thirds of the cases that occur, the act is preceded by premonitory signs, which, if attended to, will prevent the developement of the propensity.

With very few exceptions, the mental symptoms are those which are principally manifested in these cases. Lowness of spirits, a love of solitude, an indisposition to follow any occupation which requires exercise of the mind, are generally exhibited. The person's suspicions become roused; he fancies his dearest friends are regardless of his interests, or are plotting against his life. He takes no pleasure in the family circle. He may be suffering from some evident physical malady, acting through sympathy on the brain, and deranging its functions; and then he will often refer to his disease, and express his utter hopelessness of ever being cured. There is an expression of countenance generally present in a person who meditates suicide, which, if once seen, cannot easily be forgotten. Suicidal mania is easily recognised by the experienced physician. The surgeon of a large establishment in the environs of the metropolis informed me, that in six cases out of ten he could detect, by the appearance of the eye, the existence of the desire to commit self-destruction. A young gentleman, a few days previously, had been admitted into the house as a patient. The surgeon, after examining and prescribing for the lunatic, said to one of the keepers, "You must watch Mr. — — carefully, for I feel assured he will attempt his life." Everything with which he might injure himself, were he so disposed, was taken from him; but it appears that he had resolved to make away with himself, and had carefully concealed a pen-knife in his boot. On the evening of the day on which he was admitted he made a dreadful gash in his throat, but failed in injuring any large vessel. He confessed that he had determined to sacrifice his life; he said, "It has been pre-ordained that I should fall by my own hands, and I am only fulfilling my destiny by cutting my throat!" Shortly after this he was removed; and as we have been subsequently informed, sufficient care not being taken of him, he eventually succeeded in killing himself.

How difficult it is for the medical man to persuade the friends of a person who has evinced a disposition to suicide, of the absolute necessity of his being confined and carefully watched! A physician, dining with a friend, met by accident a young lady who had exhibited, for a few days previously, a shrewdness of manner that attracted the notice of those with whom she associated. He also observed a wildness and incoherence about her ideas; but what particularly struck his attention was, the peculiar expression of countenance which so often denotes the presence of suicidal mania.[59] He felt convinced in his own mind that the lady meditated self-destruction; and so firmly persuaded was he of the fact, that he seriously spoke to the gentleman at whose table he was dining on the subject, and urged him, as he was intimately acquainted with the young lady's family, to suggest the propriety of having medical advice, and of carefully watching the movements of the lady. This suggestion was treated with ridicule, and of course the subject was not broached again. Two days after the conversation took place, intelligence was brought that the lady had taken a large dose of laudanum, and had died from its effects! A little prudent caution might have saved the life of this poor unfortunate being.

In cases in which the disposition to suicide has been evinced, the patient ought to be carefully watched, and, under some circumstances, placed under restraint. Men who talk loudly of the effects of moral coercion, and who repudiate the idea of strait-waistcoats &c., have had but little practical experience of the treatment of

---

[59] "When powerful feelings or passions are in active operation, in the insane or in the sane, they draw the muscles of the face into particular forms; and, if they continue for a length of time to be greatly predominant, they impress upon the countenance an appearance indicative of the character. This is felt and acted upon unconsciously in the common intercourse of life. A good countenance is a letter of recommendation; and we have, in spite of ourselves, an unfavourable feeling towards a stranger where this is absent. Now in the generality of suicidal cases, the desponding feelings are in constant and active operation; hence there is usually a melancholy and gloomy expression of countenance. This arises from no mysterious cause peculiar to insanity, but is perfectly intelligible on common physiognomical principles; but there are numerous instances where the most experienced physician would be unable to detect, by inspection only, the slightest mark of either a disposition to suicide or insanity. The absence of this expression must not, therefore, induce us to suppose that this disposition does not exist." —Sir W. Ellis.

the insane. Moral discipline has done much good. Deeply should we regret to see the system which has been in force within our own recollection again introduced into our lunatic asylums. In endeavouring to avoid Scylla we have fallen into Charybdis. How many lives are lost in consequence of the patients not being properly secured when they have exhibited a desire to commit self-destruction.

A lady who had attempted to destroy herself was very properly sent to an asylum. Having expressed a determination to avail herself of the first opportunity for carrying her intentions into execution, she was most carefully guarded. She was never allowed to be out of sight; a trustworthy nurse always kept by her side; and in the course of time she was pronounced recovered. But as it was not considered prudent to send her home at once, she was separated from the other inmates of the house, and allowed to reside with the surgeon and matron of the establishment. Even under these circumstances it was thought better not to allow her to be wholly by herself, fearful that the disposition might again suddenly develope itself. She resided with the surgeon for some weeks, and appeared completely well. She expressed much astonishment when told that she had attempted her own life; she was apparently horrified at the idea. She was sitting with the matron one morning after breakfast; the surgeon was going round the asylum, when a child was heard to cry up stairs, as if it had received some injury. The matron immediately left the room; she was not absent three minutes, and when she returned she was astonished to find the young lady had vanished. Immediate search was made for her, but she was not to be found, when, looking behind the curtain in the parlour, the lady was discovered hanging to the cornice! In that short space of time she had succeeded in suspending herself, and was quite dead. Of course we cannot determine whether she had recovered, and this was but a sudden recurrence of the suicidal mania, or whether she had cunningly concealed her ailment for the purpose of throwing her attendant off her guard, and thus being enabled to effect her dreadful purpose. We should be more disposed to accede to the latter solution of the question, knowing the extreme cunning of such lunatics, and the ingenious stratagems they often have recourse to in order to accomplish any mischievous object they have in view.

A person who manifested indications of mental aberration was found in the act of hanging himself. Upon being detected, he promised most solemnly to abandon his rash resolution. He attempted a second time to kill himself by cutting his throat, but the wound was not fatal. He was now placed under the care of a gentleman who had devoted much attention to the treatment of insanity; and, knowing his propensity, the keeper received strict injunctions to watch his movements carefully. Everything by which he could injure himself was removed from his room, he was shaved every day by a barber, and no instrument of any kind was allowed to be in his possession. He was confined for nine months; and it appeared, from what afterwards occurred, that he had, during the whole of this period, been absorbed in the one idea of how he should contrive to commit suicide. He was discovered one morning hanging by the neck from the bedstead, quite dead. How he got possession of the cord which suspended him, puzzled everybody acquainted with the history of the case. At last the enigma was solved. It appears that parcels of books and newspapers had occasionally been sent to him by his family, tied with twine; and he had carefully, and unknown to the keeper, concealed each piece, until he had collected a quantity to constitute a cord sufficiently strong with which to hang himself. For nine months this idea had exclusive possession of his mind; and although he exhibited no apparent symptoms of insanity, he had evidently been contemplating suicide for the period already specified.

A female had made repeated attempts, during her residence in the asylum at Wakefield, to hang herself, but had been so watched that she had not succeeded. One evening, the servant, on going to remove all her clothes out of her bed-room, thought she saw something bright on the top of one of her under garments; upon examination, this was found to be a pin. She had contrived just before bed-time to take off her garter; and, knowing that her pockets as well as her clothes would all be removed, she contrived to pin it within her dress, so high up that it would not easily be perceived. Very providentially, the brightness of the metal discovered it, and she was again prevented from accomplishing her purpose. By degrees the propensity wore off; and after a residence of eighteen years in the Hanwell Asylum, Sir W. Ellis found her a few years ago, living, though upwards of eighty years of age, in a comparatively tranquil state, waiting her removal in the ordinary course of nature.

When persons determined on suicide find that they are unceasingly watched, and so carefully secured that they have no opportunity of executing their design, they will assume a most cheerful manner for days and weeks together, in order to lull suspicion; and when a favourable opportunity offers, it is never neglected.

A man who had long been in a state of despondency, and had made many attempts to hang himself, but had always been prevented, very suddenly appeared much better. He became apparently cheerful, and being desirous of employment, was sent out with a large party into the hay-field. He continued in this and other out-door occupations for some time, gradually improving. One evening, on returning from the field, when the rest of the party went in to tea, (which they were allowed when hay-making,) he told the farming man that he did not feel thirsty, and as it was very warm he would rather remain at the door. He was left there. A short time afterwards his keeper came down to inquire for him, and being told where he had been left, immediately exclaimed, "Then he has hung himself!" It was also singularly impressed upon his mind, that it was in one particular out-house that he had done it. There he went, and found him suspended and dead, as he expected.

"A noble lord," (says Dr. Rowley,) "whose family I had the honour to attend, had received, it is said, some little reproof from a great personage, concerning a military omission. It seized his lordship's mind so seriously, that on examination it was evident to me that suicide was intended. All weapons and dangerous means whatever were removed. It being a circumstance of delicacy, I sent for his lordship's son, then about eighteen, from Westminster school, communicated my apprehensions, and requested his constant attendance on his noble parent. This the young man executed for several days, and prevented the commission of the crime apprehended. In my absence a few hours in the country, a very eminent, learned, and indeed remarkably sagacious physician, but my mortal and vindictive enemy, was called in. I had, contrary to medical *etiquette*, enforced the necessity of promptly bleeding a most noble lady in an apoplexy, which saved life, but brought down invectives, hatred, and vengeance on me. Whether out of opposition to my vigilance, or from malicious motives, it would be difficult to determine, but the noble lord was liberated from all restraint, and my apprehensions treated by injurious insinuations and with contempt. Thirty-six hours had scarcely elapsed before the noble lord put a period to his existence, by a sword he had concealed, which had been a present from Prince Ferdinand: he wounded his breast in two places, but the third thrust pierced his heart. Thus perished a nobleman, whose liberality, feelings, and many virtues, did honour to human nature, and who might, in all probability, have been now living, had not medical arrogance and illiberality, merely from personal ambition, dictated error, at the risk of human destruction! *Horridum! valde horridum!"*

The physician should constantly bear in mind this important fact connected with the suicidal disposition—viz., that those determined upon self-destruction often resolve to kill themselves in a particular manner, and however anxious they may be to quit life, they have been known to wait for months and years, until they have had an opportunity of effecting their purpose according to their own preconceived notions. A man who has attempted to drown himself will not readily be induced to cut his throat, and *vice versa*. A morbid idea is frequently associated in the maniac's mind with a particular kind of death, and if he be removed from all objects likely to awaken this notion, the inclination to suicide may be removed.

An old man, upwards of seventy years of age, who had a market garden, near the asylum at Wakefield, consulted the late Sir W. Ellis as to the best mode of destroying himself, as he had made up his mind not to live any longer. He said he had thought of hanging himself, if Sir William could not recommend an easier death. The physician talked to him some time upon the heinousness of the crime he contemplated, and endeavoured to shew him that hanging was a most horrible death, from the suffocation that must be felt. His conversation was attended with little success. Finding that the chylopoietic viscera were a good deal disordered, he prescribed for him, and sent to inform his wife that he ought never to be left alone. The medicine had the effect of restoring the secretions to a healthy action, and he got better. Sir William heard no more of him for some time, when he was at length informed that he was discovered dead in a little shed in his garden, where he used to keep his tools. But so fixed was the mode in his mind, by which he was determined to accomplish his death, that, though the place was so low he could not stand upright in it, and he had not a rope or a string with which he could suspend himself, he contrived to effect his purpose by getting a willow twig, and making it into a noose, which he fastened to one of the rafters. He stooped to put his head through it, and then pushing his feet from under him, suspended himself until he died. Now, if he had not made up his mind to destroy himself in this particular way, he might have accomplished it with much greater ease by drowning himself in the pond in his garden, or by cutting his throat with his garden knife, which he always had about him; but neither of these was the mode he previously intended.

It may be practically useful to all who have the immediate care of suicidal patients to bear this in mind; and if the medical man can find out that any particular plan is contemplated, he ought to be especially careful to remove the means of accomplishing it out of the patient's reach, and to prevent him having an opportunity of carrying it into execution.[60]

"A medical friend," says Dr. Burrows, "who had much enjoyed life, and never met with any circumstances to occasion him particular disquietude, when at the age of forty-five became very dyspeptic, low-spirited, and restless. He gradually shunned society; but still, though with great reluctance, pursued his professional avocations. This depression increased so much that he often told his wife that he should consult me. (He knew very well that both his father and grandfather had destroyed themselves.)

"One morning he kept in bed much longer than usual, and a relation calling, went up, without being announced, to see him. He seemed composed, at length complained of being very faint, and upon raising him up, blood was perceived on his hands. Upon examination it was discovered, at the moment his friend entered the chamber, he was employed in opening the femoral artery; that there had been considerable hemorrhage from the small vessels he had divided. I saw him within an hour afterwards. He had recovered from the syncope, and expressed great sorrow for what he had done; described with minuteness his case; lamented he had not seen me sooner, but that he could not muster sufficient resolution; consented to place himself under my superintendence; and, in fact, to follow all my directions.

"I placed him in charge of a careful keeper. It was agreed that he should be removed into lodgings in the environs of town; and he therefore submitted to the necessary medical treatment.

"He remained two days at home, till lodgings could be procured, during which he was calm and rational; but there existed the suicidal eye, which sufficiently denoted that he was not to be trusted.

"On the third morning, his keeper, having a violent attack of rheumatism in his right arm, could not shave him, and another person was obliged to be trusted. This person, unfortunately, laid the razor on the dressing-table; and, while his face was turned away, and the keeper was heating some water a few feet from the table, the patient suddenly jumped up, seized the razor, and in a moment applied it to his throat, and effectually divided the carotid artery."

A case somewhat similar we find recorded by the same authority. Major——had been wounded at the battle of Waterloo. He had since recovered his health, but a great depression of spirits followed. The maniacal diathesis was hereditary. By degrees he became more desponding, his ideas wandered, and at length a suicidal propensity was evident. On visiting him, Dr. Burrows strongly urged the necessity of placing him under the supervision of an experienced keeper; but here, as in too many cases, his family opposed this advice, and would not permit proper restraint, but put him under the care of a nurse only. In the evening, he retired

---

[60] Ellis on Insanity.

early to bed. The nurse went to tea in his chamber, supposing her charge to be asleep. The patient watched the opportunity, jumped out of bed, seized a knife on the table, wounded, and would have effectually cut his throat, had not the nurse interposed.

"A clergyman in Warwickshire told me," says Dr. Conolly, "that he was requested, some years ago, to interfere respecting certain measures proper for securing a neighbour who had exhibited unquestionable symptoms of insanity. His neighbour, however, was not to be met with on the day when it was intended to remove him, and when he reappeared, which was either the next day or in a day or two afterwards, he was quite in a sound state, in which condition he has lived with great comfort up to the present time. On the other hand, an instance came under my own observation in which a gentleman had shewn many proofs of disordered mind for the space of three or four months, and his actions becoming dangerous, it was resolved to remove him. About two hours before I was to call for him, he was so quiet and orderly in a conversation with the old family-apothecary, that the latter gentleman rode off to the relations of the patient, relenting all the way concerning the proposed restraint, and purposing to solicit its postponement; in which attempt he was only prevented by being overtaken by a messenger before he had ridden half a mile, who came to inform him that his apparently tranquil patient had nearly blown up his house and his whole family with gunpowder, having for that purpose thrown a pound and a half of it into the fire, sitting by to see it explode. In another case, a gentleman had made repeated attempts at self-destruction, but seemed to have got well, and was no longer much looked after; yet after living comfortably at home for a little while, and having passed a cheerful evening in reading to his wife, he concluded it, when she had retired, by hanging himself in the parlour.

"These lamentable accidents are, of course, always productive of disagreeable feelings in the mind of a practitioner; but never more so than when he has been too confident of the absence of danger. It is questionable, perhaps, whether there are not, in all these cases, certain means of which prudence might avail itself, for the purpose of ascertaining the exact state of the supposed convalescent's mind, as well as the existence of such intentions in a lunatic as are inconsistent with the safety of other persons, or with the preservation of his own existence. The lunatic may maintain a very guarded silence on these matters so long as they remain quite unsuspected, but is not very well able, in general, to prevent his intentions becoming visible to those who have begun to suspect him. These intentions, too, are generally associated with certain recollections, or certain topics, or certain antipathies or prepossessions, which may be found out and brought into the conversation; in which case, the lunatic can seldom conceal his agitation, his superstitious belief, his anger, or his inly-cherished hope of full revenge. Indeed, he is often in no degree solicitous to conceal his feelings. There cannot be anywhere a more harmless person than Jonathan Martin; his manners are mild, his occupations are of the most peaceful description, his language is strikingly simple and unassuming; but take up the Bible, and you have touched the chord of his insanity; you find that, to destroy the noblest monuments of ancient piety and munificence seems to him a work to which God has especially called him. The effect of possessing a key to the excited feelings of a lunatic is, indeed, always surprising to those unaccustomed to their peculiarities. You walk with a man who seems to delight in the simplest pleasures of a state of innocence; he admires the flowers of the field and the beauty of the sky, or he dwells with satisfaction on the contemplation of whatever is generous and good; nothing can exceed the mildness of his manner: but a single word calculated to rouse a morbid train of ideas, a name, the reminiscence of a place, or any trifling inadvertency, will convert this placid being into a demon; the tones of his voice, his gestures, his countenance, his language, assume, in a moment, the expression of a fiend; and you discover that opportunity alone is wanting to effect some dreadful crime. The discovery of such a design is certainly not always so easy, but wherever suspicion exists, strict superintendence is warranted, or various degrees of restraint must be determined upon, and steadily adhered to."[61]

The following cases will shew the necessity of guarding a person by the strictest surveillance from the moment that he evinces the slightest symptom of mental alienation, when it manifests itself by incongruous expressions or attempts at self-destruction. This precept should be engraven on the mind of every medical man, and no feeling of false delicacy should prevent his communicating his suspicions and wishes the moment he considers measures of precaution necessary. In these cases, the loss of an hour may make all the difference between life and death.

M. Piorry was called to the Hôtel de Bibliothèque, where he found a man of athletic form and military appearance in a state of complete insensibility. He manifested all the indications of apoplexy or epilepsy. Some time elapsed before the physician could ascertain what was the matter; he could not obtain any satisfactory answers to his repeated questions. At last the patient made Piorry understand that he had swallowed a key. Professor Roux was sent for, who, after considerable difficulty, succeeded in extracting the foreign body from the œsophagus, along with an oblong piece of copper attached by a chain to the handle of the instrument. On the succeeding night he made fresh attempts to destroy himself; first by hanging with the bed-clothes, and, on that mode not proving successful, he endeavoured to strangle himself by squeezing two chairs against his neck. Thwarted in effecting his design, he again swallowed the key, and he was nearly dead when he was discovered, and the key extracted from his throat. He was now confined in a strait-waistcoat, and was subjected to proper medical treatment. In the course of a short period, all disposition to suicide was removed, and his mind was restored to perfect integrity.[62]

A soldier, who was greatly beloved in his regiment for his exemplary conduct and amiable qualities, became affected with suicidal melancholy, and fired a pistol into his mouth. The havoc made was dreadful; but by great exertions on the part of M. Petit, who attended the case, his life was preserved. During his confinement, he manifested great anxiety for his recovery, and expressed himself horrified that he should ever have attempted to commit self-destruction. The surgeon and his friends entertained every hope that all suicidal tendency was dissipated. The re-

[61] Indications of Insanity.
[62] Journ. Gen. de Médecine, Juillet, 1822.

sult, however, proved that the whole was a manœuvre on the part of the patient to lull suspicion to rest, and when he had succeeded by this dissimulation in throwing his friends off their guard, he put an effectual period to his existence whilst in the wards of the hospital.

The following case exhibits some practical points exceedingly worthy of record, and displays besides, in a remarkable degree, the control a lunatic disposed to suicide acquires over himself, his conversation, and conduct, when he wishes to lull suspicion to sleep. In this instance, says Dr. Burrows, who relates the particulars of the case, a most judicious physician, and those in whom he had confidence, all experienced in the phases of this wonderful malady, insanity, and its no less wonderful concomitant, suicide, were completely deceived.

A medical friend of the Doctor's, travelling over Shooter's Hill, observed a gentleman walking up it, his carriage following him. When opposite to each other, the stranger suddenly fell on his knees in the dirt, and lifted up his hands, as if in earnest prayer. The friend stopped his post-chaise at so extraordinary a sight, and soon found by his looks and manners that the poor gentleman was insane. He immediately accompanied him back to London, and placed him under Dr. B.'s care till his relations were informed of his state.

The history of the case was this:—The patient was a cavalry officer of rank, aged thirty-five, and had particularly distinguished himself at the recent battle of Waterloo. On that occasion he had two horses killed under him, and was himself wounded in four places. He was first struck on the crown of his helmet by the splinter of a shell, which wounded the scalp and stunned him; he was next shot through the fleshy part of the thigh by a grape shot, which at the same time killed his first horse; from these two wounds he lost much blood. Whilst lying under his second horse, he was pierced in the groin by a lance; and in this helpless condition he received from a French drummer, who was rifling the dead and dying, a violent blow on the temple from the butt-end of a musket, from the effects of which, he remained some time insensible. He was afterwards conveyed in a most deplorable state as a prisoner within the French lines, and though released the same evening by the victorious allies, a long while elapsed before his wounds and exhausted condition received any attention.

He inherited a predisposition to insanity, and was naturally reserved, diffident, and taciturn, but affectionate and generous.

When he recovered from his wounds, he often complained of pains in his head; and it was observed that his temper became fretful and suspicious; that he slept ill, was depressed in spirits, and courted solitude. These symptoms increased latterly. At length he imagined himself the sport of his brother officers, and many other delusions arose.

There was a moral cause likewise operating which, on a constitution that had recently received so severe a shock, no doubt greatly influenced his disorder. He had applied for promotion in consequence of his sufferings in the service. This was withheld, as he thought, ungraciously, and too long; and when he was raised a step, his mind was already too much disturbed duly to appreciate it. The anniversary of the glorious battle of Waterloo was just passed, and the recollection of it was painful to him. In this state he came to town.

He was exceedingly sober and temperate by habit; but during the day before, with a brother officer, he was persuaded to commit an unusual excess in wine, with the hope of raising his spirits.

This proved a match to the mine. It exploded, and his intellects became completely deranged.

Dr. Burrows found him with his countenance very wild, the eyes injected and pupils contracted, pulse quick and weak, tongue white, and great thirst. He had had no sleep for five nights. Sometimes exalted, violent, and loquacious; sometimes depressed and taciturn. He was rather languid, which was imputed to his having lost full twenty ounces of blood from the rupture of an hæmorrhoidal vessel.

It is not necessary to detail the medical treatment adopted, but we will proceed to those points in the case which are relevant.

He was placed in lodgings with a careful attendant. In about three weeks he was nearly well, when unluckily a whitlow formed on his finger, and as one of his delusions was that he was rotten in every part, it was the cause, besides pain, of considerable irritation, and it broke his rest; other delusions returned, but subsided with the pain of the whitlow, and he again greatly improved.

In six weeks he was so well that the Doctor took his leave, advising him to travel during the remainder of the autumn. The next day some domestic occurrence occasioned violent irritation, and he again relapsed into despondency, unattended by paroxysms of violence; but he shortly recovered.

However, instead of going into the country and varying the scene, his lady brought him into town and permitted unrestricted intercourse with his relations, &c. He grew quarrelsome, suspicious, and very low-spirited, and began to abuse his wife. It was then earnestly recommended that he should be completely separated from all intercourse with her and his connexions, but the advice was disregarded.

A boil now formed on his body. This irritated him more than the whitlow, and his delusions about his rottenness were more prominent than ever; but when the boil suppurated and discharged, his mind again improved.

No persuasion could induce his friends to give him exercise or diversion, or change the scene. He therefore sat all day brooding over his fantasies, and reading religious books; for now there was added to his delusions an impression that he was very wicked, and had neglected his religious duties. His face, too, assumed the suicidal expression.

A month afterwards, a consultation with two eminent physicians confirmed Dr. Burrows' opinion of the treatment to be pursued. But, notwithstanding this consultation, all remedial aid was neglected, and he was allowed to follow his own inclinations, both in religious matters and in totally secluding himself. In about three weeks all the symptoms were so much increased that he was sent to a private asylum. A few days afterwards, while walking out, he tried to drown himself, but was rescued by his keeper. He continued in this desponding state some months, when, rather suddenly, he appeared much better; and continuing to improve, his physician thought him well, and he returned home. Two days only had passed, when he called on the same physician, acknowledged that he was as bad as ever, and entreated earnestly that he might again be received into his house. He was so on that day. The next day he poisoned himself and died.

It proved, that he had never abandoned the desire of committing suicide; but he so well concealed it, and otherwise conducted himself, as to lead to the conclusion that he had recovered. It was, in fact, a scheme, the sole object of which was to get out and buy laudanum. Having procured a sufficient quantity, but anxious to save his wife the agony of witnessing the act he meditated, he preferred returning to the asylum to execute it.

A few general principles have been laid down in this chapter to direct the practitioner in the management of certain cases of suicidal insanity. The success of the treatment will in a great measure be dependent on the physician making himself acquainted with the minute history of each case submitted to his professional care. No particular rules can be adduced that will be applicable to all cases of this description; much must be left to the judgment of the medical man. The physician should, however, never forget that whatever apparently may be the physical disturbance going on in the system, the brain, and the brain alone, is the seat of the disease in all cases of suicide, and to the condition of that organ most particular attention ought to be paid.

CHAPTER XI.

IS THE ACT OF SUICIDE THE RESULT OF INSANITY?

The instinct of self-preservation—The love of life—Dr. Wolcott's death-bed—Anecdote of the Duke de Montebello—Louis XI. of France—Singular death of a celebrated lawyer—Dr. Johnson's horror of dying—The organ of destruction universal—Illustrations of its influence—Sir W. Scott, on the motives that influence men in battle—Have we any test of insanity?—Mental derangement not a specific disease—Importance of keeping this in view—Insanity not always easily detected—Is lowness of spirits an evidence of derangement?—The cunning of lunatics—Esquirol's opinion that insanity is always present—Moral insanity—The remarkable case of Frederick of Prussia—Suicide often the first symptom of insanity—Cases in which persons have been restored to reason from loss of blood, after attempting suicide—The cases of Cato, Sir Samuel Romilly, Lord Castlereagh, Colton, and Chatterton examined—Concluding remarks.

NATURE has ordained no law more universal in its influence than the desire which all animated beings display, and which is indeed the governing principle in the greater part of their actions, to preserve their existence, and to secure themselves from the influence of circumstances that bring it into danger. That "no man ever yet hated his own flesh, but nourisheth it and cherisheth it," is an axiom laid down in scripture, and one founded on reason and observation.[63]

One of our poets, in alluding to this subject, after declaring life to be the dream of a shadow, "a weak-built isthmus between two eternities, so frail that it can neither sustain wind nor wave," yet avers his preference of a few days', nay, a few hours' longer residence upon earth to all the fame that wealth and honour could bestow—

---

[63] "Pain is an evil; death, the deprivation of every hope or comfort in this life. No man in his senses will burn, drown, or stab himself; for these all produce what are called evils; neither can any of these actions be executed without the probability of pain in the convulsive action or struggles of death. As no rational being will voluntarily give himself pain, or deprive himself of life, which certainly, while human beings preserve their senses, must be acknowledged evils, it follows that every one who commits suicide is indubitably *non compos mentis*, not able to reason justly, but is under the influence of false images of the mind; and therefore suicide *should ever be considered an act of insanity*."—DR. ROWLEY.

> "Fain would I see that prodigal
> Who his to-morrow would bestow
> For all old Homer's life, e'er since he died till now."

"Is there anything on earth I can do for you?" said Taylor to Wolcott, as he lay on his death-bed. The *passion for life* dictated the answer, "Give me back my youth?" These were the last words of the celebrated Peter Pindar.

Dr. Johnson had a superstitious fear of death. Boswell asked him whether we might not fortify the mind for the approach of death. Johnson answered in a passion, "No, Sir, let it alone! It matters not how a man dies, but how he lives. The act of dying is not of importance; it lasts so short a time." But when Boswell persisted in the conversation, Johnson was thrown into such a state of agitation that he thundered out, "Give us no more of this;" and turning to Boswell, he said, with great earnestness, "Don't let us meet to-morrow!"

> "O thou strong heart!
> There's such a covenant 'twixt the world and thee,
> They're loath to break!"

There is an anecdote recorded of one of the favourite marshals of Napoleon, the Duke de Montebello, which finely illustrates the strength of this instinctive principle. During a battle in the south of Germany, the duke was struck by a cannon-ball, and so severely wounded that there was no hope of his surviving. Summoning the surgeon to his side, he ordered the wounds to be dressed; and when help was declared to be unavailing, the dying officer, excited into frenzy by the love of life, burned with vindictive anger against the medical attendant, threatening the heaviest penalties if his art should bring no relief. The dying marshal demanded that Napoleon should be sent for, as one who had power to save, whose words could stop the effusion of blood from the wounds, and awe nature itself into submission. Napoleon arrived in time to witness the last fearful struggle of expiring nature, and to hear his favourite marshal exclaim, as the lamp of life was just being extinguished, "Save me, Napoleon!"

The following case, which occurred in humble life, illustrates the same principle:—A man on the point of death vowed he would not die, cursing his physician, who announced the near termination of his life, and insisted that he would live in defiance of the laws of nature.

It is recorded of Louis XI. of France, that so desperately did he cling to life when everything warned him to prepare for death, that he, in accordance with the barbarous physiology of that age, had the veins of children opened, and greedily drank their blood, hoping in that way to fan the dying embers of life into a flame!

A once celebrated member of the English bar, whose strong original powers of mind had been obscured and enfeebled by the gross sensuality of his habits, in the extremity of his last illness, when the shadows of death were fast coming over him, with a blasphemous audacity, swore by his Creator that he *would not die*. In this state of morbid and impious rage he struggled out of his bed, tottered down the stairs, and fell lifeless in the passage. From the exclamation of this unfortunate man, it would seem as if he fancied that he held the reins of life in his hands, and could arrest at will the rapidity of its descending career.

Spence says, that "Salvini was an odd sort of man, subject to gross absences, and a very great sloven. His behaviour in his last hour was as odd as any of his behaviour in all his lifetime before could have been. Just as he was departing, he cried out in great passion, *"Je ne veux pas mourir, absolument!"*

> "The weariest and most loathed worldly life
> That age, ache, penury, and imprisonment, can lay on man,
> Is paradise to what we fear of death."

It is not our intention to consider this subject phrenologically. That we have all certain good and evil propensities inherent in our nature, developed in various degrees in different individuals, is admitted by the anti-phrenologist, as well as by the most zealous advocate of that science. We need no phrenology to tell us, that "the heart of man is deceitful above all things, and desperately wicked:" scripture makes us acquainted with this fact. It is useful to look at the dark as well as the bright side of human nature. Without, then, using *terms* which might be considered objectionable, there can be no doubt of the existence in the human mind of a propensity to destroy, varying in degree from the simple pleasure of viewing the destruction of human life, to the most impassioned desire to kill others or oneself. This is a natural propensity, and, when not subdued by the higher faculties of the mind, it exhibits itself in the form of unequivocal insanity. This feeling to destroy may exist in conjunction with a consciousness on the part of the individual that he is about to commit a crime opposed to the laws of God and man. Dr. Gall relates many particulars of cases in which this natural propensity became morbidly developed. A student shocked his fellow-pupils by the extreme pleasure he took in tormenting insects, birds, and brutes. It was to gratify this inclination, he confessed, that he studied surgery. A man had so strong an inclination to kill that he became an executioner; and a Dutchman paid his butcher, who furnished ships with extensive supplies of meat, for being allowed to slaughter the oxen. In these cases we see this natural feeling inordinately developed. Subject such persons to the operation of causes likely to excite this extra-developed propensity, and they will murder others or themselves.

Gall mentions the case of a person at Vienna who, after witnessing an execution, was seized with a propensity to kill; at the same time, he had a clear consciousness of his situation. He wept bitterly, struck his head, wrung his hands, and cried to his friends to take care and get out of his way. Pinel mentions the case of a man, exhibiting no apparent unsoundness of intellect, who confessed that he had a propensity to kill. He nearly murdered his wife, and then attempted several times to destroy himself.

In 1805, a man was tried at Norwich for wounding his wife and cutting his child's throat. He had been known to tie himself with ropes for a week to prevent his doing mischief to others and to himself. A man exposed to a sudden reverse of fortune was heard to exclaim, "Do, for God's sake, get me confined; for if I am at liberty I shall destroy myself and wife! I shall do it, unless all means of destruction are removed; and therefore do have me put under restraint. Something above tells me I shall do it; and I shall!"

Whenever the mind is exposed to the influence of excited feeling, and the operation of the reasoning powers are suspended, we see the faculty alluded to developed according to the constitution of the individual. On the field of battle, striking examples occur of the various energies of this inclination. One soldier at the appearance of blood experiences the intoxication of carnage; another will swoon at the same sight. Sir Walter Scott, in the poem in which he has referred to the battle of Bannockburn, alludes to the various feelings that influence the mind in the heat of an engagement; and it will be perceived that he directs particular attention to those who are influenced by no other motive than the pleasure they derive from sacrificing human life: —

> "But, oh! amid that waste of life,
> What various motives fired the strife!
> The aspiring noble *bled for fame*,
> The patriot for his country's claim;
> This knight his youthful strength to prove,
> And that to earn his lady's love;
> *Some fought for ruffian thirst of blood*;
> From habit some, or hardihood;
> But ruffian stern, and soldier good,
> The noble and the slave,
> From various cause the same wild road
> On the same bloody morning trode
> To that dark inn, the grave."

What conclusion are we justified in drawing from the facts just related? Certainly, that there is in us all a disposition to destroy, which is in some wisely and providentially restrained. If this view of the matter be correct, we do not think that we should be wrong in concluding that by far the great majority of cases of suicide result from a morbid development of this natural feeling, consequent upon a primary or secondary affection of the brain. This subject is of great interest in a medico-legal point of view, and is well deserving of serious consideration.

Is the act of suicide an evidence of mental derangement? Before this question can be satisfactorily answered, it would be necessary for us to consider that *vexata questio*—what is insanity? Have we an unfailing standard to which to appeal; an infallible *test* by which we can ascertain, with anything like a proximity to truth, the sanity of any mind? Perhaps, if we were to assert that we considered it impossible to point out the line of demarcation which separates the confines of a sane and insane condition of the mind, we might lay ourselves open to an attack. Again, were we bold enough to proclaim our non-adherence to what is considered as the orthodox faith in this matter, and assert that we viewed every departure from a healthy tone of mind, whether in its intellectual or moral manifestations, as an evidence of insanity, we might still more expose ourselves to the merciless lash of the critic; yet these are the opinions to which we should feel most disposed to give our assent. We must make a marked distinction between insanity considered as a *legal* and as a *medical* question; and it is greatly owing to our not keeping this essential difference in mind that so much useless reasoning and vituperation has arisen. The man who is daily exposed to the kind and cheering influence of friendship, and who fancies himself alone in the world, without one human being to sympathize with him in his afflictions, is as essentially mad as he is who imagines himself to be made of glass, and is fearful of sitting down lest he should injure his brittle glutei muscles. A poet of antiquity wrote a book describing the miseries of the world, and destroyed himself at the conclusion of the task.

"No man who is oppressed with grief," Crichton justly observes, "and who is constantly preyed on by mental and bodily pain, can be supposed capable of exercising his judgment at all times correctly; a fresh misfortune, imaginary or real, excites an irresistible desire of relief. Tired out, hopeless, dismayed by the threatening aspect of many a bursting cloud; discerning nothing, whichever way he looks, but a dreary and comfortless life, how can he be supposed capable of taking a clear, calm, and comprehensive view of the obligations he owes to his Creator or society, or of reflecting on the sudden vicissitudes which daily occur in human life, and on which every man may safely form some hope, even in the most distressed situation? The wretchedness of life is the only picture present to the mind of one in whom grief has terminated in such a state of deep melancholy; the only objects of comparison are the misery of existence on the one hand, and the relief he can obtain by withdrawing himself from it on the other."

Insanity results from a disease of the brain. Although after death, in many cases, no appreciable structural lesion can be detected in the cerebral mass, it would be illogical for us to conclude that the sentient organ has not been physically affected. Derangement of mind is but the effect of physical disease, and, like all other diseases, it has an early as well as an advanced stage. Medical men have not paid sufficient attention to the premonitory indications of mental alienation. Having erected an arbitrary standard of derangement in their own minds, they have been disposed to consider no deviation from mental soundness as insanity, unless it exhibited the symptoms which their preconceived ideas had led them to suppose necessary, in order to constitute that disease. They have argued as if insanity were a specific disease invariably manifesting the same phenomena, and in this way definitions have been framed, by which the soundness of the intellect has been tested. It is hardly necessary to say how fallacious all such tests must be. The brain, like every other organ, is liable to a variety of diseases, in all of which the mental faculties are more or less affected. The danger of attempting to erect an arbitrary standard of insanity is this: it induces us to overlook the incipient symptoms of mental derangement, and to consider no deviation from soundness of intellect as insanity which does not come within the scope of our definition. The early symptoms of mental aberration are as much an evidence of the presence of insanity, as when the disease is more advanced, and the indications become so apparent that no one hesitates in pronouncing the individual mad. Medical men who have maintained that the act of suicide is not invariably the result of insanity have argued as if the mental ailment was always self-evident and easily detected; whereas, those who have had any experience in the matter know full well, that occasionally there are no diseases more difficult of detection than those which relate to a morbid condition of the mind. If an act of suicide has been committed, and the individual at the moment of perpetrating it did not manifest evident symptoms of insanity, the conclusion drawn is, that he was perfectly sane at the time. That the facts of the case do not warrant this inference must be apparent to those who consider the subject in an enlarged point of view. If we examine attentively the majority of cases of suicide, we shall find that the unfortunate persons have laboured, either for some time previously or at the very moment, under depression of spirits, anxiety of mind, and other symptoms of cerebral derangement. Very few cases of suicide take place in which you cannot trace the existence of previous mental depression, produced either by physical or moral agents. It may be said that lowness of spirits is not insanity; certainly not, according to the *legal* definition of the term; but we may always be assured, that if mental anxiety or perturbation be more than commensurate with the exciting cause, it may be presumed that the individual is labouring under the incipient indications of insanity.[64] This view of the case is strengthened if an hereditary predisposition to the disease should also be present.

"It will be said," says Esquirol, "that there are individuals who, in the midst of affluence, grandeur, and pleasures, and in the full enjoyment of reason, have suddenly put an end to their existence, immediately after parting with their friends in good spirits, or after having written letters on business with perfect correctness. Can these be said to be insane when they commit suicide? Yes; most undoubtedly. Do not monomaniacs appear perfectly sane on all other subjects, till the particular idea is started which forms the burden of their hallucination? Are they not capable of curbing the expression of their delirium, and dissembling their aberration of intellect? It is the same with sane individuals, over whom the suicidal idea tyrannizes. A physical pain, an unexpected impression, a moral affection, a recollection, an indiscreet proposition, the perusal of a passage in writing, will occasionally revive the thought and provoke the act of suicide, although the individual the instant before should be in perfect integrity of mind and body."

In general, most persons actually insane wish not only to be esteemed free from the malady, but to be considered as possessing considerable intellectual endowments; hence, *real* lunatics seldom allow the existence of their lunacy; but are always endeavouring to conceal from observation those lapses of thought, memory, and expression, which are tending every moment to betray them, and of the presence of which they are much oftener conscious than is generally apprehended or believed. Alexander Cruden, when suffering under his second and last attack of mental aberration, upon being asked whether he ever was mad, replied: "I am as

[64] Lowness of spirits ought to be regarded and treated as insanity, says Ellis, and not dreaded as its forerunner. For it is at this stage that suicide is resorted to. Should this not be the case, specific hallucinations may speedily appear, and the agony of mind will be endured as a consequence of bankruptcy, the unfaithfulness of a friend, the persecutions of enemies, or the ravages of an incurable disease. No demonstration of the untenableness of such grounds, no picture of brighter and happier circumstances, will avail to refute or encourage. The sufferer clings to his hoarded misery. There is generally great loss of physical strength in cases of this kind, and the pale emaciated countenance, dull and sunken eye, and listless dejected form, tell as plainly as the querulous complaint, or the long intricate description of sorrows and anticipated evils, to what class the patient belongs.

mad now as I was formerly, and as mad then as I am now, that is to say, *not mad at any time.*"

Again, medical men who have reasoned against this opinion have forgotten entirely one peculiar, and a very remarkable feature of insanity — viz., the singular cunning of lunatics; how extremely difficult it is in many cases where *we know* the individual to be unquestionably mad, to make his delusion apparent. The case of the lunatic who indicted Dr. Monro for confining him in his asylum has often been cited. He brought an action against the Doctor at Westminster; and, although the man was subjected to a most severe examination and cross-examination, his insanity could not be detected. The trial was on the eve of being concluded, when Dr. Sims entered the court, and knowing the man's peculiar delusion, he was requested to ask him a question. He did so, and his insanity instantly became apparent. He brought another action against Dr. Monro in the city of London, and, knowing that he had failed before by acknowledging his love for an imaginary princess, so remarkable a degree of cunning did he exhibit that one of the severest examinations to which a man was ever subjected in a court of justice could not induce the lunatic to disclose the delusion under which he was known to labour. This curious feature of insanity must be taken into consideration in forming an estimate of the presence of derangement in cases of suicide, and we must not hastily conclude, because insanity is not *self-evident*, that it does not exist.

A merchant, fifty-five years of age, of a strong constitution, although of a lymphatic temperament, mild and gentle in his disposition, the father of a numerous family, and who had acquired a considerable fortune in business, experienced some domestic troubles, not sufficiently serious, however, to affect any one of a resolute character. About a year ago, he formed a large establishment for one of his sons, and shortly afterwards became very active, and expressed, contrary to his usual habits, the delight which he felt at his increasing prosperity. He was also more frequently absent from his warehouse and business than usual. But notwithstanding these trifling changes, neither his family, nor any of his friends or neighbours, suspected any disorder of his reason. One day, whilst he was from home, a travelling merchant brought to his house two pictures, and asked fifty louis for them, which he said was the price agreed on by a very respectable gentleman who had given his name and address. His son sent away both the pictures and the seller. On his return, the father did not mention his purchase; but the children began the conversation, alluding to the roguery of the merchant, and their refusal to pay him. The father became very angry, asserting that the pictures were very beautiful, that they were not dear, and that he was determined to purchase them. In the evening, the dispute became warmer, the patient flew into a passion, uttered threats, and at last became delirious. On the next day, he was confided to Esquirol's care. His children, frightened at their father's illness, and alarmed at the purchase which he had made, looked through their accounts; and great was their astonishment at seeing the bad state of their books, the numerous blanks which they presented, and the immense deficiency of cash. This irregularity had existed for more than six months. Had this discussion not taken place, one of the most honourable mercantile houses would have been compromised in a few days; for a bill of exchange of a considerable amount had become due, and no means had been taken to provide for it.

A patient has been known to weep, and affect the deepest contrition for attempting suicide, when it has been proved that all the time he was meditating on the means of accomplishing his design. A workman was admitted into a French hospital, having a third time attempted his life. He appeared deeply mortified and broken-hearted that he should have suffered a relapse, and was much affected by the remonstrances of his physician. He promised faithfully, in tears, to abandon his rash resolve. Ten minutes afterwards, whilst on his road home, he perceived a piece of cord; he seized it, made a noose, put his head into it, and suspended himself from the branch of a tree, where he was found dead! Cases illustrative of the same fact are mentioned in another part of this work.

Again, we must bear in mind that insanity is often as much a disease of the *moral* as of the intellectual faculties, and that it is possible for the intellect to be perfectly sound, and yet for insanity to be present. Moral derangement has not met with that consideration from the profession which its importance demands. Insanity often consists in a vitiated condition of the moral principle, independently of any delusion of the intellect; and in many cases of suicide, if we investigate their history, we shall find that the alienation has been of this character. A man, whose disposition naturally disposed him to vice, fancied that he had been guilty of committing a nameless offence, and, whilst labouring under this idea, blew out his brains. In this case, the intellect was unaffected; the derangement consisted in a perversion of the moral powers. Senile insanity, which has been recognised in our courts of law, is a derangement of the moral constitution. In cases of this description, it is possible for the person to be conscious of his infirmity, and to confess, with great apparent regret, his inability to control his feelings. "I am impotent, and not fit to live," said a man, and accordingly cut his throat. If we admit the existence of an insanity which consists solely in a perversion of the moral powers, then we should hesitate in pronouncing *ex cathedrâ* that insanity is not present because no derangement of the intellectual faculties can be perceived.

Dr. T. Mayo observes, that "no intellectual delusion need be present when self-destruction is coveted. But there must be an extinction of that moral sense which revolts from it on grounds independent of fear. Owing, however, to the systematic neglect of moral symptoms, the suicide is seldom recognised as possessing this destructive tendency until he has made an attempt upon his life; often, therefore, until all measures must be too late."

A very common feature of moral mania is a deep perversion of the social affections, whereby the feelings of kindness and attachment that flow from the relations of father, husband, and child, are replaced by a perpetual inclination to tease, worry, and embitter the existence of others. The ordinary scene of its manifestations is the patient's own domestic circle, the peace and happiness of which are effectually destroyed by the outbreakings of his ungovernable temper, and even by acts of brutal ferocity. Frederic William of Prussia, father of Frederic the Great, undoubtedly laboured under this form of moral mania; and it furnishes a satisfactory explanation of his brutal treatment of his son, and his utter disregard of the feelings or comfort of any other member of his family. About a dozen years before his death, his health gave way under his constant debauches in drunkenness; he became hypochondriacal, and redoubled his usual religious austerities. He forbade his family to talk of any subject but religion, read them daily sermons, and compelled them to sing, punishing with the utmost severity any inattention to these exercises. The prince and his elder sister soon began to attract a proportionate share of his hostility. He obliged them to eat and drink unwholesome or nauseous articles, and would even spit in their dishes, addressing them only in the language of invective, and at times endeavouring to strike them with his crutch. About this time he attempted to strangle himself, and would have accomplished his design had not the queen come to his rescue. His brutality towards the prince arrived to such a pitch that he one morning seized him by the collar as he entered his bed-chamber, and began to beat him with a cane in the most cruel manner, till obliged to desist from pure exhaustion. On another occasion, shortly after, he seized his son by the hair, and threw him on the ground, beating him till he was tired, when he dragged him to a window, apparently for the purpose of throwing him out. A servant hearing the cries of the prince, came to his assistance, and delivered him from his hands. Not satisfied with treating him in this barbarous manner, he connived at the prince's attempts to escape from his tyranny, in order that he might procure from a court-martial a sentence of death; and this even he was anxious to anticipate by endeavouring to run him through the body with his sword. Not succeeding in procuring his death by judicial proceedings, he kept him in confinement, and turned all his thoughts towards converting him to Christianity. At this time, we first find mention of any delusion connected with his son, though it probably existed before. In his correspondence with the chaplain to whom he had entrusted the charge of converting the prince, he speaks of him as one who had committed many and heinous sins against God and the king, as having a hardened heart, and being in the fangs of Satan. Even after he became satisfied with the repentance of the prince, he shewed no disposition to relax the severities of his confinement. He was kept in a miserable room, deprived of all the comforts and many of the necessaries of life, denied the use of pens, ink, and paper, and allowed scarcely food enough to prevent starvation. His treatment of the princess was no less barbarous. She was also confined, and every effort used to make her situation thoroughly wretched, and though, after a few years, he relaxed his persecution of his children, the general tenour of his conduct towards his family and others evinced little improvement in his disorder, till the day of his death.[65]

In considering this point it is important to remember that *the attempt at self-destruction is* OFTEN *the* FIRST *distinct overt act of insanity*. A young lady of delicate constitution, but previously in apparent health, started up one day from the tea-table, rushed to the window, and endeavoured to throw herself out. It required several persons to restrain her until a strait-waistcoat could be procured. She remained insane from that time until the day of her death, with very partial glimmerings of reason. "Fortunately," says Mr. Chevalier, who relates the case, "her life was not long protracted."

---

[65] Vide Lord Dover's Life of Frederick, and Ray on Med. Juris.

It has been inferred, that when an unsuccessful act of suicide has been committed, and the person expresses his regret for what he has been guilty of, that we are justified in concluding that the mind was sane when the suicide was attempted. The effort which Sir Samuel Romilly is said to have made to stop the hemorrhage after having cut his throat, has been cited by a celebrated living authority as an evidence of his previous sanity.[66] We must bear in mind that many cases of suicide result from derangement of mind dependent on cerebral congestion.

In such cases, we can imagine a person insane when the act of self-destruction is attempted, and sane immediately afterwards. The loss of blood which a person would sustain from an extensive wound of the throat, particularly when, as is often the case, some large vessel is wounded, would instantly relieve the brain of the superabundant blood which had been oppressing it, and deranging its manifestations, and thus producing a return of sanity. That this was the fact in Sir Samuel Romilly's case is evident from its history. There cannot be a shadow of doubt that he was insane when he cut his throat; and his apparent desire to live after the act was committed, may be attributed to the relief which he had derived from the loss of blood.

Mr. T. Miller, of Spalding, in a fit of delirium, cut his throat so dreadfully that after languishing three days, he died. He manifested during this interval the utmost contrition for his offence, declaring he knew not what he had done until he found the blood streaming from his wound. He dictated his will, and talked rationally with his friends till his dissolution.[67]

A merchant in the city, not many months back, met with some losses in business. His mind became affected to a certain extent; he felt a strong desire to kill himself; but being a man of education and enlarged capacity, he fought most resolutely against this inclination. He had been exposed during one day to the influence of circumstances which caused great mental depression. He said to his head-clerk, previously to his leaving his counting-house, that his head felt heavy and oppressed, and he had a *presentiment* that something would happen before the morning. The clerk suggested the propriety of his having medical advice, but he did not think proper to do so. In this state he went to bed. In the middle of the night he awoke in a state of extreme agitation; no language could convey an adequate idea of his feelings, and suicide was the only act which held out the hope of relief. In this state he rose from his bed, called up the servants, and commanded them to run for the surgeon. A professional gentleman who lived close by was soon in attendance, and the moment he entered the room the patient exclaimed, "Bleed me, or I shall cut my throat!" The operation was instantly performed, and as the blood flowed from the vein the patient exclaimed, "Thank God! I have been saved from committing self-murder." Every disposition to suicide was immediately removed.

The following is an extract of a letter found in the pocket of Captain Aitkins, of the Pembroke Fusileers, who committed suicide:—"As some inquiry may be

[66] Dr. J. Johnson.
[67] Hill on Insanity.

instituted as to the cause of my death, I think it necessary to state that it was inflicted by my own hand, partly from pecuniary embarrassment, and partly from the effect of *strong nervous malady*, which has fixed itself on my spirits so as to render life insupportable." In this case we have no hesitation in asserting, that if the brain could have been relieved of the unnatural weight which oppressed it, this poor man would not have stained his hand with his own blood.

In many cases the delusion of the intellect is so self-evident that no one questions the existence of insanity. A respectable Scotch merchant, near Pimlico, committed suicide by cutting his throat. He fancied the devil was in him; he asserted he could feel him in his throat. On examining his room after his death, two wills were discovered, in one of which he desires his executors to employ a surgeon to open his body, that the devil might be found, secured, and destroyed; and in this way, he says, he will be prevented from injuring any one else.

Many other cases could be cited in which the act of suicide was clearly traceable to mental derangement, were it considered necessary further to illustrate this point. Much evil has resulted from the opinions which the profession have entertained relative to the absence of insanity in cases of those who have exhibited a disposition to destroy themselves. In this matter, the principle which the great Edmund Burke applied to politics is equally applicable to medicine—"We had better be blamed for too anxious apprehension, than be ruined by too confident a security."

It is a safe doctrine always to presume the presence of insanity in those who have exhibited a desire to commit suicide. A person who has once attempted to take away his life cannot be trusted, notwithstanding he manifest the usual evidences of a sane intellect. It is astonishing to consider the ingenious tricks and stratagems to which a person whose mind is bent on self-destruction will have recourse in order to effect his purpose. We find recorded the case of a woman who was tried for her life, and who, in order that she might escape from the hands of the executioner, applied a hundred leeches to her body, hoping to bleed to death. Another female exposed herself to a swarm of bees; and we read of an apothecary who endeavoured to beat out his brains with his own pestle.

A builder, who had been found fault with by his employer, became melancholy, and finally determined upon self-destruction. He hurried to a steep part of the high road, where vehicles of all descriptions were compelled to put on the drag in the descent. Here he waited until a heavily loaded wagon reached the spot, when he seized hold of one of the wheels that was not locked, and applying his body to the circumference, was instantly crushed.

A woman cut her throat severely, but not fatally. Her friends could not be prevailed on to believe that she was insane. She recovered, but shewed such evidences of that unhappy condition, through the whole progress of her cure, as were sufficiently unambiguous to every competent judge. She had speculated unsuccessfully in the lottery, and it was insisted that the rash act was solely to be ascribed to her disappointment in this venture. Soon after her recovery, and when her affairs had assumed a more comfortable train, she went up one day into her bed-room, and being thought to stay longer than was necessary, a person went to see after her, and found her sitting before a dressing-glass, with a basin under her chin, and a knife in her hand, cutting her throat again, as deliberately as a surgeon would have performed an operation. She recovered this time also, and afterwards made a third and successful attempt.

A maniac who was extremely turbulent, and had evinced a strong propensity to destroy himself, was confined, and everything taken from him which could be imagined in any way capable of being instrumental for such a purpose. He was re-marked on one occasion to be unusually quiet, and on his keeper looking through an aperture in his apartment, he discovered him scooping out his eyes with a bit of broken china found by him in the mattress, which he had torn to pieces; and with his face full in the glare of the sun, he had completely accomplished this horrid act before the door could be opened to secure him.

A gentleman of some political consequence in France had an attack of apo-plexy, from which he recovered by copious bloodletting. Some years afterwards, he had a fall from his horse, and was wounded severely in his head, the injury occasioning fever and delirium of some weeks' duration. After this accident, he evinced some marks of mental aberration. He threw up his post under govern-ment, and retired to his chateau in the country, for the purpose of concocting, as he said, a scheme for *uniting the people of all nations*. To prepare a suitable edifice for this philanthropic union, he began to pull down his chateau; but being inter-rupted by his friends, he came to Paris, and one day jumped off the Pont-Neuf into the middle of the Seine. He swam manfully, and reached the shore in safety. He was so proud of this exploit that he considered himself invulnerable, and began next day to run in the way of carriages or fiacres he met in the street, calling to the drivers that they need not mind him, as he could not be injured! He was seized and carried home, but in a day or two jumped out of the chamber window into the street. He was then placed in M. Esquirol's establishment, and considered as an incurable maniac.

During the French revolution, a case of mania without delirium gave rise to an extraordinary scene at the Asylum de Bicêtre. The mob, after the massacre of the prisons, broke like madmen into the above hospital, under pretence of emanci-pating certain victims of the old tyranny, whom it had endeavoured to confound with the maniacal residents of that house. They proceeded in arms from cell to cell, interrogating the prisoners, and passing such of them as were manifestly insane. A maniac, bound in chains, arrested their attention by the most bitter complaints which he preferred, with apparent justice and rationality. "Is it not shameful," said he, "that I should be bound in chains, and confounded with madmen." He defied them to accuse him of any act of impropriety or extravagance. "It is an instance of the most flagrant injustice!" He conjured the strangers to put an end to such op-pression, and to become his liberators. His complaints excited amongst the armed mob loud murmurs and imprecations against the governor of the hospital. They immediately sent for that gentleman, and, with their sabres at his breast, demand-ed an explanation of his conduct. When he attempted to justify himself, they im-posed silence upon him. To no purpose did he adduce, from his own experience, similar instances of maniacs who were free from delirium, but at the same time extremely dangerous from their outrageous passions. They answered him only with abuse; and had it not been for the courage of his wife, who protected him with her own person, he would have been sacrificed to their fury. They commanded him to release the maniac, whom they led in triumph with reiterated shouts of "Vive la République!" The sight of so many armed men, their loud and confused shouts, and their faces flushed with wine, roused the madman's fury. He seized with a vigorous grasp the sabre of his next neighbour, brandished it about with great violence, and wounded several of his liberators. Had he not been promptly mastered, he would soon have made them repent their ill-timed humanity. The savage mob then thought proper to lead him back to his cell, and, with shame and reluctance, yielded to the voice of justice and experience.

Many modern and ancient cases of suicide have been referred to in support of the opinion that insanity is not necessarily present under such circumstances. The conclusions drawn from the history of ancient cases, such as Cato, Cleopatra, Cassius, &c., cannot fairly be made use of in the present inquiry; and yet if we examine these instances, which have been so triumphantly brought forward as incontrovertible proofs that it is possible for a person with a mind perfectly unclouded and free from even the semblance of aberration to commit suicide, we shall discover that they are not such good illustrations in support of the doctrines which they who cite them are anxious to uphold.

The suicide of Cato has often been referred to, and is considered a most apt and conclusive instance in point. We admit this case is one of great importance, inasmuch as it has been held up as an example to others of a man who sacrificed his own life to promote the interests of his country. How many have been induced to plunge recklessly into another world in imitation of the conduct of the Roman hero!

Was Cato perfectly sane when he sacrificed his life? We are disposed to think not. His whole conduct immediately preceding the last fatal act of his life evinces the extreme mental agitation under which he laboured; despair had taken possession of his faculties; the ambition and the hopes of years were prostrated in a moment to the dust, and to escape from a long life of tyranny, he perished on his own sword.

Many modern cases have been cited as evidence of the coolness and collectedness which many have exhibited in the act of suicide. The Rev. Mr. Colton, the accomplished author of "Lacon," is said to have been sane when he committed self-destruction. He shot himself with a pistol after having written the following apophthegm: "When life is unbearable, death is desirable, and suicide justifiable." The last few weeks of Colton's life were embittered by acute mental and physical suffering. He was involved in great pecuniary difficulties, and was dependent for the necessaries of life on the charity of his friends. Independently of this, he laboured under a very painful disease, and it was when exposed to this combination of misery that he committed suicide. His biographer states that there was no doubt of Colton's insanity at the time of his death; it was evident to all who were about him. The evidence in Sir Samuel Romilly's case is as strongly corroborative of his derangement as in that of poor Colton's. At the time, he was suffering from the loss of a wife to whom he was most dotingly attached, and the cerebral derangement was so apparent that his physician ordered him to be cupped in the nape of the neck a short period previously to his killing himself. Lord Castlereagh's insanity was also clearly manifested. His whole conduct on the day he cut his throat led irresistibly to the conclusion that he was not in his right senses. His strange manner was noticed some time previously in the House of Commons. The Duke of Wellington saw the necessity of medical advice, and had a physician sent to him; in fact, the evidence was as strong as evidence could be, and no one at the time questioned the correctness of the verdict. There were many peculiar circumstances connected with his lordship's early history which ought to be borne in mind before we conclude that he was of sane mind at the moment of his suicide.

It is now more than thirty-five years ago that the following singular circumstance occurred to the Marquis of Londonderry: He was on a visit to a gentleman in the north of Ireland. The mansion was such a one as spectres are fabled to inhabit. The apartment, also, which was appropriated to his lordship was calculated to foster such a tone of feeling from its antique character; from the dark and richly carved panels of its wainscot; from its yawning chimney, looking like the entrance to a tomb; from the portraits of grim men and women arrayed in orderly procession along the walls, and scowling a contemptuous enmity against the degenerate invader of their gloomy bowers and venerable halls; and from the vast, dusky, ponderous, and complicated draperies that concealed the windows, and hung with the gloomy grandeur of funeral trappings about the hearse-like piece of furniture that was destined for his bed. Lord Londonderry examined his chamber; he made himself acquainted with the forms and faces of the ancient possessors of the mansion as they sat upright in their ebony frames to receive his salutation; and then, after dismissing his valet, he retired to bed. His candle had not long been extinguished when he perceived a light gleaming on the draperies of the lofty canopy over his head. Conscious that there was no fire in his grate; that the curtains were closed; that the chamber had been in perfect darkness but a few minutes previously, he supposed that some intruder must have entered into his apartment; and, turning round hastily to the side from whence the light proceeded, he, to his infinite astonishment, saw not the form of any human visitor, but the figure of a fair boy surrounded by a halo of glory. The spirit stood at some distance from his bed. Certain that his own faculties were not deceiving him, but suspecting he might be imposed on by the ingenuity of some of the numerous guests who were then inmates of the castle, Lord Londonderry advanced towards the figure; it retreated before him; as he advanced, the apparition retired, until it entered the gloomy arch of the capacious chimney, and then sunk into the earth. Lord Londonderry returned to his bed, but not to rest; his mind was harassed by the consideration of the extraordinary event which had occurred to him. Was it real, or the effect of an excited imagination? The mystery was not so easily solved.

He resolved in the morning to make no allusion to what had occurred the previous night, until he had watched carefully the faces of all the family, to discover whether any deception had been practised. When the guests assembled at breakfast, his lordship searched in vain for those latent smiles, those conscious looks, that silent communication between parties, by which the authors and abettors of such domestic conspiracies are generally betrayed. Everything apparently proceeded in its ordinary course; the conversation was animated and uninterrupted, and no indication was given that any one present had been engaged in the trick. At last, the hero of the tale found himself compelled to narrate the singular event of the preceding night. He related every particular connected with the appearance of the spectre. It excited much interest among the auditors, and various were the explanations offered. At last, the gentleman who owned the castle interrupted the various surmises by observing that "the circumstance which had just been recounted must naturally appear very extraordinary to those who have not been inmates long at the castle, and are not conversant with the legends of his family;" then, turning to Lord Londonderry, he said, "You have seen the Radiant Boy. Be content; it is an omen of prosperous fortunes. I would rather that this subject should not again be mentioned."[68]

The case of Chatterton—

> "The marvellous boy,
> The sleepless soul that perish'd in his pride"—

has been adduced; but no one acquainted with the history of this unfortunate youth would doubt for one moment that he was insane. Chatterton possessed naturally acute sensibilities; he was unquestionably a man of genius. When the forgery of Rowley's poems was detected, his mind received a severe shock; friend after friend forsook him. All his bright and cheering hopes were levelled to the earth; his character for integrity was gone; the world, which had been so eager to court his society and friendship, turned its back upon him; misfortunes followed in rapid succession, until he was frenzied by mental agony and physical suffering. At the time of his death he was in want of the common necessaries of life, realizing the affecting picture of the poet—

> "Homeless, near a thousand homes he stood,
> And near a thousand tables pined and wanted food."

Under such circumstances, it is not surprising that poor Chatterton's mind should have been overthrown, and that he should have been led to commit suicide. A few days before his death, he wrote to his mother in these terms:—"I am about to quit for ever my ungrateful country. I shall exchange it for the deserts of Africa, where tigers are a thousand times more merciful than man." A very important fact connected with Chatterton's case ought to be borne in mind—viz., that insanity was in his family.

We have entered at some length into the consideration of this question, because we felt it to be one of great importance. In forming an estimate of the condition of a person's mind who has committed suicide, the coroner and jury should

---

[68] This was no doubt an hallucination of the senses. On another occasion, when in the House of Commons, Lord Castlereagh fancied he saw the same "Radiant Boy." Does not this fact establish that his lordship's senses were not always in a healthy condition? It is possible that when impelled to suicide he laboured under some mental delusion.

make particular inquiries into the following points:—First, as to state of mind for some time prior to the act. In many, and in fact, in all cases, if proper evidence can be obtained, it will be discovered that the person has laboured under depression of spirits, either resulting from physical or mental causes. Inquiry should be instituted as to the presence of any disease of the stomach or liver which may have operated injuriously on the mind. In many cases it will be found that the suicide has received at some period of his life a blow on his head, giving rise to cerebral injury, which may remain latent for a great length of time, and suddenly manifest itself. Is insanity, particularly suicidal insanity, in the family? What was the person's natural character? Was he liable to sudden bursts of passion? Had his mind been dwelling on the subject of suicide? Was he monomaniacal, or remarkable for any peculiar eccentricity? All these various but important questions should be carefully sifted, should the coroner entertain any doubts as to the presence of mental derangement in such cases. In another chapter we have considered the unjustifiableness of a jury ever returning a verdict of *felo-de-se*.

CHAPTER XII.

SUICIDE IN CONNEXION WITH MEDICAL JURIS-PRUDENCE.

The importance of medical evidence—The questions which medical men have to consider in these cases—Signs of death from strangulation—Singular positions in which the bodies of those who have committed suicide have been found—The particulars of the Prince de Condé's case—On the possibility of voluntary strangulation—General Pichegru's singular case—The melancholy history of Marc Antonie Calas—How to discover whether a person was dead before thrown into water—Singular cases—Admiral Caracciolo—Drowning in a bath—The points to keep in view in cases of suspicious death—Was Sellis murdered?—Death from wounds—The case of the Earl of Essex.

MEDICAL men are frequently called upon in our courts of law to give evidence in cases where it is doubtful whether persons found dead were murdered or committed suicide. The questions involved in these judicial inquiries are of great public importance, and it is the sacred duty of medical men, for the sake of their own characters, and for a much higher consideration—for the ends of justice, to make themselves thoroughly conversant with all the evidence which can be brought to bear in the elucidation of such important questions. Our criminal annals are replete with illustrations in which individuals accused of the atrocious crime of murder have been saved from a dreadful and ignominious death by medical evidence. Cases also are recorded in which death has been ascribed to suicide, but which after investigation have been proved to have been effected by other hands. In doubtful cases of this description, the evidence of the medical man is of the highest importance; without it, in the great majority of cases, justice would be defeated.

In the cases of persons found hanging, two questions naturally suggest themselves to the mind:—1. Whether the individual was suspended before or after death. 2. Whether it was an act of suicide or murder. It is possible, and such cases have occurred, that a person may have been hanged up after having been murdered, or may have endeavoured to destroy himself by firearms, or by cutting his throat, and suspend himself afterwards, not being able to effect his purpose in any other way. In the first case we might mistake murder for suicide; and in the second, suicide for assassination. The following are the signs of death from strangulation:—The countenance is livid and distorted; the eyes protrude, and are often suffused with blood; the tongue projects and is wounded by the teeth. If the rope be placed below the cricoid cartilage, the tongue will protrude; but if it presses above the thyroid cartilage, the tongue will not be seen in the position described. It was formerly the generally received opinion that persons who were hanged died of apoplexy; but the experiments of Sir B. Brodie and other physiologists clearly prove that death is owing to suffocation. The livid or depressed circle which the rope is said to make round the neck is pronounced by M. Klein to be an uncertain sign; he saw fifteen cases of suicide in which it was not discovered. Remer, of Breslaw, who has recently directed his mind to the consideration of this important point, found, out of one hundred cases of persons who died from strangulation, eighty-nine with sugillation on the neck in an evident manner. In addition to the signs mentioned, others have been enumerated. The fingers are said to be found bent, the nails blue, hands nearly closed, with swelling of the chest, shoulders, arms, and hands.

If the body be not suspended, but touches, more or less, the ground or floor, while the cord is not tight enough for the purpose of strangulation, and there be no manifestations of any other means of death, there can hardly be room to doubt as to self-murder. It is true that the mere resting of the toes takes away but little of the character of suspension, but we may meet with stronger cases. A few years ago, a man, aged seventy-five, destroyed himself at Castle Cary, in the morning, by fixing a cord round his neck while sitting on the bed-side, and leaning forward till his purpose was accomplished. His wife, who had for years been bedridden, and was therefore not likely to have been very fast asleep, was in the room during the transaction, and knew nothing of what was going on. A prisoner hung himself in a gaol by fastening the cord to one of the window-bars, and pushing himself away from it with his arm.

Persons have both wounded and hung themselves. This may be effected by placing the cord in a wrong position, which would protract the person's sufferings, and compel him to struggle and make violent efforts to kill himself. Ballard relates, that a young priest, having first cut his throat to a certain extent, hung himself with his robe.[69] In cases like these there can be little difficulty in ascertaining the real cause of death.

In a memoir published in a French journal,[70] there are related several instances of self-destruction by hanging, where the bodies were found in the most extraordinary positions and attitudes. A man was discovered in a granary hanging by a cotton handkerchief, made fast to a rope which stretched across; the knees were bent, so that the legs formed a right angle backwards; the feet were suspended on a heap of grain, over which the knees hung at a distance of a few inches. A prisoner was found suspended in a vertical position, with his heels resting on a window-stool. An Englishman, a prisoner in Paris, hung himself in his cell, which was an apartment with an arched roof, and at the lower part of it was a grated window, the highest part of which was not near the height of a man. Nevertheless,

[69] Notes to Metzger.

[70] Annales de Hyg. pub. et de Méd. Lég. tom. v. p. 156.

he hung himself to this grating, and was found almost sitting down, with his legs stretched out before, and his hips within a foot and a half of the ground. Another case is related of a man whose attitude was similar to the case first described. He had suspended himself to a large iron pin driven into the wall to support the bed-curtains, and his feet, bent at a right angle, rested on the bed, while his knees approached it within a few inches. A female suspended herself so low that, in order to accomplish her purpose, she was obliged to stretch out her legs, one before resting on the heel, the other behind resting on the toes. A female was found stretched at the foot of her bed, the legs, thighs, and left hip lying on the floor; the upper part of the body was raised, and suspended by a cord fixed to the neck, and fastened to the hospital bed.

A patient in La Charité was found one morning hanging by the rope which was attached to the head of his bed. He had fastened this by a loop round his neck, but his body was so retained, that when discovered he was on his knees by the side of his bed.

In 1832, at the west end of the town, a man was found hanging in his room, with his knees bent forwards and his feet resting upon the floor. He had evidently been dead for some time, since cadaverous rigidity had already commenced. The manner in which this man had committed suicide was as follows:—He had made a slip knot with one end of his apron, (he was a working mechanic,) and having placed his neck in this, he threw the other end of the apron over the top of the door, and shutting the door behind him, he had succeeded in wedging it in firmly. At the same moment he had probably raised himself on tip-toe, and then allowed himself to fall; in this way he died. The weight of his body had apparently sufficed to drag down a part of the apron, for it seemed as if it had been very much stretched.

In October, 1833, a gentleman who was employed as an assistant in a respectable school in the neighbourhood of London, was discovered by some of his pupils, one morning, in a sitting posture, on a dark part of a staircase of the house. Upon examining further, it was ascertained that he was completely dead, and that he was suspended to the banisters by a cravat firmly tied round his neck. The deceased had evidently made two similar attempts at self-destruction before he succeeded, as part of a silk pocket-handkerchief and his braces were found suspended to other parts of the banisters. It seemed scarcely possible to those who discovered him that the deceased could really have accomplished suicide by hanging in such a situation, for his body was resting entirely on the stairs, and, making every allowance for the slipping of the ligature by which he was suspended, still his feet must have been throughout in contact with the stair.

There have been few medico-legal investigations of late years which have excited greater interest than the case of the Duke de Bourbon, in France.

On the 27th August, 1830, the duke was found suspended in his bed-room, in the chateau of St. Leu. An inquest was held the same morning on the body, and from the evidence of the witnesses, as well as from the reports of the physicians and surgeons who examined it, a verdict was returned to the effect that the duke had committed suicide in a fit of temporary insanity. This event did not excite much notice until the contents of his will were made public.

The deceased, it appears, had made his will in favour of the Baroness de Feuchéres, a female who had lived with him for some years, bequeathing to her the whole of his immense estates, and leaving the Duke d'Aumale, the youngest son of the king of the French, residuary legatee. The Princes de Rohan, heirs by collateral descent to the deceased, thus finding themselves deprived of an expected inheritance, attempted to set aside the will, alleging that undue influence had been exercised over him. The cause came on for hearing before the First Chamber of the Civil Tribunal of Paris, in December, 1831, and excited considerable attention, not so much in consequence of the dispute concerning the validity of the will, as of the question which was raised during the trial, — whether the duke had committed suicide, or whether he had been murdered, and afterwards suspended, in order to defeat the ends of justice.

The facts of the case, collected from the *procés verbaux*, are as follows: — The deceased had naturally partaken of the alarm which had diffused itself throughout France in consequence of the events of the revolution of 1830. Some of his most intimate friends declared that, for some time previously to his death, his mind had been filled with the most gloomy forebodings as to what this new order of things would bring about. On the morning of the 27th, his servant went, as usual, to his bed-room door about eight o'clock; but receiving no answer on knocking, he became alarmed. Madame de Feuchéres then accompanied the valet to the door of the room, which was fastened on the inside; and receiving no reply after calling to the duke in a loud voice, she ordered it to be broken open. On entering the apartment, the body of the deceased was found suspended from the fastening at the top of the window-sash by means of a linen handkerchief, attached to another which completely encircled the neck. The head was inclined a little to the chest; the tongue protruded from the mouth; the face was discoloured; a mucous discharge issued from the mouth and nostrils; the arms hung down; the fists were clenched. The extremities of both feet touched the carpet of the room, the point of suspension being about six feet and a half from the floor; the heels were elevated, and the knees half bent. The deceased was partly undressed; the legs were uncovered, and had some marks of injury on them. Among other points of circumstantial evidence, it was remarked that a chair stood near the window to which the deceased was suspended, and the bed looked as if it had been lain on.

The medical witnesses, who examined the body soon after its discovery, stated that they found it cold, and the extremities rigid, from which they inferred that the deceased had been dead eight or ten hours. This would have fixed the time of his death at midnight of August 26th. The body underwent a second examination, a report of which was furnished to the legal authorities, on the following day. Five medical men were present at the inspection; and they gave it as their opinion, from the *post mortem* appearances—1st, that the deceased had died by hanging; and, 2ndly, from the absence of all marks of violence or resistance about the person or clothes of the deceased, and other facts, that he had destroyed himself. They considered that the contusion on one arm, and the excoriations observed on both legs, must have arisen from the rubbing of these parts against the projecting rail of the chair near the window. The mark on the neck of the deceased they described to be large, oblique, and extending upwards to the mastoid process.

General evidence was given to shew that the duke had meditated self-destruction, and had conversed about it with some of the witnesses. On the morning of the 28th, some fragments of paper, which had been written on, were taken from the grate of his chamber; these were carefully put together by one of the legal inspectors; and among a few disjointed sentences, indicating despair and a dread of impending danger, were the following:—"It is only left for me to die in wishing prosperity to the French people and my country. Adieu for ever!" Here followed his signature, and a request to be interred at Vincennes, near the body of his son, the Duke d'Enghien. It is necessary to observe, that no noise or disturbance was heard in the bedroom on the night of the deceased's death.

On the other side it was contended that the duke was not unusually melancholy before his death; that the supposition of suicide was inadmissible in a moral point of view, and indeed was physically impossible, from the circumstances. One person argued that he could not have made the knots seen in the handkerchiefs; another, that he could not have reached so high above his head to have suspended himself, and that the chair could not have been used in any manner to assist him; while a third affirmed, that a person might be suspended in the position in which the body was discovered, without death ensuing. The circumstance of the door being fastened on the inside, was accounted for by supposing that the bolt had been pushed to from the outside. The duke had been heard to condemn suicide; he had made an appointment for the following day; and had attended to many little circumstances, such as winding up his watch the night previously, and noting his losses at play;—facts which were forcibly urged as being opposed to the supposition of his having destroyed himself.

To combat the medical evidence, it was assumed that the deceased was strangled or suffocated, and was afterwards hanged, by assassins. Several schemes were devised by the medical witnesses on this side of the question, to account for the manner in which the supposed murder was committed. According to some, a handkerchief might have been tightened round the deceased's neck by one assassin, while another forcibly held his legs under the bed-clothes, by which the lesions already described would have been produced; or instead of being strangled by a handkerchief, he might have been suffocated by a pillow placed over his mouth.

The body might then have been dragged across the room to be suspended; and if during this time the hand of one of the assassins had been rudely thrust between the cravat and the neck, the excoriation and mark seen on the skin might be easily accounted for.

The counsel for the appellants remarked, that the want of a line in writing, to withdraw from all suspicion his attendants, and even Madame de Feuchéres, was remarkable, as this *latter precaution* had suggested itself *to almost every suicide*. He condemned those engaged in the anatomical examination of the body, as having been guilty of culpable mismanagement. He ridiculed the idea that the duke, as reported by the two physicians consulted, had probably come to his death through asphyxia by strangulation. He contended that all the appearances on the skin of the neck, where no ecchymosis, *as is usual in persons hung alive*, was visible, *shewed that death had preceded the hanging of the body.*[71]

Conflicting as the evidence was in this case, we think no impartial mind, after maturely considering all the physical facts and moral circumstances connected with the Prince de Condé's death, can entertain any other opinion than that he sacrificed his own life. The case is one of great interest; and the minute particulars detailed in the French journal are worthy of the perusal of every medical man.

It has been doubted whether voluntary strangulation was possible, but we have too many cases on record to allow us to question the probability of such an occurrence. An individual was found strangled in a hay-loft by a handkerchief which had been tightened by a stick. A Malay, who, on board of a man-of-war in the East Indies, had made repeated attempts to commit suicide, at last effected his purpose in the following manner:—He tied a handkerchief round his neck, and with a small stick twisted it several times, and then secured it behind his ear, to prevent its untwisting. Jealousy was the cause assigned for the suicide.

General Pichegru was found strangled in prison during the consulate of Buonaparte. The case gave rise to various suspicions. The body was found lying in bed on the left side, in an easy attitude, with the knees bent, and the arms lying down by the side, with a black silk handkerchief twisted tightly round the neck, by means of a stick passed under it. The cheek was torn by the ends of the stick in its rotations. It was established that he had been guilty of suicide.

A very important lesson is to be learned from the history of the following case, which Dr. Beck has published in his "Medical Jurisprudence." This is but one of many cases in which the innocent have been accused, and have suffered for crimes of which it has been subsequently proved they were innocent.

Marc Antoine Calas was the son of John Calas, a merchant of Toulouse, aged seventy years, of great probity, and a Protestant. He was twenty-eight years of age, of a robust habit, but melancholy turn of mind. He was a student of law, and becoming irritated at the difficulties he experienced (in consequence of not being a Catholic) concerning his licence, he resolved to hang himself. This he executed by fastening the cord to a billet of wood placed on the folding doors which led from his father's shop to his storeroom. Two hours after, he was found lifeless. The parents unfortunately removed the cord from the body, and never exhibited it to shew in what manner his death was accomplished. No examination was made. The people, stimulated by religious prejudice, carried the body to the town-house, where it was the next day examined by two medical men, who, without viewing the cord, or the place where the death had been consummated, declared that he had been strangled. On the strength of this, the father was condemned by the parliament of Toulouse, in 1761, to be broken on the wheel. He expired with pro-testations to Heaven of his innocence.

---

[71] We have availed ourselves of Dr. Taylor's translation of the particulars of the prince's death, which are recorded with much minuteness in the "Annales d'Hygiène Publique, et de Médecine Légale."

Reflection, however, returned when it was too late. It was recollected that the son had been of a melancholy turn of mind; that no noise had been heard in the house while the deed was doing; that his clothes were not in the least ruffled; that a single mark only was found from the cord, and which indicated suspension by suicide; and in addition to these, that the dress proper for the dead was found lying on the counter. Voltaire espoused the cause of the injured family, and attracted the eyes of all Europe to this judicial murder. The cause was carried up to the council of state, who, on the 19th May, 1765, reversed the decree of parliament, and vindicated the memory of John Calas.[72]

Many cases occur in which it is impossible to decide whether the person was dead before being thrown into the water. The attention of the jurist ought to be directed to the condition of the ground in the neighbourhood of the pond, to ascertain whether any signs exist of a struggle having taken place. In the case of Mr. Taylor, who was murdered at Hornsey, in December, 1818, marks of footsteps, deep in the ground, were discovered near the New River; and on taking out the body, *the hands were found clenched, and contained grass, which he had torn from the bank*. The appearance of wounds on the body will often lead to, or assist in, the formation of a correct opinion, as to the cause of death. These facts are, however, very often fallacious. Instances have occurred in which persons determined upon suicide have endeavoured to kill themselves with sharp instruments, and not effecting their purpose, have subsequently thrown themselves into the water. Again, persons may, in the act of drowning themselves, receive severe injuries, by being propelled against rocks and stakes by the force of the current.

A few years ago, a man, who had leaped from each of the three bridges with impunity, undertook to repeat the exploit for a wager. Having jumped from London Bridge, he sunk and was drowned. When the body was discovered, it appeared that both his arms were dislocated, in consequence of having descended with them in an horizontal instead of a perpendicular position. Persons have been discovered drowned with ligatures on their hands and feet, and the circumstance has naturally excited a suspicion as to whether they had committed suicide or had been murdered. Numerous cases prove that suicides do, occasionally, adopt such precautions, in order to ensure death. In June, 1816, the body of a gauging-instrument maker, who had been missing for some days from his home, was discovered floating down the Thames. On being taken out of the water, *the wrists were found tied together and made fast to his knees*, which were in like manner secured to each other. He had been deranged for two years. The cord was recognised as one which had been attached to his bed. He could swim well, and it was presumed that he had so tied himself, in order to prevent his using his legs and arms should his courage fail him after having plunged into the water.

A man, with his wife and child, was reduced to great distress. On a certain day, he took an affectionate leave of his family, declaring he would not return until he had procured some employment by which he should be able to buy bread for them. On the following day, he was found drowned in the New River, with his

---

[72] Foderé, vol. iii. p. 167; from the Causes Célèbres. See also Grimm's Historical and Literary Memoirs, (from 1753 to 1769,) vol. ii. pp. 41, 117, and 166.

hands and legs tied. A card with his address was found in his pocket.

A gentleman was found in the Seine, at Paris, having his feet, wrists, and neck, tied with a cord. His neck, limbs, and hands, were bound by means of a rope with slip-knots, in order to put it out of his power to aid himself when in the water, and thereby to render certain the execution of his suicide.

In the year 1832, the body of Elizabeth Martin was found dead in the water. A man of the name of Bayley was accused of the murder. They had been quarrelling, and were seen struggling with each other at the banks of the pond. He declared that she had fallen in accidentally. Her face was found turned downwards towards the bottom of the pond, *and one of her hands was found to be in her pocket*. The judge properly observed, that if the woman had fallen into the water as the prisoner stated, that she would have, undoubtedly, taken her hand from her pocket for the purpose of extricating herself. The man was convicted of the murder, and executed.

There has been much discussion as to whether bodies sink or swim when thrown into the water after having been killed. Considerable discrepancy of opinion exists on this point. It has been maintained that strangled persons will float more readily than others, as many facts prove. Caracciolo, Admiral of the Neapolitan navy, was hanged by sentence of a court-martial. The body was committed to the deep in the usual manner; and thirteen days afterwards, while the king was walking on the deck of Lord Nelson's ship, he suddenly exclaimed, with a yell of horror—*"Viene! viene!"* The admiral's corpse, breast-high, was seen floating towards the ship. The shot which had been attached to the feet for the purpose of sinking not being sufficiently heavy. This phenomenon may have arisen from the evolution of gaseous matter, after the process of putrefaction had commenced, which notoriously renders the body specifically lighter than water.

The apparitions that appeared at Portnedown Bridge, after the Irish massacre, and which excited such commotion at the time, were accounted for in a similar manner. It appears that, about twilight in the evening, a number of spirits became visible; one assumed the shape of a naked woman, waist-high, upright in the water, with elevated and closed hands, and looking as awful a spectre as the most superstitious person would wish to behold. Various sounds were also heard proceeding from the river, which caused no little alarm. The sounds were mere delusions, but that bodies were seen floating upright in the water there cannot be a doubt.

"One day," says Clarke, "leaning out of the cabin-window, by the side of an officer, who was employed in fishing, the corpse of a man, newly sewed up in a hammock, started half out of the water, and continued its course with the current towards the shore. Nothing could be more horrible; its head and shoulders were visible, turning first to one side, then to the other, with a solemn and awful movement, as if impressed with some dreadful secret of the deep, which from its watery grave it came upwards to reveal. Such sights became afterwards frequent, hardly a day passing without ushering the dead to the contemplation of the living, until at length they passed without exciting much observation.[73]

In October, 1829, a female, who was an in-patient of St. Luke's Hospital, was found dead in the bath of the institution. It appears that, for some time previously, she had been permitted the privileges allowed to patients exhibiting indications of convalescence, and had obtained access to the nurse's room, in which the key of the bath was deposited. One afternoon, she secretly possessed herself of this key, and then immediately proceeded to make arrangements for the accomplishment of her purpose. In order to deceive the vigilance of the nurse, who was accustomed to lock the patients up at bed-time, she took off her clothes and disposed them about the room, in the usual manner, as if she had undressed. She then made up a bundle to resemble the human figure, and placed it inside the bed, filling her nightcap with handkerchiefs. So accurate was the deception that the other patients, who slept in the room with the deceased, readily answered that they were all present. The lunatic, after these preparations, must have stolen cautiously down to the bath. She was found, the next morning, dead, lying stretched out with her face downwards. The water of the bath was not deep, and, indeed, it is presumed, she must have forcibly maintained the position in which her body was found, in order to have effected her purpose. The door of the bath-room was locked inside, and the key was found in the deceased's pocket.

In a small village of Warwickshire, in the year 1800, a young gentleman suddenly disappeared on the evening previous to his intended marriage. After a lapse of some days, his body was found floating in a mill-stream, and it was generally concluded that he had committed suicide, though the cause for such a rash act could not be conjectured. Upon stripping the body, some marks of a suspicious nature were discovered upon the throat. A surgeon was sent for to decide whether death had taken place from any other cause than drowning, who, after a minute examination, gave it as his opinion that he had died by strangulation. Suspicion now fell upon a man of bad character, who had been seen the night the gentleman was first missed, running in great haste from the direction in which the body was afterwards found. He was apprehended, but, no evidence of guilt being elicited by the examination, was discharged, and the fate of the unfortunate young man remained buried in mystery. Ten years afterwards, the person suspected was convicted of sheep-stealing, and sentenced to transportation. While on board the hulks, he made a voluntary confession of having destroyed him, and declared that such was his remorse, and the horror of his conscience, that he earnestly desired to expiate his crime on the scaffold. He was tried for the alleged offence entirely on his own evidence, which was as follows:—

Upon the evening of the fatal event, he was stealing potatoes from a field-garden belonging to the deceased, whom he unexpectedly saw coming over the gate to secure him, upon which he jumped over the hedge on the opposite side, and ran across the field to make his escape. The gentleman pursued him, and being an active young man, nearly overtook him; upon which he (the prisoner) attempted to leap the mill-stream, but the bank on the other side giving way, he fell back into the water. The young gentleman, instantly plunging into the water after him,

---

[73] Travels in Asia, Africa, &c.

strove to secure him. A desperate struggle now ensued, and the deceased had at one time got the prisoner down under him in the water, by which he was half drowned. At length he succeeded in overturning his antagonist, and, seizing him by the throat, held him fast in this manner under water, till he seemed to have no more power. He then left him, sprang out, and made his escape.

The judge gave it as his opinion that the case amounted only to excusable homicide, and the man was acquitted.

In forming an opinion as to the cause of death in doubtful cases of suicide, the following important points ought to be carefully kept in view:—

1st. If the person had for some time laboured under melancholia; had met with losses, disappointments, or had suffered any acute chagrin.[74] 2nd. If any of his family, associates, or connexions, had any interest in his death. 3rd. The season of the year should be taken into consideration; for we have observed, without being able to assign the reason, that suicide is more frequent during the solstices and the equinoxes. 4th. If the patient, instead of complaining, remains quiet, seeks for solitude, and refuses medical aid. And 5th. If there be any writing (as those who destroy themselves ordinarily express their last opinions or will) it will be one of the most satisfactory proofs that they have made away with themselves. Remains of poison found in their pockets, or in the apartment, are but an equivocal proof, and one which may attend upon homicide as well as on suicide.[75]

In the course of judicial investigations, medical men are frequently called upon to decide in cases of suspicious death whether wounds discovered on the bodies of the deceased were self-inflicted. Before deciding questions of this character, the medical witness ought to take into consideration the following points:—1st, The situation of the wound; 2nd, its nature and extent; 3rd, the direction of the wound; and 4th, the moral circumstances connected with the case.

Generally speaking, those who commit suicide do not wound themselves on the posterior parts of the body; therefore injuries detected in such situations naturally excite suspicions as to the mode of death. The throat and chest are commonly selected when cutting instruments are used. When death has resulted from the discharge of a weapon introduced into the mouth, Dr. Smith says it may be taken for granted that the case is one of suicide. It is, however, possible, even under such circumstances, for a person to be assassinated in this way. When death has been caused by firearms, the fingers and hands of the deceased should be carefully examined, in order to detect the presence of discoloration. In several instances, a murder has been discovered by a careful examination of the wadding. In two cases on record, the wadding being examined, it was discovered to have been torn from paper found in the possession of the parties on whom suspicion had rested.

Some time back, the body of a man was found lying on the high-road. The throat was severely cut, and he had evidently died from hemorrhage. A bloody knife was discovered at some distance from the body; and this, together with the circumstance of the pockets of the deceased having been rifled, led to a suspicion

[74] To which may be added, anticipation of punishment, or disgrace from misconduct.
[75] Méd. Légale, iv. § 948; and Smith on Med. Jurisprudence.

of murder. This idea was confirmed when the wound was examined. It was cut, not as is usual in suicide, by carrying the instrument from before backwards, but as the throats of sheep are cut. The knife had passed in deeply under and below the ear, and had been brought out by a semi-circular sweep in front, all the great vessels of the neck, with the œsophagus and trachea, having been divided from behind forwards. The nature of the wound rendered it at once improbable that it could have been self-inflicted; and it further served to detect the murderer, who was soon afterwards discovered, and executed.

With reference to the *extent* of the wound, the celebrated Earl of Essex's case has often been quoted. He was found dead in the Tower, in 1683, and it was the generally received opinion that he had been murdered by persons hired by the Duke of York, afterwards King James II. Upon examining the wound, it was found that the jugular vessels, trachea, and œsophagus, were cut through to the very neck-bone. The verdict was suicide. In 1688, the matter was revived, and before a committee of the House of Lords,[76] it was proved that the razor with which the wound was inflicted was found on the left side of the body, while it was known that the Earl was left-handed. The edge of the razor was found notched; and it was also proved that the cravat worn by the deceased was cut through, and his right hand was wounded in five places.

As there was much political feeling mixed up with this case, it was difficult to arrive at the truth. That many persons who have cut their throats have divided the neck to the vertebræ is a well-known fact. In the case of Mr. Calcraft, all the large vessels in the neck were divided, and the throat was cut through to the vertebral column.

In the case of Sellis, much stress was laid by Sir E. Home on the wound being *regular*; he observes, *"any struggle would have made it irregular."* Although there were points connected with this remarkable case which naturally tended to excite suspicion, we cannot but declare that the Duke of Cumberland most clearly vindicated himself from the foul charge which party feeling and private malevolence had endeavoured to establish against him.

Many doubtful cases may be decided by taking into consideration the moral circumstances connected with them. A girl was discovered dead. Suspicion rested upon her mother, who had severely beaten the child. It was, however, clearly proved that the girl had been repeatedly heard to declare her intention to commit suicide. Persons should be examined as to the state of mind of the party found dead; whether he or she laboured under an hereditary predisposition to suicidal insanity, or had been exposed to the influence of causes likely to cause melancholy or a depressed state of feeling. If all these points be carefully considered, a fair conclusion may be arrived at in the majority of cases that occur, and which are made the subject of judicial investigation.

---

[76] The committee made no report. Lord Delamere undertook to draw it up, but before he did so, parliament was prorogued. Bishop Burnet, who has given the particulars of the case with great minuteness, says, he had no doubt that the Earl of Essex committed suicide. He was subject to fits of deep melancholy, and maintained the lawfulness of suicide. This is also Hume's opinion.

CHAPTER XIII.

STATISTICS OF SUICIDE.

Number of suicides in the chief capitals of Europe from 1813 to 1831—Statistics of death from violence in London from 1828 to 1832—Number of suicides in London for a century and a half—Suicides in Westminster from 1812 to 1836—Suicide more frequent among men than women—Mode of committing—Influence of age—Effect of the married state—Infantile suicides—M. Guerry on suicides in France—Cases—Suicide and murder—Suicide in Geneva.

In Great Britain, owing to the neglect of statistical science, much difficulty has been experienced in obtaining anything like correct data respecting the number of suicides committed annually. For the details given in this chapter we are indebted to various authorities. Every work has been consulted which it was supposed would throw some light on the subject.

Number of Suicides in the chief Capitals of Europe.

Places.	Periods.	Suicides.	Proportion to Population.	
Berlin	1813-1822	360	1 in	750
Copenhagen	1804-1806	100	1 —	1,000
Naples	1828	330	1 —	1,100
Hamburg	1822	59	1 —	1,800
Berlin	1799-1808	60	1 —	2,300
Paris	1836	341	1 —	2,700
Milan	1827	37	1 —	3,200
Berlin	1788-1797	35	1 —	4,500
Vienna	1829	45	1 —	6,400
Prague	1820	6	1 —	16,000
Petersburg	1831	22	1 —	21,000
London	1834	42	1 —	27,000
Naples	1826	13	1 —	173,000
Palermo	1831	2	1 —	180,000

Statistics of Suicide & Deaths from Violence in general, in London.

	1828.	1829.	1830.	1831.	1832.
Suicide	41	35	25	48	52
Executed	1	26	7	6	10
Murdered	6	4	2	5	2
Poisoned	7	7	4	7	4
Found dead	15	6	13	5	5
Drowned	150	36	97	131	149
Burnt	47	53	61	35	36
From famine	1	0	0	1	1
From intoxication	7	3	4	0	1
From suffocation	10	10	5	5	5

Number of Suicides in London during a Century and a half.

From 1690 to 1699	236	From 1760 to 1769	351
— 1700 — 1709	278	— 1770 — 1779	339
— 1710 — 1719	301	— 1780 — 1789	224
— 1720 — 1729	478	— 1790 — 1799	274
— 1730 — 1739	501	— 1800 — 1809	347
— 1740 — 1749	422	— 1810 — 1819	363
— 1750 — 1759	363	— 1820 — 1829	381

Suicides in Westminster, from 1812 to 1836.

(Extract from Report of Medical Committee of the Statistical Society of London. April, 1837.)

"The first statement to which the Committee will draw the attention of the Council is an account of the number of persons, male and female, who have committed suicide, and upon whom inquests have been held, within the city and liberty of Westminster, in each month, from January, 1812, to December, 1836, procured from Mr. Higg, the deputy coroner of Westminster; with other statements which the Committee had prepared from it.

"The Committee deems it right to premise that caution must be used in drawing too general inferences from these statements, on account of the comparatively small number of cases to which they refer. The average annual number of suicides upon which inquests have been held in Westminster does not probably exceed one per cent. of the total number annually committed in Great Britain; hence the number committed in Westminster during twenty-five years, amounting to 656, is only about twenty-five per cent. of the whole number annually committed in

Great Britain.

"For some conclusions, however, they afford sufficient data, and these the Committee will proceed to notice.

"It appears from the following abstract, No. 1, that suicides in Westminster are most prevalent in the three months of June, July, and March; but that the excess is on the part of the males, as the greatest number of female suicides was in January, September, and November. September, August, and October exhibit the smallest number of male and of total suicides; but February, March, and April, the smallest number among females.

No. 1.

A Statement of the total number of Suicides of each Sex committed in West-minster in each month during the twenty-five years, from 1812 to 1836; also the per centage proportion of the whole number committed in each month; and the proportion which the number of each sex bears to the other.

Total Number of Suicides from 1812 to 1816.			Per Centage Proportion committed in each Month.			Per Cent. Proportion of Male to Female.	
	Male.	Female.	Total.	Male.	Female.	Total.	Male and Female.	
January	35	20	55	7.3	11.2	8.4	64	36
February	39	12	51	8.2	6.8	7.8	77	23
March	52	11	63	10.9	6.2	9.6	83	17
April	40	11	51	8.4	6.2	7.8	79	21
May	41	15	56	8.5	8.4	8.5	73	27
June	60	15	75	12.6	8.4	11.4	80	20
July	50	16	66	10.5	9.0	10.1	76	24
August	30	15	45	6.3	8.4	6.9	67	38
September	30	18	48	6.3	10.1	7.4	62	38
October	28	15	43	5.9	8.4	6.5	65	35
November	32	17	49	6.7	9.6	7.4	65	35
December	41	13	54	8.5	7.3	8.2	76	24
	— —	— —	— —	— —	— —	— —	—	—
Total	478	178	656	100.	100.	100.	73	27

"The last two columns in the above account shew more precisely the proportion of female to male suicides in each month.

"The following statement shews the number of times, during the twenty-five years, that no suicide was committed during each month:—

February		Not once.	July		Twice.	April	}	Four times.
January	} Once		May	} Three times.		October		
March			August			September	}	Five times.
June			December			November		

"From No. 2 it appears that the average annual number of suicides in Westminster has been increasing in each quinquennial period; but No. 3 shews that it has actually decreased with reference to the increase which has taken place in the population.

No. 2.

A Statement of the Average Annual Number of Suicides, Male and Female, in each Quinquennial Period; also, the proportion per cent. which the two Sexes bore to each other in each period.

Periods of Years.	Average Annual Number.			Proportion of each Sex.	
	Male.	Female.	Total.	Male.	Female.
1812 to 1816	18.2	7.6	25.8	70	30
1817 — 1821	15.0	5.2	20.2	74	26
1822 — 1826	16.4	7.4	23.8	69	31
1827 — 1831	22.0	7.8	29.8	78	22
1832 — 1836	24.0	7.9	31.9	76	24
	—	—	—	—	—
Average of Total	19.1	7.1	26.3	73	27

No. 3.

A Statement of the Population of the City and Liberty of Westminster, according to each census, and the proportion which the number of Suicides in the Quinquennial Period immediately following each census bore to the population.

Dates of Census.	Population.	Suicides.		Proportion of Suicides to the Population.
		Quinquennial Periods.	Average Annual Number.	One in
1811	160,801	1812 to 1816	25.8	6,232
1821	181,444	1822 — 1826	23.8	7,623
1831	201,604	1832 — 1836	31.6	6,379
	— — —	— — — — —	— —	— —

Average	181,283	..	27.06	6,700

"It must, however, be taken into consideration that suicides committed in Westminster may not belong to the population of the district, for that the proximity of the river, and other causes existing in Westminster, may attract persons residing in other parts of the town. Hence an increase or decrease of facilities for committing suicide in the surrounding districts, such as the formation of a canal, &c., will naturally affect the number of such deaths in Westminster."[77]

It has been clearly established that suicide is less frequent among women than men. In early life, death by hanging is preferred; in middle life, firearms are had recourse to; and in more advanced years, strangulation again becomes the fashionable mode of terminating life.

Years of Age.		Pistol.	Hanging.
Between	10 and 20[78]	61	68
—	28 — 30	283	51
—	49 — 50	182	94
—	60 — 70	150	188
—	80 — 90	161	256

In an analysis of 525 cases of suicide in Prussia, the following was the result:—

Hanging	234
Shooting	163
Drowning	60
Cutting throat	17
Stabbing	20
Jumping out of window	19
Poison	10

[77] This is confirmed by the fact that within the jurisdiction of the metropolitan police, the two districts in which the greatest number of suicides were committed or attempted, in 1836 or 1837, were those of the Regent's Park and Stepney, through both of which the Regent's Canal runs. This circumstance tends to shew that drowning is the mode of suicide most frequently resorted to in London, and that a canal offers greater facilities for that purpose than the river.

[78] The disposition to suicide may be manifested very early in life. M. Falret knew a boy, twelve years old, who hanged himself because he was only twelfth in his class. A similar case occurred at the Westminster school about seventeen years ago. Harriet Cooper, of Huden Hill, Rowly-Regis, aged ten years and two months, upon being reproved for a trifling fault, went upstairs, after exhibiting symptoms of grief by sighing and sobbing, and hung herself with a pair of cotton braces from the rail of a tent bed. A girl named Green, eleven years old, drowned herself in the New River, from the fear of correction for a trifling fault. Dr. Schlegel states, on the authority of Casper, that in Berlin, between the years 1812 and 1821, no less than thirty-one children, of twelve years of age and under, committed suicide, either because they were tired of existence or had suffered some trifling chastisement.

Opening artery   2

—

525

Marriage is to a certain extent a preventive of suicide; it has been satisfactorily established that among the men two-thirds who destroy themselves are bachelors.

In M. A. Guerry's able "Essai sur la Statisque Morale de la France," published in 1833, we find some valuable statistical facts relating to suicide in France.

It appears on evidence of the most authentic description, that, from the year 1827 to that of 1830, there were committed throughout France no less than 6900 suicides! that is to say, an average of nearly 1800 per annum! It should, however, be remembered, that this calculation is founded only upon judicial documents, in which are included merely those cases of suicide in which death has followed, or in which legal proceedings were taken; so that it is not improbable that many more attempts were made to perpetrate this crime of which the public is quite ignorant.

Taking up this fact, let us consider that the number of crimes against the person amounts yearly in France to 1900. Now, it appears that more than 600 of these crimes consist of attempts on the lives of others; so that the conclusion cannot be resisted, that every time an individual in France meets with a violent death, in any other way but by accident or mere homicide, there are three chances to one that he has committed suicide.

M. Guerry makes a transition to the geographical position of this crime throughout the several arbitrary divisions, and he finds the state of the case to be as follows:—

Out of every hundred suicides which take place on the average every year, there are committed in the

Suicides.

Northern	division	51
Southern	—	11
Eastern	—	16
Western	—	13
Central	—	9

Another view of the proportion of suicides in France is, that which takes place in the number of them, as compared with the amount of the population. It is as follows:—

Suicides in proportion to Population.

Northern	division	1 in	9,853
Eastern	—	1 in	21,734
Central	—	1 in	27,393

Western	—	1 in	30,499
Southern	—	1 in	30,876

It is proper to bear in mind, that in the single department of the Seine, there are perpetrated every year nearly the sixth part of the whole number of suicides which take place in all the eighty-six departments of France. It is said, however, that the greater portion of those persons who commit suicide in this department are altogether strangers to the capital. We come, then, to this conclusion, that of the thousand individuals who are guilty of the crime of suicide, no less than five hundred and five take place in the department of the north; one hundred and sixty-eight occur in the southern division; sixty-five in the western; and fifty-two in the central; a distribution which shews that there is, if not the same proportion, certainly the same order, as the distribution of suicides in the five divisions in respect of the amount of population.

In the explanation which is appended to the table just alluded to, the author shews, that of the suicides committed in the department of the Seine, where they are most numerous, there appears to be one suicide for every 3,600 the inhabitants; whilst in the department of the Haute Soire, where the crime is less frequent, this proportion does not amount to more than one in 163,000 inhabitants.

A singularly curious inference is to be drawn from the consideration of the facts presented in another of M. Guerry's graphic illustrations—viz., that which arises from the circumstance, that from whatever confine of France an inquirer proceeds to the capital, he will find, as he approaches it, that the number of suicides increases by a regular gradation; so that in those departments which are near the Seine and Maine, the traveller will discover that more suicides have been committed than in those more remote from the metropolis, such as the departments of the Lower Seine, of Aube and Soiret. The same observation applies as forcibly to Marseilles, which is in some measure to be considered the capital of certain departments in the south of France. The more these districts are in the vicinity of Marseilles, the greater the amount is there of suicides as compared with the number of the population.

A curious fact has been elicited in the examination of the French registers of crime, from which it appears that those divisions of the kingdom of France in which the most frequent attempts have been made to commit murder are those divisions exactly where the crime of suicide is most rare; and it has been further proved that precisely the reverse of this law takes place in other departments; namely, that where suicides are numerous in proportion to the population, there the number of murders committed by individuals on others is considerably diminished. One peculiarity is mentioned by M. Guerry as being connected with cases of suicide, which is, that we are much oftener enlightened as to the cause of it than we are upon the motives of most other crimes, and that it is rarely the case that any person sets about the crime of self-destruction without leaving in writing, or in some other way, the expression of his last wishes, together with an explanation of the causes of the rash act, which he most generally seeks to justify.

Holcroft, in speaking of the number of suicides in Paris, observes, "I am not well informed on the subject, but I doubt if as many suicides be committed through all Great Britain *in a year, as in Paris alone in a month*. It is the practice of the French police to stifle inquiry and conceal facts, whenever they are of a disagreeable nature; for they tax its omnipotence, to something little short of which it pretends: all things are under its protection; its eye is everywhere; the assaulted cannot sink; the culprit cannot escape; its guardian arm is stretched out so effectually to save that none are in danger. Such are its high claims and the daily assertion it repeats; they are the necessary results of despotism, which, ever on the alarm, will in everything interfere.

"The Parisians are in general themselves so ignorant that the things which they see produce only a momentary impression; none but men of superior minds collect facts and deduce consequences; the rest discern with great quickness, but they forget with greater; and it is chiefly from this forgetfulness that their gaiety of heart is derived.

"In England, misfortunes, so far from being concealed, are sought after with eagerness by people who are paid for the bad news they bring, and by whom it is sometimes greatly exaggerated. If the tale do not astonish, it is scarcely worthy to be reported in our newspapers, and the tales in these newspapers circulate through Europe. This is a benefit when truth is not falsified.

"Of the suicides which are daily happening in France, I, who read the daily journals, saw only two noticed; and these I was surprised to see. One was an officer in the army who pistolled himself at the public office of the war minister; and the other a poor wretch who, at the moment before he threw himself from the upper story of one of the high houses in Paris, called out in mercy to the passengers, *Garde l'eau!* the phrase used by the Parisians when they throw water out of a window. I was told of another suicide of the same kind, and with the same humane caution, while I was at Paris.

"I likewise saw the body of a man borne through the streets, who, after having breakfasted at a hut in *les Champs Elysées*, put an end to his existence. Before doing so, he told the people that he had been a subaltern officer of a regiment then reduced; and that all means of procuring a livelihood was lost.

"Nine conscripts who had for a time concealed themselves, but who were at last discovered, being determined not to serve, encouraged each other rather to die, and voluntarily ended life by drowning themselves together.

"I was passing *le Pont des Tuileries* after dark, and saw a man surrounded by other men. They had deterred him on the bridge from jumping over; but they could not prevail on him to tell his name, or to go home. He appeared to be determined in his purpose; the only resource they had was, at last, to commit him to the guard; but unless his state of mind could be altered, safety like this was but merely temporary.

"Another evening, on the same bridge, and about the same hour, a woman, standing near the centre parapet, attracted my attention by her look, and manner in which she seemed to be examining the river. I stopped; she desisted, but did not remove. I was uncertain what her intentions might be, and she appeared to shun notice. Two other passengers, guessing my doubts, halted; but either their fears were not so strong as mine, or their patience was less; they stood a few minutes and left. I felt as if I did not dare to go, yet could not decide how to act, from the fear of doing wrong. At length the woman moved towards the end of the bridge, and I was obliged to leave her to her fate. I was not certain her intentions were ill; to have charged her with such might deeply have insulted her. I walked home, however, in a most dissatisfied state of mind; at one minute, proving to myself I could not act otherwise, and at another, making self-accusations for having deserted the duties of humanity.

"The number of suicides that really happen in Paris must exceed, no man can say how much, those that are actually known. The bodies exposed at *La Morgue* are most of them brought from *St. Cloud*; the distance to which by water must be above three, perhaps four miles. At the bridge of *St. Cloud* the fishermen nightly spread their nets; and in the morning, with the fish, these bodies are drawn up; but as an old inhabitant of *St. Cloud*, whom I strictly questioned on the subject, assured me the nets were only suffered to be down a stated number of hours, according to the season, certainly not upon an average half a day; and in proof of what he said, he observed to me that this regulation must take place, or the navigation of the river would be impeded. Hence, by the most moderate calculation, the number of bodies that escape the nets must at least equal the number of those that are caught.

"I was told that the government had lately refused the accustomed fee to the fishermen for each corpse they brought, and that they would not continue to drag up the dead bodies, affirming that the money they had before received was insufficient to pay the damage their nets had sustained."

The following statistical facts with reference to suicide in Geneva may be relied upon:—

By the laws of the canton, each case of violent death is investigated by a police magistrate, and the documents are sent to the "Procureur-Generale," and carefully preserved. M. Prevost has examined these documents, collected between 1825 and 1834 inclusively, with a view to investigating the causes of suicide, and of diminishing them if possible. The following are the most important results:—

1.—*Age.*

Ages.	No. of Cases in 10 years.	Men.	Women.
From 50 to 60	34	25	9
20 to 30	30	22	8
60 to 70	19	10	9
30 to 40	18	15	3
40 to 50	15	13	2
70 to 80	9	6	3
10 to 20	5	3	2
80 to 90	3	1	2

From this table it appears that suicides are most frequent between 50 and 60 years of age. The age when the passions are the strongest (from 20 to 30) is, as might be expected, high in the scale; that of youth and old age low, from the young being strangers to the cares of life, and the old few in number when compared with the population.

2.—*Sex, and State of Marriage or Celibacy.*

There are more suicides among men than women, in the proportion of 95 to 38, or about three to one; and more unmarried than married, or in the state of widowhood, in the proportion of 70 to 63, or about seven to six. Notwithstanding this, the female suicides are more numerous among the married and widows than among the unmarried, in the proportion of 21 to 17. But among men the proportions are reversed,—that is, 42 to 53; so that, on the whole, suicides are more frequent among the unmarried than amongst those who are or have been married. This will not surprise those who know the energy, courage, and patience of women under misfortune; men more readily give way to despair, and to vices consequent upon it. Men also have means of destruction, as firearms, &c., more readily at hand.

3.—*Occupations.*

The number of suicides are in proportion to the number of the individuals engaged in various trades, except among the agricultural population, where the proportion is very small. Thus the agricultural population of the canton is 18,000, among whom, during ten years, there have been but ten suicides; whereas, if they had been in the same proportion to the whole number as was found in other occupations, they would have amounted to thirty-nine. Constant occupation and hard yet healthy work render them less sensible to the cares of life. There is also a somewhat larger proportion of suicides among the educated classes, who are engaged in literary pursuits or the higher branches of commerce.

4.—*Religion.*

The relative proportion of Protestants to Catholics in the canton of Geneva is, according to the census of 1834, as 77 to 56. Thus—

Of 133 inhabitants there are,		Of 133 cases of suicide there are,	
Protestants	77	Protestants	107
Catholics	56	Catholics	26
	——		——
	133		133

This result should attract the attention of those who are interested in the moral and religious education of Protestants.

5.—*Means of Destruction.*

Drowning	55
Firearms	31
Strangulation	18
Voluntary falls	15
Cutting instruments	7
Poison	7
	——
	133

In a small province, with a lake and two rapid rivers, it is not surprising that drowning should be the most frequent mode of suicide; next to this is death by firearms, which is accounted for by all the men having firearms, as they are in the militia. Whilst the men have used firearms and cutting instruments, the women have almost alone had recourse to poisons and voluntary falls.

6.—*Seasons.*

The seasons sensibly influence the number of suicides. There are more almost constantly in April. Of 133 suicides there were in—

April	19	March	10
June	17	November	9
August	17	September	6
July	15	January	5
October	14	February	5
May	13	December	3

The spring appears to have an unfavourable effect; and during the great heats, there are more suicides than during the cold weather. It is curious that many suicides happened on the same day or week. Thus, on April 9th, 1830, there were two suicides, and several others on the previous and subsequent days; on the 20th of May, 1830, there were two suicides; on the 28th and 29th of March, 1831, two; and the same on the 3rd and 4th of July of the same year. On the 20th of April, 1833, there were two; and on the 5th of July, 1833, two others. Some atmospheric changes may account for this, though meteorological tables did not satisfactorily explain them.

7.—*Presumed Motives.*

Physical disease	34	Bad conduct. Drunkenness	10
Insanity	24	Fear of punishment. Remorse	6
Losses of property	19	Disappointment in love	6
Domestic grief	15	Gambling	4

| Melancholy without known cause | 13 | Mysterious | 2 |

8.—Relation of Suicides to Population and to Deaths.

The number of suicides is to the whole number of deaths as 1 to 90-1/8; and to the whole population as 1 to 3·985; the mean population of the canton during the last ten years being 53,000—

In 1825	6	Suicides.
1826	6	"
1827	9	"
1828	13	"
1829	13	"
1830	16	"
1831	18	"
1832	12	"
1833	24	"
1834	16	"

—————

133

From this table it appears that the number of suicides has gradually increased from six as high as twenty-four in eight years. The last year, it decreased to sixteen; and it is fervently hoped that this deduction may be maintained, and that the increase may not be so frightfully rapid as it appears to have been. It must, however, be taken into account, that the population was, in 1822, 51,113, and in 1834, 56,655. The police also are more active, and inquests are held more regularly.

CHAPTER XIV.

APPEARANCES PRESENTED AFTER DEATH IN THOSE WHO HAVE COMMITTED SUICIDE.

Thickness of cranium—State of membranes and vessels of brain—Osseous excrescences—Appearances discovered in one thousand three hundred and thirty-three cases—Lesions of the lungs, heart, stomach, and intestines—Effect of long-continued indigestion.

As in cases of insanity, the morbid appearances discovered in the bodies of suicides are varied and contradictory. Nothing has yet been detected which can lead the pathologist to a correct conclusion as to the nature of the organic change which precedes and accompanies the suicidal mania.

The cranium has in many cases been found preternaturally thick, and in others the reverse. Greeding and Gall give their testimony in favour of the skull's thickness. Out of 216 examined, a preternatural thickness of cranium was found in 167. Out of 100 who died of furious mania, 78 had the skull thick, and 20 very thin. Out of 30 fatuous patients, 21 had thick crania, and six thin. The thickness of the cranial bones in melancholy and maniacal patients, and in old people, was supposed by Dr. Gall to be connected with diminished size of the brain, to which the inner table of the cranial bone accommodated itself; and together with this thickness, he considered there was also thickness of the membranes, and ossification of the blood-vessels.

Malformations of the cranium are often detected. Osiander relates the case of an old man who had suffered for a considerable time from dreadful headache, and who, weary of life, hanged himself. On examining the head, small osseous excrescences were found near the carotid foramen. Lancisi refers to a case of hypochondriasis and suicide, in which, after death, a sharp long excrescence was found near the apex of the lambdoid suture.

From an examination of the particulars of 1333 cases of persons who have committed suicide, and who have been examined after death, the following analysis is made. The particulars of the cases referred to are recorded in the works of Pinel, Esquirol, Falret, Foderé, Arntzenius, Schlegel, Burrows, Haslam, &c.

Thickness of cranium	150
No apparent structural change	100
Bony excrescences	50

Tumours in brain	10
Simple congestion	300
Disease of membranes	170
Disease of lungs	100
Softening of brain	100
Appearances of inflammation in brain	90
Disease of stomach	100
Disease of intestines	50
Disease of liver	80
Suppressed natural secretions	15
Disease of heart	10
Syphilitic disease	8
	— —
	1333

Accretions of the membranes of the brain are often found in suicides. The dura mater is often ossified, and the pia mater inflamed, and the arachnoid thickened. Osiander considers congestion of the vessels of the brain a frequent cause of suicide.

Auenbrugger refers to the case of a man who had suffered for a long duration severe headache, and who committed suicide. After death, a fissure was found in the middle of the pons varolii.

Lesions of the lungs are among the common morbid appearances in the bodies of lunatics. Esquirol states that one fourth of the melancholic die of consumption.

The heart is sometimes found seriously disorganized. The stomach, liver, and intestines, are the most frequent seats of morbid phenomena in these cases. It is difficult, however, to say whether they ought to be considered as the effect or cause of the suicidal disposition. In many cases of gastric disease, the brain is also found organically affected. How is it possible for us to say which organ was primarily affected? The stomach, intestines, and liver, may be originally the seat of the irritation, and the brain may be sympathetically deranged. This is often the case. Again, the patient may have laboured under a severe mental ailment, which may give rise to disease of the splanchnic viscera. Severe and long-continued indigestion, from whatever cause it may originate, will, in certain dispositions, produce the suicidal mania. Very few cases are examined in which we are not able to detect some disease of the gastric organ or its appendages.

It is not our wish to throw discredit on, or to underrate the value of, morbid anatomy; but, with reference to the peculiar branch of inquiry now under investigation, we must confess that very little practical importance can be attached to the structural lesions which the industry and scalpel of the anatomists have enabled them to discover in the bodies of those who have committed suicide. The morbid appearances are so varied and capricious that they cannot lead to a sound conclusion as to the exact seat of the disease. In many cases, the brain is apparently free from structural derangement; and yet, reasoning physiologically, we must believe that in every case the sentient organ must be affected, either primarily or secondarily. There are many instances in which there cannot be a doubt but that the cerebral organ is the seat of the disease, but in which, after death, no vestige of the malady can be discovered!

CHAPTER XV.

SINGULAR CASES OF SUICIDE.

Introduction—Contempt of death—Eustace Budgel—M. de Boissy and his wife—Mutual suicides from disappointed love—Suicide from mortification—Mutual suicide from poverty—A French lady while out shooting—A fisherman after praying—Determination to commit if not cured—Extraordinary case of suicide after seduction—Madame C. from remorse—M. de Pontalba after trying to murder his daughter-in-law—Young lady in a pet—Sir George Dunbar—James Sutherland while George III. was passing—Lancet given by a wife to her husband to kill himself—Servant girl—Curious verses by a suicide—Robber on being recognised—A man who ordered a candle to be made of his fat—After gaming—Writing whilst dying—From misfortune just at a moment of relief—Curious papers written by a suicide—By heating a barrel in the fire—By tearing out the brains—Sisters by the injunction of their eldest sister—Mutual from poverty—Girl from a dream—Three servants in one pond—Indifference as to mode—By starvation—A man forty-five days without eating—Mutual of two boys after dining at a restaurateur's—By putting head under the ice—By a pair of spectacles—By jumping amongst the bears—Young lady from gambling—Verses by a suicide—To obtain salvation—A lover after accidentally shooting his mistress—Mutual attempt at suicide—M. Kleist and Madame Vogle—Richard Smith and wife—Love and suicide—Bishop of Grenoble—Suicide in a pail of water—Mutual of two soldiers—Lord Scarborough—A man who advertised to kill himself for benefit of family—The case of Creech, and the romantic history of Madame de Monier—Suicide of M — —, after threatening to kill his brother—Two young men—Two lovers—Homicide and suicide from jealousy—Cure of penchant for—Attempt to, prevented—Man in a belfry—Attempt at—The extraordinary case of Lovat by crucifixion.

In the preceding chapters we have detailed the history of many remarkable cases of self-destruction. It is melancholy to consider that the principle of life with which God has endowed us for high and noble purposes should have been sacrificed with that apparent coolness and self-possession which was manifested in many of the instances recorded in this work.

"How we abuse that article our life! Some people pluck it
Out with a knife; some blow it up with powder; others duck it;—
One thing is sure, and Horace
Has already said it for us,—
Sooner or later, all must kick the inevitable bucket."

A gladiatorial contempt of death is becoming one of the most alarming features of the time; in this respect we appear ambitious to imitate the conduct of the French sophists, and seek, in acts of desperation, a notoriety that nothing else can give us. In investigating, as we have endeavoured to do, the motives that have led to this heinous offence, we have in many cases been unsuccessful in tracing the act to any definite principle. Either no reasons have been assigned or the accounts of the cases transmitted to us have been imperfect. These individuals stand apart from the rest of the world, and exhibit an anomaly in the last act of life totally irreconcilable to all acknowledged principles of reason and human action. Eccentric in their lives, they have been desirous of manifesting the ruling passion strong in death. This mental idiosyncracy may be, and no doubt often is, the result of original constitution, aided in its development by the moral atmosphere in which the person is placed, as well as by education and other circumstances which are known to influence the formation of the mind and character.

The singular facts adduced in this chapter are only brought forward as evidence of that anomalous condition of the mind referred to which leads to suicide; at the same time the instances will afford to the metaphysician valuable materials to assist him in his investigations into the philosophy of the human understanding. Some of the cases related, of course, admit of elucidation, but the majority will be found to puzzle the ingenuity even of those who pride themselves on their capacity of understanding what is beyond the ken of ordinary mortals.

Eustace Budgel was a man of much literary fame at the beginning of the last century, the relation and friend of Addison, and a distinguished writer in the periodical publications of that day. He was born to a good fortune, and held a considerable place under government whilst Addison lived, who kept him in some order as to his political character. But having lost all court favour after Addison's decease, and being a man of great expense and vanity, having also sunk a large sum of money in the South Sea scheme, and having involved himself in a number of fruitless litigations, he became highly distressed in his circumstances. This, added to the chagrin of disappointed ambition and to other matters, determined him to make away with himself. He had always thought but lightly of revelation, and after Addison's death became an avowed free-thinker, which laxity of principle strongly concurred in disposing him to adopt this fatal resolution. Accordingly, after having been visibly agitated and almost distracted for several days, he took a boat, and ordered the waterman to go through London bridge. While the boat was under the bridge, Budgel threw himself overboard, having had the previous caution to fill his pockets with stones. This happened in the year 1737. It was said to have been Budgel's opinion, "that when life becomes uneasy to support, and is overwhelmed with clouds and sorrows, man has a natural right to deprive himself of it, as it is better not to live than to live in pain." A man of unsettled principles easily persuades himself into the notion of suicide when he is actually suffering from some violence of his passions, even though he had not imbibed it before. For whenever the passions attempt to reason, it is only on the delusive suggestions of their own perturbed feelings. The morning before Budgel carried his deadly intentions into execution, he endeavoured to persuade his daughter to accompany him in his death. His only argument to her was, that her life was not worth holding; but she thought otherwise, and refused to concur in the sacrifice. A slip of paper was left on his writing-table, containing these few words, as an apology for his rash act:—

> "What Cato did and Addison approved
> Cannot be wrong."

Monsieur de Boissy, a French dramatic writer and satirist, being reduced to great indigence, resolved to commit suicide. As he considered this action in no other light than as a friendly relief from further misery, he not only persuaded his wife to bear him company, but prevailed on her not to leave their child of five years old behind them, to the mercy of that world in which they had experienced so little sympathy and happiness. Nothing now remained but to fix on the mode of their death. They at length agreed to starve themselves. This not only seemed to them the most natural consequence of their condition, but also saved them from committing a violence either on their child, themselves, or each other, of which perhaps neither Boissy nor his wife found themselves capable. They determined therefore to wait with unshaken constancy the arrival of death under the meagre form of famine; and accordingly they shut themselves up in the solitude of their apartment, where, on account of their distresses, they had little reason to dread the interruption of company. They began, and resolutely persisted in their plan of starving themselves to death with their child. If any one called by chance at their apartment, they found it locked, and receiving no answer, it was concluded that nobody was at home. A friend, however, from that kind of instinct perhaps with which the spirit of friendship abounds, began to apprehend that something must be much amiss with Boissy, as he could neither find him at home, nor get intelligence concerning him. Under much anxiety he returned once more to his apartment; and, whether from hearing any groans from within, or suspecting something was wrong, he ventured to break open the door. Boissy and his wife had been so much in earnest, that it was now three days since they had taken any sustenance, and they were so far on their way to their intended home, that they were in sight, as it were, of the gates of death. The friend, entering into the room where this scene of death was going forward, found the miserable pair in such a situation as to be insensible of his intrusion. Boissy and his wife had no eyes but for each other, and were not sitting in, but rather supported from falling on the ground by two chairs set opposite to each other. Their hands were locked together, and in their ghastly looks was painted a kind of rueful compassion for their child, which hung at the mother's knee, and seemed as if looking up to her for nourishment, in its natural tenaciousness of life. This group of wretchedness did not less shock than afflict his friend. But soon collecting from circumstances what it must mean, his first care was not to expostulate with Boissy or his wife, but to engage them to receive his succours, in which he found no small difficulty. Their resolution had been taken in earnest. They had got over the worst, and were in sight of their port. Their friend, however, took the right way of reconciling them to live by making the child join in the intercession. The child, who could have none of the prejudices or reasons they might have for not retracting, held up his little hands, and in concert with him entreated his parents to consent to live. Nature did not plead in vain. They were gradually restored to life, and provided with everything that could make them in good humour with its return.

Euphrosine Lemoine was the daughter of a bourgeoise of the Faubourg St. Antoine. She loved, and had admitted to secret interviews, a young cabinetmaker of the neighbourhood. Her parents, however, had long intended her to marry Mr. B— —, a man of some property. She reluctantly consented — pronounced the "*fatal yes;*" and the young man prudently left Paris for some years. In 1836 he yielded to the desire of once more seeing her he had loved. They met, and the husband was dishonoured. This was followed by an elopement; but the husband, who still loved his wife in spite of her crimes, discovered their retreat, and by the intervention of friends and of the police a reconciliation was effected — in vain. They again eloped, but only to perish together; and they were found dead, eight days after, locked in each other's arms, in a miserable apartment they had hired for the purpose. Before the suicide, one of them had sketched with coal on the wall of their retreat two flaming hearts, and beneath, this inscription — "We have sworn eternal love, and death, terrible death, shall find us united."

A boatman discovered in the Seine a mass which the stream seemed to roll along with difficulty; he found it was two bodies, a young woman about twenty, tastefully dressed, and a young man in the uniform of the eighth hussars. The left hand and foot of one victim were laid to the right hand and foot of the other. A bit of paper, carefully wrapped up in parchment to preserve it from the water, told their names and motives: —

"O you, whoever you may be, compassionate souls, who shall find these two bodies united, know that we loved each other with the most ardent affection, and that we have perished together, that we may be eternally united. Know, compassionate souls, that our last desire is, that you should place us, united as we are, in the same grave. Man should not separate those whom death has joined.

(Signed),
"Florine. Goyon."

Some years ago, a light was observed in the church of Rueil. This singular appearance occasioned a search; on the approach of the authorities the light was extinguished, but a woman's stays were found on the pavement. The beadle of the church was met, apparently much agitated. On a further search, the proprietress of the stays was found concealed in a press under the *draps mortuaires*, (the parish pall.) The unhappy man, on the detection of this profanation, drowned himself.

M. Malglaive, a half-pay officer, lately employed in a public office, had suffered some unexpected pecuniary losses. One of his friends received a note from him by the twopenny post, requesting him to call at his lodgings, where he would find a packet addressed to him. On proceeding there, and opening the packet, he found a letter in these words:—

"When you shall have received this letter, my poor Eleanore and I will be no more. Be so good as to have our door opened; you will find our eyes closed for ever. We are weary of misfortunes, and don't see how we can do better than end them. Satisfied of the courage and attachment of my excellent wife, I was certain that she would adopt my views, and take her share in my design."

These young people (for the husband was but thirty-four and the wife twenty-eight) had taken the most minute precautions to render the effect of the fumes of charcoal certain; but a brace of loaded pistols was placed on the night table, to be used if the charcoal had failed.

Madame de F— — killed herself in the park of her chateau, with *her own* fowling-piece, which she took out on pretence of going shooting, as she was in the habit of doing. She loaded it with six balls, and placing the muzzle to her breast, discharged it. The only cause assigned is the vexation she and M. de F— — felt at her having no children to inherit their large fortune.

A fisherman with a large family, residing at Vellon d'Auffes, near Marseilles, had been driven by domestic trouble to form a design of suicide, which he had long announced. One Sunday he climbed a high rock in the neighbourhood, where, in the sight of his friends below, with a crucifix in his hands, he was evidently saying his last prayer, preparatory to suicide. One of the neighbours, guessing his intentions, reached the spot suddenly, and seized him; a struggle ensued on the edge of the precipice; the unhappy man prevailed, and, escaping from the arms of his friendly antagonist, flung himself over.

Voltaire relates the particulars of the following singular case:—An Englishman of the name of Bacon Morris, a half-pay officer, and a man of much intellect, called on Voltaire at Paris. The man was afflicted with a cruel malady, for which he was led to suppose there was no cure. After a certain number of visits, he one day called on the philosopher, with a purse and a couple of papers in his hand. "One of these papers," he said, addressing Voltaire, "contains my will, the other my epitaph; and this bag of money is intended to defray the expenses of my funeral. I am resolved to try for fifteen days what can be effected by regimen and the remedies prescribed, in order to render life less insupportable; and if I succeed not, I am determined to kill myself. You will bury me in what manner you please; my epitaph is short." He then read it; it consisted of the following two words from Petronius, "Valete, curæ"—"Farewell, care." "Fortunately," says Voltaire, "for him and myself, who loved him, he was cured, and did not kill himself."

Two young people—Auguste, aged twenty-six, and Henriette, aged eighteen—had long loved each other, but the parents of the girl would not consent to the match. In this difficulty the young man wrote to Henriette:—

"Men are inexorable. Well, let us set them at defiance. God is all-powerful; our marriage shall be celebrated in his presence; and to-morrow, if you love me, we will write, in our blood, at the foot of the cross, our marriage vow."

This proposition turned the weak girl's head, and she consented. They proceeded one night to a field near St. Denis, where there was a cross. On their way they made incisions in both their arms, to procure the blood in which the following *acte de mariage* was written:—

"O great God, who governs the destinies of mankind, take us under thy holy protection! As man will not unite us, we come on our knees to implore thy sanction to our indissoluble union. O God, take pity on two of thy poor children! Assemble all thy heavenly choir, that on so happy a day they may partake our transports, and be witnesses of the holy joy that shines in our hearts. O God! O ye angels of heaven and saints of Paradise! look down upon a happiness which even the blessed may envy.

"And you, shades of our parents, come to this affecting ceremony, come and give us your approbation and your blessing. It is in the presence of you all that we, Pierre Auguste and Marie Henriette, swear to belong to each other, and to each other only, and to be faithful to each other to the hour of dissolution. Yes, we swear it—we swear it with one voice. You are our witnesses, and we are united for life and for death.

(Signed in letters of blood),
"PIERRE AUGUSTE.
"MARIE HENRIETTE."

The very day after this visionary marriage it was dissolved by the suicide of the unfortunate Henriette. The moment her fault had become irreparable, her betrayer abandoned her, and the poor creature threw herself into the Seine. On the body was found the foregoing singular *acte de mariage*, to which she had subjoined, with a feeble hand, the following note:—

"He has dishonoured me—the monster! He deceived me by pretences which went to my heart; but it is he who is to be pitied—wretch that he is!"

A young woman, of a highly honourable commercial family, put an end to herself, overwhelmed with the idea of having forfeited the esteem of her husband. *Rosalie* had from her youth been destined to be the wife of M. C——, a gentleman of her own station in life. Their union, though not distinguished by any transports of love, was soberly and rationally happy, and they had two children.

Unfortunately, Madame C—— was obliged by affairs of business to go into the country while her husband remained in Paris. During this absence, she appears to have formed a guilty passion, (the circumstances of which have not been revealed;) but on her return home, the remorse of her conscience so preyed upon her spirits as to be at last unsupportable, and, after a long and painful struggle, she resolved upon suicide. Just before the fatal act, she wrote a long letter to her sister, of which we can only spare room for the most striking passages:—

"I have resolved to terminate my existence to-day; but I have not had, during the whole morning, resolution to leave my poor little children, who are unconscious of their mother's agony.... Forgive, my dear sister, the grief that my death is about to cause you. If my excellent husband has offended you, forgive him....

If I had appreciated his worth, I should not be the wretch I am: my negligence towards him began my misfortune, but I had nothing to reproach myself with till my fatal journey to Sarcelles—that journey was my ruin!... If I had your virtues, I should have been the happiest of women; but I allowed myself to be bewildered by a sentiment which I had not before known, and in my culpable frenzy I was guilty before I intended it. O, my God! may my repentance be accepted, and may thy goodness inspire my husband with a peculiar, an exalted degree of parental affection for those unhappy and innocent children. Protect them, O, my God, and grant that they may not curse the memory of their unhappy mother, who was guilty without intending it.

"And you, O my dearest Louis, forgive your wretched wife, who offers you this her last farewell."

One may judge the consternation which this affecting letter spread in the family. The sister, on receiving this letter, hastened with Dr. Bouillet to Mr. C—— 's house: it was too late—they found the poor woman in the last agonies of death, whilst her little children were playing about the adjoining room, indulging in the sports of their age.

M. de Pontalba was one of the great proprietors of France. His son had been a page of Napoleon's, and afterwards a distinguished officer, aide-de-camp to Marshal Ney, and a protégé of the Duke of Elchingen. He married the daughter of Madame d'Almonaster, and for some time they lived happily; but on the death of her mother, Madame de Pontalba began to indulge in such extravagances that even the enormous fortune of the Pontalbas was unequal to it. This led to some remonstrance on the part of her husband, on the morning after which she disappeared from the hotel, and neither he nor his children had any clue to her retreat. At last, after an interval of some months, a letter arrived from her to her husband, dated New Orleans, in which she announced that she meant to apply for a divorce; but for eighteen months nothing more was heard of her, except by her *drafts* for money. At last she returned, but only to afflict her family. Her son was at the Military Academy of St. Cyr. She induced him to elope, and the boy was plunged in every species of debauchery and expense. This afflicted, in the deepest manner, his grandfather, who revoked a bequest he had made him of about £4,000 a year, and seemed to apprehend from him nothing but future ruin and disgrace. The old man, eighty-two years of age, resided in his Chateau of Mont Levéque, whither, in October, 1834, Madame de Pontalba went to attempt a reconciliation with the wealthy senior. The day after her arrival she found she could make no impression on her father-in-law, and was about to return to Paris, when old M. de Pontalba, observing a moment when she was alone in her apartment, entered it with a brace of double-barrelled pistols, locked the door, and, approaching his astonished daughter-in-law, desired her to recommend herself to God, for that she had but few minutes to live; but he did not even allow her one minute—he fired immediately, and two balls entered her left breast. She started up and fled to a closet, her blood streaming about, and exclaiming that she would submit to any terms, if he would spare her. "*No, no! You must die!*" and he fired his second pistol. She had instinctively covered her heart with her hand; the hand was miserably fractured by the balls, but it saved her heart. She then escaped to another closet, where a third shot was fired at her without effect; and at last she rushed in despair to the door, and while M. de Pontalba was discharging his last barrel at her, she succeeded in opening it. The family, alarmed by the firing, arrived, and she was saved. The old man, on seeing that she was beyond his reach, returned to his apartment, and blew out his brains. It seemed clear that he had resolved to make a sacrifice of the short remnant of his own life, in order to release his son and his grandson from their unfortunate connexion with Madame de Pontalba. But he failed—none of *her* wounds were mortal; and within a month after, Madame de Pontalba, perfectly recovered, in high health and spirits, radiant, and crowned with flowers, was to be seen at all the fêtes and concerts of the capital.

A wealthy inhabitant of St. Denis arrived from a long journey, in which he had occasion to carry a brace of pistols; these he deposited, loaded, on a table in his bed-chamber, and sat down to dinner with his family and some friends, invited to celebrate his return. Hardly had dinner begun when a discussion arose between the father and his eldest daughter, about twenty years of age. This young woman had always shewn great jealousy of her younger sister, of whom she pretended her father was fonder than of her. On this occasion the same feeling broke out, and after some strong exhibition of ill-temper on her part, her father said, "Nay, if you are sulky, you had better go to bed." The girl got up immediately, went to her father's bed-room, took one of the pistols, shot herself, and expired in a few hours in great agony.

Sir George Dunbar, Baronet, Major in the 14th Light Dragoons, quartered at Norwich, unhappily got involved in a dispute with his fellow officers. He was a man of quick sensibility, which may have betrayed him into error on the occasion; but whichever party was to blame, the quarrel was of a most violent nature, and he returned home much bruised from blows received in the scuffle. The next day, repairing to the mess-room, he declared to the other officers, "That, if he had offended any of them, he was ready to make an apology; or, if that was not thought sufficient, to give them honourable satisfaction." This proposal was refused, and the officers insisted "That he must sell out, for that, as he had abused the whole regiment, nothing else would or could satisfy them." To this, Sir George replied, "That he would live and die in the regiment, of which he had been an officer for twenty years, and that a pistol should end the dispute." Here ended all communication, but the business made a most deep impression on his mind. For two successive days he neither took food nor slept; and his melancholy appearance filled his family with the most lively apprehensions. Lady Dunbar locked up his razors, pistols, &c., and watched him with unceasing vigilance. Her distress at seeing him so wretched was very great, and in the night she moaned very much, and was quite restless. Sir George said, "Maria, you disturb me; I will get up;" which he immediately did, put on his watch-coat, and laid down on the floor. Lady Dunbar then endeavoured to conceal the anguish of her mind, in hopes to pacify him, and, being overcome with watching, fell asleep. Sir George, as soon as he perceived it, left the room, and at about five or six in the morning walked out. Her ladyship, when she awoke, being much alarmed at his absence, eagerly inquired for him, and was told he had taken a morning walk, having a violent headache, and thinking the air would do him good. This, however, proved only a pretence; for he had gone to purchase a case of pistols, and stood by while the bullets were casting, which, with the pistols, he brought home, concealed under his watch-coat. On his return, he went to Lady Dunbar, who took hold of his hand, observing at the same time, "How cold you are!" To which he answered, "Yes; I shall be better presently." She then proposed to make breakfast, but he declined it, saying he had a letter to write first, and that he would ring to let her know when he had finished it. He then parted from her, after pressing her hand very hard; went to his study, wrote his will, and instantly after blew out his brains. Lady Dunbar, who heard the report of the pistol, ran down into the room, and fell insensible on his body, which lay extended on the floor, and from which she was taken up covered with his blood, and immediately removed to a friend's house. They were a very happy couple, and she had accompanied him in all his campaigns.

As George III. was passing in his carriage through the park to St. James's, a gentleman dressed in black, standing in the green park, close to the rails, just as the carriage came opposite to where he stood, was observed to pull a paper hastily from his pocket, which he stuck on the rails, addressed to the king, threw off his hat, discharged a pistol in his own bosom, and instantly fell. Though surrounded with people collected to see the king pass, the rash act was so suddenly perpetrated, that no one suspected his fatal purpose till he had accomplished it. He expired immediately. In his left hand was a letter addressed "To the coroner who shall take an inquest on James Sutherland." This unfortunate gentleman was judge-advocate at Minorca during the governorship of General Murray, with whom he had a law suit which terminated in his favour. The general, however, got him suspended and recalled. This, and the failure of some applications to government, had greatly deranged his mind. He was very genteelly dressed, but had only two-pence and some letters in his pocket; the letters were carried to the Secretary of State's Office. He left a singular paper behind him, expressive of being in a sound mind, and that the act was deliberate.

The following case is mentioned by Dr. A. T. Thomson, as illustrative of the extraordinary determination often exhibited by those resolved on self-destruction. A gentleman, who had long enjoyed an unblemished reputation, was appointed the treasurer of a society; but having unfortunately fallen into pecuniary difficulties, he not only applied the funds of the society to his own purposes, but forged some bills. As the punishment of the latter crime was penal at that period, on being arrested, he made an attempt upon his life, but did not succeed. His prior good character, and the respect in which he had been held, prevented him from being immediately sent to jail; and he was permitted to remain in the custody of the officer of justice who arrested him. The attempt which he had made upon his life rendered it requisite that every implement which could be employed by the suicide should be withheld from him; but in other respects, as much indulgence was extended to him as possible, under the circumstances of the case. His wife also was permitted to visit him, but she was searched before entering his apartment. He was locked up every night, and he was awoke in the morning by an officer, at a certain hour. On the third morning after his arrest, the officer, as usual, entered his room, and called to him, but received no answer; he then approached the bed, and found that his prisoner was dead. A medical man was immediately sent for. It appeared that this gentleman had studied anatomy, and knew how to use a lancet; and as he had a thorough conviction that he should be hanged, he had persuaded his wife to bring a lancet to him in her mouth. After being locked up for the night, he undressed himself, and opened the femoral artery, the blood from which he allowed to flow into the pan of the night chair, until, as was supposed, he became faint. He then bound a handkerchief round the upper part of the thigh, and placed himself in bed, in the position in which he was discovered. Notwithstanding his great loss of blood, he contrived so effectually to stem the further flow, that none was seen on the floor of the room, and only a few spots on the sheets of the bed."

A servant girl of Mursley, Bucks., committed suicide while her master and his men were weeding in the field, by taking a cord and tying it tight round the upper part of her left thigh, and with a fleam and stick used in bleeding cattle, making a deep incision through the artery. She bled to death before any assistance could be procured.

John Upson, of Woodbridge, in Suffolk, a glover, who was committed to the castle for felony a few days before, hanged himself in his own room with a garter. The following verses were written in a prayer-book lying by him: —

> "Farewell, vain world, I've had enough of thee,
> And now am careless what thou say'st of me;
> Thy smiles I court not, nor thy frowns I fear,
> My cares are past, my heart lies easy here.
> What faults they find in me take care to shun,
> And look at home: enough is to be done.

"June 26, 1774. Poor John the Glover."

Mr. Brower, a print-cutter, near Aldersgate-street, was attacked on the road to Enfield by a single highwayman, whom he recollected to be a tradesman in the city, and called him by his name. The robber immediately shot himself through the head.

The case of a man is recorded in a French paper who burnt with one of the strongest passions of which we ever heard an account. His mistress having proved unfaithful to him, he called up his servant, informed him that it was his intention to kill himself, and requested that, after his death, he would make a candle of his fat, and carry it lighted to his mistress. He then wrote a letter, in which he told her that as he had long burnt for her, she might now see that his flames were real; for the candle by which she would read the note was composed of part of his miserable body. After this he committed suicide.

Lieutenant Colonel Mautren, of the Prussian Hussars, having been stripped, at the gaming table, of all his property, even to his watch and the rings he wore, returned home. Next day he disposed of his commission; and having offered marriage to a respectable female whom he had seduced, a clergyman was sent for, and the ceremony performed. He then retired to a private room, and while some friends were felicitating the bride on her good fortune, the report of a pistol announced the catastrophe that had taken place. The company hastened to the room; but the Colonel was no more. On the table was a letter to his wife, mentioning the cause of his death and inclosing the amount of the sale of his commission.

The particulars of the following case were read by M. Gerard de Gray, at the *Société de Médecine*. A young man, having spent in the capital all his finances, returned home to recruit his purse; but failing in his object, he resolved to put an end to himself. He made no secret of his determination. On the 16th of August he carried it into execution. His bed-room was about nine feet square, and a little more than six in height. On every aperture in it by which the air might possibly have admittance, he pasted paper, and about five in the afternoon lighted a brazier of coals, which he set on the floor close by his bed. He then left the apartment, carefully closing the door after him. At six, he said to an old lady, "My brazier is now ready—I go to die." On the following morning, the family having become alarmed, the door of the chamber was forced open. An insupportable vapour issued from the place, and the body of the unfortunate youth was found stretched across the bed. On the floor, the brazier still occupied the place already mentioned; it was of considerable capacity, and seemed to have been lighted with paper. Near the body were placed two volumes of an old Encyclopædia; one of them at the foot of the bed, open at the article Ecstasy; the other near the right hand displayed the article Death. On the latter volume was a pencil and a bit of paper, with the words, *Je meurs avec calme et bonheur*, clearly written, with the date annexed; but beneath that there appeared, in characters very difficult to be read, the following words: *Au moment de l'agonie j'aurais voulu m'être procuré une sensation agréable*. It would appear that the deceased immediately on writing the scrawl, had fallen into the position in which he was found. The attitude did not betoken any struggle at the last moment; yet it seems probable, from the signs of sickness of the stomach, and the mention of agony in the last phrase, that life did not become extinct without some painful sensations.

Madame Augine having been personally attached to the late Queen of France, expected to suffer under the execrable tyranny of Robespierre. She often declared to her sister, Madame Campan, that she never would wait the execution of the order of arrest, and that she was determined to die rather than fall into the hands of the executioner. Madame Campan endeavoured, by the principles of morality and philosophy, to persuade her sister to abandon this desperate resolution; and in her last visit, as if she had foreseen the fate of this unfortunate woman, she added, "Wait the future with resignation; some fortunate occurrence may turn aside the fate you fear, even at the moment you may believe the danger to be greatest." Soon afterwards the guards appeared before the house where Madame Augine resided, to take her to prison. Firm in her resolution to avoid the ignominy of execution, she ran to the top of the house, threw herself from the balcony, and was taken up dead. As they were carrying her corpse to the grave, the attendants were obliged to turn aside to let pass the cart which conveyed Robespierre to the scaffold!

In the year 1600, on the 10th of April, a person of the name of William Dorrington threw himself from the top of St. Sepulchre's church, in London, having previously left on the leads or roof a paper of which the following is a copy:—

"Let no other man be troubled for that which is my own fault; John Bunkley and his fellows, by perjury and other bad means, have brought me to this end. God forgive it them, and I do. And, O Lord, forgive me this cruel deed upon my own body, which I utterly detest, and most humbly pray him to cast it behind him; and that of his most exceeding and infinite mercy he will forgive it me, with all my other sins. But surely, after they had slandered me, every day that I lived was to me a hundred deaths, which caused me rather to die with infamy than to live in infamy and torment.

"Oh, summa Deitas, quæ cœlis et superis presides, meis medere miseris, ut spretis inferis, letis superis, reis dona veniam.[79]

"Trusting in his only passion and merits of Jesus Christ, and confessing my exceeding great sins, I say—'Master, have mercy upon me!'"

This paper was folded up in form of a letter, and indorsed, "Oh, let me live, and I will call upon thy name!"

Thomas Davers, who built at a vast expense a little fort on the River Thames, near Blackwall, known by the name of Davers's Folly, after passing through a series of misfortunes, chiefly owing to an unhappy turn of mind, put an end to his miserable life. Some few hours before his death, he was seen to write the following card:—"Descended from an ancient and honourable family, I have, for fifteen years past, suffered more indigence than ever gentleman submitted to; neglected by my acquaintance, traduced by my enemies, and insulted by the vulgar, I am so reduced, worn down and tired, that I have nothing left but that lasting repose, the joint and dernier inheritance of all.

> "Of laudanum an ample dose
> Must all my present ills compose;
> But the best laudanum of all
> I want (not resolution) but a ball.

"N. B. Advertise this. T. D."

A farmer near Allandale, in Northumberland, procured a gun-barrel, which he loaded with powder and shot, and having placed the stock end in the fire, he leaned with his belly against the other. In this position he awaited the dreadful moment. When the barrel became hot, an explosion took place, by which he was shot through the body. He had, some time before, been in the habit of excessive drinking, which had impaired his intellects, and probably produced a derangement which led to the commission of the deed.

Mr. Henry Grymes, of Virginia, U. S., whilst labouring under the influence of delirium, broke his skull with a stone. After having shattered it, he took out a piece about three inches long, and two broad. Concluding that this would not put a period to his existence, he thrust his fingers into his head, and tore out a considerable quantity of his brains. Instead of immediate death, *he instantly returned to*

---

[79] "Oh, supreme God, who inhabitest the highest heavens, heal my afflictions; as with the wretched in hell, the joyful in heaven, shew mercy to the guilty."

the full exercise of reason! walked home, and lived to the second evening following. He appeared very penitent and rational to the last moment of his life; and in the meantime gave to his friends the above statement of the horrid transaction. The cause of this derangement is believed to have been a disappointment in marriage. Through the whole of his life he supported an unsullied character.

"A blacksmith charged an old gun-barrel with a brace of bullets, and, putting one end into the fire of his forge, tied a string to the handle of his bellows, by pulling which he could make them play whilst he was at a convenient distance, kneeling down; he then placed his head near the mouth of the barrel, and moving the bellows by means of the string, they blew up the fire, he keeping his head, with astonishing firmness and horrible deliberation, in that position till the further end of the barrel was so heated as to kindle the powder, whose explosion instantly drove the bullets through his brain. Though I know this happened literally as I relate it, yet there is something so extraordinary, and almost incredible, in the circumstance, that perhaps I should not have mentioned it, had it not been well attested, and known to the inhabitants of Geneva, and to all the English there."[80]

A Hanoverian, eighty years of age, resided at a country house near Berne, with his five daughters, the eldest of whom was aged thirty, and the youngest sixteen. The family were of very retired habits, but were governed chiefly by the eldest sister, who was noted for her imperious disposition, and opposition to religion. A young Englishman, who had been for some time an occasional visitor to the house, became smitten with one of the daughters; and one fine evening, as the five sisters were taking the air in a carriage in the avenues of the Eugi, they met him in his cabriolet, accompanied by a friend. After parading up and down for some time, an exchange of vehicles was proposed to and accepted by the young ladies, one of whom accompanied the Englishman, and his friend entered the carriage with the ladies. A similar change was again effected, until the Englishman found himself with the object of his affections, with whom he immediately decamped. The others, thinking he had returned to the house by another road, gave themselves no uneasiness, but continued their road homewards. On arriving, however, they found he had not returned. The eldest sister, becoming alarmed, sent and informed the police that her sister had been run away with; and the next day, news having been received that the runaways were at Fribourg, she immediately set out for that place, accompanied by one of her sisters. Before her departure, she told the two who remained, that if she did not return by a certain hour, it would be a proof that their family was dishonoured; in which case, it became the duty of them all to renounce life. She required, and even extorted, from them a solemn oath, that they would drown themselves if they (the two elder sisters) did not return at the hour mentioned. On arriving at Fribourg, and finding their sister, whom they could not persuade to return home, they two resolved upon putting their resolution into effect; for which purpose they repaired to the banks of the Sarine; but the younger, on arriving, finding her courage fail, exclaimed, "Kill me, sister; I can never throw myself into the river." The eldest drew out a dagger, and was about to perpetrate the deed, when a peasant coming up, interrupted the design. She immediately

[80] Dr. Moore's Travels through France, vol. i. let. 32.

despatched the peasant to prevent her other two sisters from putting their oath into effect; but the precaution was too late. After having prepared every necessary for their aged father during the day, they dressed themselves in their best apparel, and, on arriving at the banks of the Aar, fastened themselves with a shawl, and, embracing each other, precipitated themselves into the river, in which position their bodies were found some time afterwards.

The particulars of the following extraordinary case we find recorded in the Annual Register for 1823. It appears that a man of the name of Spring and his paramour, Mary Gooch, had agreed to commit mutual suicide. For that purpose a large dose of laudanum was purchased; but the dose which Spring took was not sufficient for his purpose, and he recovered. The poor woman was successful in killing herself. The following is the evidence given by Spring at the coroner's inquest: —

"John Spring said, that he was present with the deceased in bed when she died, about seven o'clock on Friday morning; that she did not die in agony; that on the Wednesday evening the deceased and witness came to an agreement to buy some laudanum to take together, that they might both be found dead together in the same bed; that on the Thursday morning, he (the witness) went to the chemist's and bought some laudanum; he thinks four ounces; that when he came in, Mary Gooch said, 'Your heart has failed you; you have not bought it for me;' that she got up and felt witness's pocket. The deceased said, 'You have got something here.' Witness replied, 'Oh, that will soon do our business, if we take it.' She said, 'Have you any money left of what I gave you to buy it with?' Witness said, 'Yes, there are some halfpence.' The deceased said she would purchase some oranges with them, to take after it, and would send for them; that she sent a boy of Webb's, who returned with two oranges; that the deceased peeled them; that she took two wine glasses off the shelf, and placed hers on the box, and said, 'Now let us take it.' She poured half into one glass, and half into another. One glass she kept to herself, and the other she gave to witness. The deceased said, 'Let us take hold of each other's hands.' Witness said, 'No, my dear; if we do, we shall not take it; let us turn back to back, and take it.' Deceased and witness turned their backs to one another, and drank the contents of the glasses. After they had drunk the laudanum, the deceased said, 'What shall we do with the bottle?' Witness said, he would go and throw it away. She said, she would in the mean time wipe the glasses. He threw away the bottle, and the deceased had wiped the glasses by the time he came back. The deceased said, 'Let us go to bed.' They both went to bed together. The deceased afterwards got out of bed, placed a chair against the door, to fasten it, and drew the window blinds. The deceased then said, 'Now we shall die happily together.' This was between two and three o'clock. He asked the deceased how she came by the money she had given him; the deceased said, 'That is of no consequence, and does not signify;' the deceased and witness conversed together about various things, till eight o'clock. She said, she had sent her gown to her aunt's, and that the money came from her. The laudanum did not take any effect till about two; she then began to sleep. The witness was sick about four, and the deceased was awake at that time. The deceased was not sick at all, and fell into a sound sleep at six. The witness awoke her between six and seven; the deceased then said, 'How large your eyes look!' Witness said to her, 'Mary, I am afraid my laudanum will take no effect.' The deceased said, 'Oh dear! if I should die without you, and you are taken before a court of justice, I shall not die easy.' Witness told her she might be quite happy, for, if it did not take effect, he would get up and buy some that would, as he would die with her. The deceased said, 'My dear, pray give me that blue muslin handkerchief, that I may have it in my hand when I die. Pray, don't you take anything; but let me die, and you will get over.' She then laid her head on the shoulder of the witness, and died almost immediately. The body began to grow cold by the time he came in from the town, about half-past eight. The deceased had been in a bad state of mind ever since he had known her. She always appeared to wish to die, and had attempted to destroy herself before, when the witness was at a fair. About a month previous, the deceased having come home in an unhappy state of mind, got up about twelve at night, took a linen line, pinned her cap over her head, and went out of the house, taking a small chair with her. She had one end of a rope about her neck, and was about to throw it over the arm of an apple-tree, when he overtook her, brought her in, and took the rope from her. The deceased, all Wednesday evening, was very anxious to die, and wished witness to die with her. On Thursday, she expressed a desire that they should both die together. The witness had known the deceased ever since Michaelmas Bury fair. She had been very anxious about the payment of the half-year's rent; the witness said, he could go to his friends and get it; deceased said, 'If you go away, I shall be afraid that you will not come back again.' It was not from want that they committed the act; it had been in contemplation some time."

A young lady, at a boarding school near Birmingham, had been set a task, and felt indignant at being obliged to learn it out of an old book, while some of the other scholars were indulged with new ones. She went next day to an old woman in the neighbourhood, and told her "that she had had a singular dream,—that she was dead, and had been carried to her grave by such and such young ladies," naming some of her companions and young friends; and asked the old woman what she thought of it; who replied, "that she put no faith in dreams." A few days after, when going a walk with the other scholars, she loitered behind, and making her escape from the party, drowned herself in a pool near the school. She left her hat (or bonnet) on the edge of the pool, wherein was pinned a letter for her parents, entreating their forgiveness of such a rash act. She therein requested to have for her bearers those whom she had said she dreamed had carried her to her grave; and enclosed some locks of her hair as mementos of friendship. She was only about eleven years of age, and the daughter of very respectable parents in the neighbourhood.

Sophia Edwards and Mary West, two female-servants, in the family of the Rev. John Gibbons, of Brasted, in Kent, were left in care of the house for some weeks, in consequence of the absence of their master and mistress. During this time they had the misfortune to break some articles of furniture, and to spoil four dozen of knives and forks, by incautiously lighting a fire in an oven where they had been placed to keep them from rust. The unfortunate girls, however, bought other knives and forks. Upon the return of Mr. and Mrs. Gibbons, the servants were severely reprimanded for what had happened, and one of them received notice to leave her place. They both appeared to be very uncomfortable for two days afterwards; and, on the second day, the footman heard them in conversation respecting Martha Viner, a late servant in the same family, who had drowned herself in a pond in the garden, and observing one to the other, that she had done so through trouble. The elder then said to the younger—"We will have a swim to-night, Mary!" The other replied—"So we will, girl." The footman thought they were jesting, and said—"Ay, and I will swim with you!" Sophia Edwards replied—"No, you shan't; but I will have a swim, and afterwards I will haunt you." After this conversation, they continued about their work as usual, and at six o'clock asked the footman to get tea for them. While he was in the pantry for that purpose, he heard the kitchen door shut; and on his return into the kitchen, they were both gone. The footman afterwards thought he heard them upstairs, and therefore took no notice of their absence, until eight o'clock, when he told his master and mistress. Search was made for them about the house, garden, and neighbourhood, during the whole night; and early next morning, the same pond was dragged which had so recently been the watery grave of Martha Viner, when both their bodies were found in it, lying close to each other.

The following whimsical instance of indifference as to the mode of suicide is related in Sir John Hawkins's History of the Science and Practice of Music, vol. v. 7:—"One Jeremiah Clarke, organist of St. Paul's, an. dom. 1700, was at the house of a friend in the country, from whence he took an abrupt resolution of returning to London. His friend having observed marks of great dejection in his behaviour, and knowing him to be a man disappointed in love, furnished him not only with a horse, but a servant to take care of him. A fit of melancholy seizing him on the road, he alighted and went into a field, in the corner whereof was a pond, and also trees; where he began to debate with himself, whether he should then end his days by hanging or drowning. Not being able to resolve on either, he thought of making what he looked on as chance, the umpire. He tossed a piece of money into the air, which came down on its edge and stuck in the clay. Though the determination answered not his wishes, it was far from ambiguous, as it seemed to forbid both methods of destruction; and would have given unspeakable comfort to a mind less disordered than his. Being thus interrupted in his purpose, he returned, and mounting his horse, rode on to London, where, in a short time after, he shot himself.

Falret relates the case of an apothecary who, on receiving a reproof from his sweetheart, went home and blew out his brains, having first written the following sentence on his door—"When a man knows not how to please his mistress, he ought to know how to die."

A German merchant, aged thirty-two, depressed by severe reverses of fortune, came to the resolution of starving himself to death. With this view he repaired, on the 15th of September, 1818, to an unfrequented wood, where he constructed a hut of boughs, and remained, without food, till the 3rd of October following. At this period, he was found, by the landlord of a public-house, still alive, but very feeble, speechless, and insensible. Broth, with the yolk of an egg, was administered to him; he swallowed some with difficulty, and died immediately.

In the pocket of the unfortunate man was found a journal, written in pencil, singular of its kind, and remarkable as a narrative of his feelings and sentiments. It commences in these words:—"The generous philanthropist, who shall one day find me here after my death, is requested to inter me; and in consideration of this service, to keep my clothes, purse, knife, and letter-case. Moreover observe, that *I am no suicide*, but have died of hunger, because through wicked men I have lost the whole of my very considerable property, and am unwilling to become a burden to my friends." The ensuing remark is dated September 17th, the second day of abstinence:—"I yet live; but how I have been soaked during the night, and how cold it has been. O God! when will my sufferings terminate! No human being has for three days been seen here; only some birds." The journal continues, "And again, three days, and I have been so soaked during the night, that my clothes to-day are not quite dry. How hard this is no one knows, and my last hour must soon arrive. Doubtlessly, during the heavy rain, a little water has got into my throat; but the thirst is not to be slaked with water; moreover, I have had none even of this for six days, since I am no longer able to move from the place. Yesterday, for the first time during the eternity which, alas! I have already passed here, a man approached me within eight or ten paces. He was certainly a shepherd. I saluted him in silence, and he returned it in the same manner; probably, he will find me after my death!"

"Finally, I here protest before the all-wise God, that, notwithstanding all the misfortunes which I have suffered from my youth, I yet die very unwillingly, although necessity has imperiously driven me to it. Nevertheless, I pray for it. Father, forgive him; for he knows not what he does! More I cannot write for faintness and spasms; and this will be the last. Dated near the forest, by the side of the Goat public-house.

"Sept. 29, 1818.   J. F. N."

It is evident, from the above account, that consciousness and the power of writing remained till the *fourteenth* day of abstinence. The operation of famine was aggravated by mental distress, and still more by exposure to the weather. This, indeed, seems to have produced his most urgent sufferings. Subsequent to the common cravings and debility of hunger, his first physical distress appears to have been the sensation of cold; then cold and thirst; lastly, faintness and spasm. In this case we find no symptoms of inflammation. A want of nervous energy, arising from the reduction in the quantity or quality of the blood, appears to have been the principal disease. The effort of swallowing, and the oppression of food on the exhausted stomach, completed the catastrophe.[81]

There is an extraordinary instance of suicidal design recorded, and which is worth noticing, were it only to shew the extent to which the human powers can sustain life unaided by proper nourishment, even though the intelligent principle be subverted.

An officer, having experienced many mortifications, fell into a state of deep

---

[81] Hufeland's Journal.

melancholy. He resolved to die of famine; and he followed up his resolution so faithfully that he passed forty-five days without eating anything, except on the fifth day, when he asked for some distilled water, in which was mixed a quarter of a pint of spirits of aniseed. This lasted him three days. Upon being told that this quantity of spirit was too much, he then took in each glass of water no more than three drops of it, and the same quantity of fluid lasted him thirty-nine days. He then ceased drinking, and took nothing at all daring the last six days. On the thirty-sixth day, he was obliged to recline on a couch. Every request to induce him to break his resolution was useless, and he was regarded as already lost, when chance recalled within him a desire to live. Having seen a child with a slice of bread and butter, the sight excited in him so violent an appetite that he instantly asked for some soup. They gave him every two hours some spoonsful of rice bouillie, and by degrees more nourishing diet, and his health, though slowly, was established.[82]

Two young men, mere youths, entered a *restaurant*, bespoke a dinner of unusual luxury and expense, and afterwards arrived punctually at the appointed hour to eat it. They did so, apparently with all the zest of youthful appetite and glee. They called for champagne, and quaffed it hand-in-hand. No symptom of sadness, thought, or reflection of any kind, was observed to mix with their mirth, which was loud, long, and unremitting. At last came the *café noir*, the cognac, and the bill; one of them was seen to point out the amount to the other, and then burst out afresh into violent laughter. Having swallowed each a cup of coffee to the dregs, the *garçon* was ordered to request the company of the *restaurateur* for a few minutes. He came immediately, expecting, perhaps, to receive the payment of his bill, minus some extra charge which the jocund but economical youths might deem exorbitant.

Instead of this, however, the elder of the two informed him that the dinner had been excellent, which was the more fortunate, as it was decidedly the last that either of them should ever eat; that for his bill, he must of necessity excuse the payment of it, as, in fact, that neither of them possessed a single sous; that upon no other occasion would they have thus violated the customary *etiquette* between guest and landlord; but that finding this world, with its toils and its troubles, unworthy of them, they had determined once more to enjoy a repast of which their poverty must for ever prevent the repetition, and then take leave of existence for ever! For the first part of this resolution, he declared that it had, thanks to the cook and his cellar, been achieved nobly; and for the last, it would soon follow, for the *café noir*, besides the little glass of his admirable cognac, had been medicated with that which would speedily settle all their accounts for them.

The *restaurateur* was enraged. He believed no part of the rhodomontade but that which declared their inability to discharge their bill, and he talked loudly in his turn of putting them into the hands of the police. At length, however, upon their offering to give up their address, he was induced to allow them to depart.

On the following day, either the hope of obtaining his money or some vague fear that they might have been in earnest in the wild tale that they had told him, induced this man to go to the address they had left with him; and he there heard that

[82] Hist. de l'Acad. Roy., 1769.

the two unhappy boys had been that morning found lying together, hand-in-hand, on a bed hired a few weeks before by one of them. When they were discovered, they were already dead and cold.

On a small table in the room lay many written papers, all expressing aspirations after greatness that should cost neither labour nor care, a profound contempt for those who were satisfied to live by the sweat of their brow, sundry quotations from Victor Hugo, and a request that their names and the manner of their death might be transmitted to the newspapers.

Many are the cases of young men, calling themselves friends, who have thus encouraged each other to make their final exit from life, if not with applause, at least with effect. And more numerous still are the tales recounted of young men and women found dead, and locked in each other's arms, fulfilling literally, and with most sad seriousness, the destiny sketched so merrily in an old song—

> "Gai, gai, marions-nous—
> Mettons-nous dans la misère;
> Gai, gai, marions-nous—
> Mettons-nous la corde au cou."[83]

A woman drowned herself by breaking a hole in the ice of a pond sufficiently large to admit her head, which she put into the water, so that her body remained quite dry.

A Greenwich pensioner, who had his allowance stopped from some misconduct, committed suicide by stabbing himself with his spectacles, which he sharpened to a point for that purpose.

A man, with a determination to sacrifice his life, threw himself among the bears in the *Jardin du Roi*, in Paris. A bear sprung immediately upon him, and before he could be rescued from Bruin's grasp, he was so mutilated that he died a few hours afterwards. Prior to his death he expressed much pleasure at having effected his purpose.

A young lady, at the age of nineteen, was extremely beautiful, in possession of a large fortune, and by no means deficient in understanding or wit; but was immoderately fond of play. She soon gambled away her whole fortune. Reflections on the past became bitter; anticipation of the future alarming; melancholy increased, and weariness of life succeeded. Being at Bath, in the year 1731, she was seen to retire to her chamber with her usual composure, and was found in the morning hanging by a gold and silver girdle to a closet door. Her youth, beauty, and distress, rendered her an object of pity to every one but a near relation, who, on hearing of her death, was inhuman enough to exclaim, in a punning style— "Then she has tied herself up from play."

On the morning of her death she left these lines in the window:—

> "O death, thou pleasing end of human woe!
> Thou cure for life! thou greatest good below!
> Still mayst thou fly the coward and the slave,

---

[83] Paris and the Parisians, by Mrs. Trollope.

And thy soft slumbers only bless the brave."

On reading which a gentleman wrote thus:—

"O dice, ye vain diverters of our woe!
Ye waste of life! ye greatest curse below!
May ne'er good sense again become your slave,
Nor your false charms allure and cheat the brave."

A man whose name and connexions were unknown, was found dead in his chamber at an inn, in Kent, with the following paper lying beside him:—

Lost to the world, and by the world forsaken,
A wretched creature,
Who groaned under a weary life
Upwards of thirty years, without knowing
One happy hour.
And all
In consequence of one single error,
Committed in early days,
Though highly venial
As being the mere effects of juvenile folly,
And soon repented of.
But, alas!
The poor prodigal
Had no kind father that would take him home,
And welcome back his sad repentant virtue
With fond forgiveness and the fatted calf.
Here
He sinks beneath his mighty load of ills,
And with
His miserable being lays them down,
Heart-broken,
At the age of fifty.
Tender reader, give him a little earth
For charity.

A middle aged Frenchman, decently dressed, hanged himself in a public-house in Old Street Road. A letter written in French was found in his pocket, setting forth that some years ago, he dreamt he was to die that day, if not, he was to be damned; and therefore, for the salvation of his soul, he had thought it necessary to put an end to his life.

A young gentleman, living in London, had paid his addresses to an agreeable young lady, won her heart, and obtained the consent of her father, to whom she was an only child. The old gentleman had a fancy to have them married at the same parish church where he himself had been, at a village in Westmoreland; and they accordingly set out alone, the father being at the time indisposed with the gout, in London.

The bridegroom took only his man, and the bride her maid; and when they arrived at the place appointed, the bridegroom wrote the following letter to his wife's father:—

"Sir,—After a very pleasant journey hither, we are preparing for the happy hour in which I am to be your son. I assure you the bride carries it, in the eyes of the vicar who married you, much beyond her mother; though he says, your open sleeves, pantaloons, and shoulder-knot, made a much better shew than the finical dress I am in. However, I am contented to be the second fine man this village ever saw, and shall make it very merry before night, because I shall write from thence, Your most dutiful son,

"T. D."

"P. S. The bride gives her duty, and is as handsome as an angel. I am the happiest man breathing."

The bridegroom's servant knew his master would leave the place very soon after the wedding was over, and seeing him draw his pistols the night before, took an opportunity of going into his chamber and charged them.

Upon their return from the garden they went into that room, and, after a little fond raillery on the subject of their courtship, the bridegroom took up one of the pistols, which he knew he had unloaded the night before, presented it to her, and said, with the most graceful air, whilst she looked pleased at his agreeable flattery, "Now, madam, repent of all those cruelties you have been guilty of towards me; consider, before you die, how often you have let a poor wretch freeze under your casement. You shall die, you tyrant! you shall die with all those instruments of death about you,—with that enchanting smile, those killing ringlets of your hair!"

"Give fire," said she, laughing. He did so, and shot her dead. Who can speak his condition? But he bore it so patiently as to call up his man. The poor wretch entered, and his master locked the door upon him. "Will," said he, "did you charge these pistols?" He answered, "Yes;" upon which his master shot him dead with the undischarged instrument of death. After this, amidst a thousand broken sobs, piercing groans, and distracted motions, he wrote the following letter to the father of his dead mistress:—

"Sir,—Two hours ago, I told you truly I was the happiest man alive. Your daughter lies dead at my feet, killed by my own hand through a mistake of my man's charging my pistols unknown to me! I have murdered him for it. Such is my wedding-day. I will follow my wife to her grave; but before I throw myself upon my sword, I command my distraction so far as to explain my story to you. I fear my heart will not keep together till I have stabbed it. Poor, good old man, remember that he who killed your daughter died for it! In death I give you thanks, and pray for you though I dare not pray for myself. If it be possible, do not curse me. Farewell for ever!

"T. D."

This being finished, he put an end to his life. The body of the servant was interred in the village where he was killed; and the young couple, attended by their maid, were brought to London, and privately interred in one grave, in the parish in which the unhappy father resided.

The following case occurred in England not many years ago. A young couple, the wife aged sixteen and the husband nineteen, discovered, a few months after marriage, that money was much more easily spent than procured; and being unable to live in the style they wished, they determined, after having held a long consultation on the subject, that their best and only remedy was at once to put an end to their imaginary miseries by committing suicide. After dinner, the husband attended his usual business, and brought home with him at tea-time a quarter of a pound of sugar of lead, for the purpose of executing their design. The whole of this poison was dissolved in a pot of coffee, and carefully strained and sweetened, to render it more palatable. The young man then deliberately wrote a letter, explaining the circumstances to his father, to whom he had previously sent a message, requesting him to call in the evening. At the time appointed the husband and wife drank off the poison, and then, embracing each other, laid down to die. When they were discovered, all that they could be induced to say was the word "poison." Medical assistance was immediately procured, but no persuasions could induce them to take an antidote, both of them heroically resolving to die. The young woman, however, reconsidered the point, and began to think that death was not so agreeable a thing as she first supposed; but, retaining her feelings of obedience strong in death, imploringly said to her husband, when she was pressed to take the medicine offered, "Shall I take it, dear?" To this he gave a direct negative, enforcing it with an oath; but her love of life triumphed over her sense of obedience to the commands of her lord, and she consented to swallow the antidote. The husband, however, was not so willing to venture upon the cares and vexations of the world, and obstinately persisted in dying; but as this was not thought prudent, he was made by physical force to swallow the medicine, and was restored to life, and is still in the land of the living.

Instances of mutual suicide are by no means uncommon on the Continent, and were not unknown in ancient times. The inhabitants of England have not become as yet romantic enough for these exhibitions. The case of M. Kleist, the celebrated Prussian poet, and Madame Vogle, may be fresh in the minds of our readers. Madame Vogle, it is said, had suffered long under an incurable disorder; her physicians had declared her death inevitable; she herself came to a resolution to put an end to her existence. M. Kleist, the poet, and a friend of her family, had also determined to kill himself. These two unhappy beings, having confidentially communicated to each other their horrible resolution, resolved to carry it into effect at the same time. They repaired to the inn at Wilhemstadt, between Berlin and Potsdam, on the borders of the Sacred Lake. For one night and one day they were preparing themselves for death, by putting up prayers, singing, drinking wine and rum, and concluded by drinking sixteen cups of coffee. They wrote a letter to M. Vogle, to announce to him the resolution they had taken, and to beg him to come as speedily as possible, for the purpose of seeing their remains devoutly interred. After having despatched the letter to Berlin, they repaired to the bank of the Sacred Lake, where they sat down opposite to each other. M. Kleist then took a loaded pistol and shot Madame Vogle through the heart,—she instantly fell back dead; he then reloaded the pistol, and applying the muzzle to his own head, blew out his brains.

A horrid scene of mixed murder and suicide, accompanied with great calmness in its execution, was exhibited in the year 1732, in the family of one Richard Smith, a bookbinder. This man being a prisoner for debt within the walls of the King's Bench, was found hanging in his chamber, together with his wife; and their infant of two years old lay murdered in a cradle beside them. Smith left three letters behind him, one of which was addressed to his landlord, in which he says:—"He hopes effects enough will be found to discharge his lodgings, and recommends to his protection his ancient dog and cat." A second was addressed to his cousin Brindley, and contained severe censure on the person through whose means he had been brought into difficulties, with a desire also that Brindley would make the third letter public, which was as follows:—

"These actions, considered in all their circumstances, being somewhat uncommon, it may not be improper to give some account of the cause; and that it was an inveterate hatred we conceived against poverty and rags, evils that through a train of unlucky accidents were become inevitable. For we appeal to all that ever knew us, whether we were idle or extravagant, whether or no we have not taken as much pains to get our living as our neighbours, although not attended with the same success. We apprehend the taking our child's life away to be a circumstance for which we shall be generally condemned; but for our own parts we are perfectly easy on that head. We are satisfied it is less cruelty to take the child with us, even supposing a state of annihilation as some dream of, than to leave her friendless in the world, exposed to ignorance and misery. Now in order to obviate some censures which may proceed either from ignorance or malice, we think it proper to inform the world, that we firmly believe the existence of an Almighty God; that this belief of ours is not an implicit faith, but deduced from the nature and reason of things. We believe the existence of an Almighty Being from the consideration of his wonderful works, from those innumerable celestial and glorious bodies, and from their wonderful order and harmony. We have also spent some time in viewing those wonders which are to be seen in the minute part of the world, and that with great pleasure and satisfaction. From all which particulars we are satisfied that such amazing things could not possibly be without a first mover,—without the existence of an Almighty Being. And as we know the wonderful God to be Almighty, so we cannot help believing that he is also good—not implacable, not like such wretches as men are, not taking delight in the misery of his creatures; for which reason we resign up our breath to him without any terrible apprehensions, submitting ourselves to those ways which in his goodness he shall please to appoint after death. We also believe in the existence of unbodied natures, and think we have reason for that belief, although we do not pretend to know their way of subsisting. We are not ignorant of those laws made *in terrorem*, but leave the disposal of our bodies to the wisdom of the coroner and his jury, the thing being indifferent to us where our bodies are laid. From hence it will appear how little anxious we are about a *'hic jacet.'* We for our part neither expect nor desire such honours; but shall content ourselves with a borrowed epitaph, which we shall insert in this paper:

'Without a name, for ever silent, dumb;
Dust, ashes, nought else is within this tomb;
Where we were born or bred it matters not;
Who were our parents, or have us begot.
We 'were, but are not.' Think no more of us,
For as we are, so you'll be turn'd to dust.'

"It is the opinion of naturalists, that our bodies are at certain stages of life composed of new matter; so that a great many poor men have new bodies oftener than new clothes. Now, as divines are not able to inform us which of those several bodies shall rise at the resurrection, it is very probable that the deceased body may be for ever silent as well as any other.

(Signed,)
"RICHARD SMITH,
"BRIGET SMITH."

A lady and gentleman visited an hotel in the neighbourhood of Paris, and ordered dinner to be prepared in a private room. The lady, who appeared only nineteen years of age, was most magnificently attired. The gentleman was observed to pay her marked attention, and addressed her with the most endearing epithets. The dinner consisted of every luxury of the season. After drinking a large quantity of wine, the gentleman requested that they should not be disturbed, and he was heard to lock the door. Half an hour afterwards, a report of a pistol was heard in the room. The master of the hotel was alarmed. The assistance of the police was obtained, and the door of the room in which the lady and gentleman had dined forced open. The lady was found on the floor dead, and the gentleman a short distance from her, in the last struggle of death. Two pistols were found near the bodies. It appeared that they had agreed to commit mutual suicide, and each being provided with a loaded pistol, fired at and killed each other. On the table was found a piece of paper, on which were written with a pencil the following words:—"We, H***d and Maria **, were enamoured of each other. Circumstances beyond the control of man prevent our alliance. We have no alternative but separation or death; and believing death to be one eternal dream of bliss, we, after much meditation, have determined to kill each other. We affix our signatures to this document.

"H***D,
"MARIA **."

Two devoted lovers, disappointed in obtaining the consent of their parents to their union, resolved upon dying. They experienced some difficulty in deciding how to effect their purpose. The lady expressed an abhorrence of pistols, and the gentleman was equally repugnant to the rope. After much hesitation, they agreed to throw themselves into the river, and stated their intention to a friend, who, thinking they were merely joking, observed—"Well, I think you will find the water very cold; I should advise you to put on warm clothing before you jump in." In the evening they were missing, and on searching the river, they were discovered, tied to each other, quite dead.

The suicide of Sir R. Croft has often been alluded to. He attended the late Princess Charlotte in her confinement, and her much lamented death, although not owing to any want of skill on his part, preyed much on his mind, and drove him to the rash act. He fancied he saw the spirit of the princess glide through his room. The sight of an open razor on the table first suggested the idea of self-destruction to him. He was a physician of great skill, and was much beloved by all who knew him.

A bishop of Grenoble affords an instance of suicidal ingenuity. He took a rod on which his bed-curtains hung, and suspended it across by a stick, which communicated with the trigger of his fowling-piece. He then sat quietly down, with his feet hanging over the rod, and placing the muzzle of the gun in his mouth, held it fast. He had nothing more now to do than to drop his leg upon the rod, when the gun went off, and three bullets entered his brain.

The fortitude which suicides display is amazing. A servant girl of the Dean of — —, who had always borne a most excellent character, was accused by the family of theft. She immediately repaired to the wash-house, immersed her head in a pail of water, and was found dead in that position. What must have been the courage of this poor creature, who, when writhing under the lash of a false accusation, kept her head under water, despite the horrible sense of suffocation that must have come on!

A French soldier of the name of Bordeaux, being determined to put an end to his life, persuaded a comrade, called Humain, to follow his example. They both repaired to an inn at St. Denis, and bespoke a good dinner. One of them went out to buy some powder and balls. They spent the day (Christmas) together with great cheerfulness, called for more wine; and, about four o'clock in the evening, blew out their brains, leaving some empty bottles, their will, a letter, and half-a-crown, in addition to the amount of their bill.

The following letter was addressed by Bordeaux to the lieutenant of his troop, and was as follows: —

"Sɪʀ, — During my residence at Guise, you honoured me with your friendship. It is time to thank you. You have often told me that I appeared displeased with my situation. I was sincere, but not absolutely true. I have since examined myself more seriously, and acknowledge that I am disgusted with every state of man, the whole world, and myself. From these discoveries a consequence should be drawn, — if disgusted with the whole, renounce the whole. The calculation is not long, — I have made it without the aid of geometry. In short, I am about putting an end to the existence that I have possessed for near twenty years, fifteen of which have been a burden to me; and from the moment that I have ended this letter, a few grains of powder will destroy this moving mass of flesh, which we vain mortals call the king of beings. I owe no one an excuse. I deserted. That was a crime; but I am going to punish it, and the law will be satisfied. I asked leave of absence from my superior officers, to have the pleasure of dying at my ease. They never condescended to give me an answer. This served to hasten my end. I wrote to Bord to send you some detached pieces I left at Guise, which I beg you will accept. You will find that they contain some well chosen literature. These pieces will solicit for me a place in your remembrance. Adieu, my dear lieutenant! Continue your esteem for St. Lambert and Dorat. As for the rest, skip from flower to flower, and acquire the sweets of all knowledge, and enjoy every pleasure.

> 'Pour moi, j'arrive au trou,
> Qui n'echappe ni sage ni fou,
> Pour aller je ne sais où.'

"If we exist after this life, and it is forbidden to quit it without permission, I will endeavour to procure one moment to inform you of it; if not, I shall advise all those who are unhappy, which is by far the greater part of mankind, to follow my example. When you receive this letter, I shall have been dead at least twenty-four hours.

With esteem, &c.
"BORDEAUX."

Lord Scarborough exhibited the same nonchalance in the act of killing himself as he did when he resigned his situation as master of the horse. He was reproached in the House of Peers with taking the king's part because he had a good place at court. "My Lords," said he, "to prove to you that my opinion is independent of my place, I resign it this moment." He afterwards found himself in a perplexing dilemma between a mistress whom he loved, but to whom he had promised nothing, and a woman whom he esteemed, and to whom he had promised marriage. Not having sufficient resolution to decide which to choose, he killed himself to escape the embarrassment.

Perhaps the coolest attempt at self-destruction on record, the *chef d'œuvre* of a suicide, is one related by Foderé. An Englishman advertised extensively that he would on a certain day put himself to death in Covent Garden, for the benefit of his wife and family. Tickets of admission a guinea each.

Voltaire states that Creech, the translator of Lucretius, wrote on the margin of the manuscript, "Remember to hang myself after my translation is finished," and he accordingly did so.[84] Zimmerman asserts that he committed suicide in order to escape from the contempt of his countrymen, in consequence of the ill-success that attended the translation of Horace, which followed Lucretius. Mr. Jacob, however, observes, in reply to the statement of Zimmerman, that Creech did not hang himself until seventeen years after the appearance of his Horace. His death was attributed at the time to some love affair, or to his morose and splenetic temper.

The history of the unfortunate *Madame de Monnier* is full of interest. It has been asserted that her death was the result of an ardent passion for Mirabeau; but we think it has clearly been established that, at the time of her suicide, she had abandoned all claim to his affection, and had formed a strong attachment to a person who, although highly respectable in point of rank, was very inferior to herself. It is well known that Mirabeau had a *liaison* with Madame de Monnier, the wife of the Marquis de Monnier, whom she abandoned. After residing seven years with

[84] Voltaire observes, that if Creech had been translating Ovid, he would not have committed suicide.

her seducer, mutual jealousies and suspicions arose, and all intercourse between them ceased. After the death of her husband, the Marquis de Monnier, she became enamoured of M. Edme. Benoit de Poterat, a retired captain of cavalry, a widower, thirty-five years of age. The lovers were mutually captivated, and they agreed to marry. Before this happy event, however, could be arranged, the ill health of M. de Poterat forced him to quit the country, and Madame de Monnier resolved to terminate her own existence. She often conversed with her intimate friend Dr. Ysabeau on the effects of suffocation from charcoal wood. She asked whether death necessarily ensued? The doctor replied, that when suffocation was gradual and incomplete, instances had been known of persons saved by the instinctive effort of introducing air into the room. On the death of M. de Poterat, which took place on the 8th of September, 1789, Madame de Monnier was overcome with grief. Dr. Ysabeau and his wife did all they could to console her, but without effect. Being alone one day, she collected her papers, tied them in bundles, sealed them, wrote a letter containing her last directions, and entered a closet, the smallness and closeness of which she considered well suited to the design she had long resolved to carry into execution. She then closed and carefully calked the door and the window. Two chafing dishes full of charcoal, which she had just lighted, were then placed by her, one on each side of the arm chair upon which she seated herself. In order to prevent her purpose from being counteracted by any instinctive effort of nature, she bound her legs, first under and then above her clothes. She then tied one of her arms to the chair, and fixed the other, and in this position calmly awaited death. When it was discovered that she had attempted suicide, M. Bousseau, Procureur du Roi of the Bailliage, proceeded to the house, attended by a surgeon, who, without adopting the most simple means of resuscitation, commenced opening the body, on the supposition that she was *enceinte*. In the meanwhile, a messenger was dispatched for Dr. Ysabeau, who rode full gallop towards Madame de Monnier's house; but he arrived too late; the operation had been performed, and life was extinct. From the symptoms which were present before the ignorant and barbarous surgeon commenced the operation, Dr. Ysabeau expressed a firm belief that he could have restored her to animation.[85]

M. — —, aged twenty-seven, a native of Burgundy, who was equally favoured by nature and by fortune, fell passionately in love with a young lady. For a long time he solicited in vain the consent of his parents to the match, but at length love triumphed. Scarcely a month had elapsed after his marriage, when he was seized with a lowness of spirits, a disgust of life, and a frightful desire to commit suicide. Everything which the tenderness of a young and loving wife, and the solicitude of the whole family, by whom he was loved, could suggest, was done to disperse these gloomy ideas, and reconcile him to life; but the unfortunate fellow was too deeply sunk in his melancholy. He at length quitted Burgundy, and went to Paris with his brother to consult a physician. The day after he had arrived, he went to M. Esquirol, made known his sad state to him, assuring him that his weariness of

[85] We refer our readers, for a minute and deeply interesting account of this unfortunate woman's career, to a work from which we have gleaned the above facts; the particulars of her life will be perused with great interest. — Videi> "Memoirs of Mirabeau, by himself," vol. iii. chap. xi.

life was not the result of any physical disease, of any disappointment, or of any moral pain; affirming, on the contrary, that he was surrounded with nothing but subjects of contentment. His brother confirmed this declaration. He left M. Esquirol, and promised to return the next day and commit himself to his care in his establishment. The next day arrived, the young man went out at six o'clock in the morning, purchased a pair of pistols, and returned at seven. He then proposed to his brother to set out together for Rouen; but he reminded him of the promise he had given to M. Esquirol, adding, to prevent his changing his mind, that he had months suitable to go. At that instant M. — — took out his two pistols, and placing the mouth of one of them at his brother's forehead, said, "If you do not consent to go with me immediately, I will instantly blow out your brains with this pistol, and afterwards kill myself with the other." The brother, on hearing this, fell at his feet in a swoon, and when he recovered, he no longer saw his unfortunate relative who had threatened him, and he trembled lest he should have gone to some secret place to terminate his life. He at once gave notice to the police, and demanded that the most active of their body should be sent in search of him. On his part, he neglected nothing which could give him any clue to his discovery; he inquired of his friends and his acquaintances, but heard nothing of him until the next day, when he received intelligence from the police that the body of a man shot through the head, had been found in the forest of Seuart. It was that of his unfortunate brother.

M. Escousse, author of a drama called Faruck le Maure, about twenty, and M. Lebras, about fifteen, both united by the closest ties of friendship, and each of a melancholy turn of mind, committed suicide at Paris. They had often complained of the miseries of this world, and talked of the necessity of quitting it. M. Escousse wrote the following note to his friends:—"I shall expect you at half-past eleven o'clock; the curtain will be raised; come, and we will at length arrive at the *dénouement*." The young Lebras arrived at the appointed time, the charcoal was ignited, and the two friends expired together.

A young woman of Marseilles, remarkable for her beauty, formed a connexion with a cabinetmaker, whose parents objected to their union. They were found quite dead, clasped in each other's arms, having been suffocated by a quantity of burning charcoal. They were both dressed in the most elegant manner, and must have spent many hours at their toilet preparing for their last adieu.

The following case related by Gall cannot easily be paralleled. The first lieutenant of a company in which a man named Prochaska served became enamoured of the wife of the latter; but she resisted all his entreaties. The officer, irritated by this obstinacy, was guilty of some injustice to the husband. Prochaska appeared dejected and morose, but the following day he appeared at the dinner table and seemed quite tranquil. A few days afterwards he and his wife attended the confessional and took the sacrament. He dined in good spirits, and took a few glasses of wine. In the evening, he and his wife went out to walk, and he expressed himself in terms of great affection for her. He asked her, however, if she had made a candid and full confession to the priest; and on being answered in the affirmative, he coolly plunged a poniard in her breast; seeing that she was not instantly dispatched, he cut her throat across, in order to release her from her sufferings. He now repaired to his house, and seizing his two children, who were in bed asleep, he actually hacked them in pieces with a hatchet. Having committed these three murders, he repaired to the main guard, and with the most perfect coolness and deliberation detailed the whole particulars of the bloody deed. He concluded in these words:—*"Let the lieutenant now make love to my wife if he pleases!"* Shortly after this, he stabbed himself to the heart.

A young lady threatened, without ceasing, to kill herself, and made many attempts at it. An old uncle with whom she lived, tired by her repeated menaces, proposed a walk in the country; and taking her to the brink of a piece of water, he commenced undressing himself. "Now, niece," said he, "throw yourself into the water, and I will follow after you." He continued pressing her, and pushed her towards it; but after some struggling, she cried out that she was unwilling to die, and would never more talk of killing herself.

A young woman, married to a churlish husband, and who, although the mother of many children, was unhappy in domestic life, determined to fall by her own hands. She threw herself into a part of the river sufficiently deep for the execution of her project, but a man, passing by, drew her out, and compelled her to go home. The necessary attentions were paid her, and she recovered; but it was observed that she stood in much dread of water, and felt a pain even in going into a bath. She, besides, had a fit of melancholy at the time in which she endeavoured to drown herself. This fit lasted two or three months; it was followed by a month of great excitement, and then she remained calm during the remainder of the year.

The bell of the church at Fressonville, in Picardy, was heard to sound at an unusual hour, and in a very extraordinary manner. The people hastened to make inquiry, and found a man suspended from the clapper. He was immediately cut down, and after some time restored to life. No motives are assigned for the act.

A person of melancholy temperament, and who detested his parents on account of their injustice towards him, had recourse to the chase as a diversion from his domestic sorrows. One day, being weary, he lay down in the shade by the side of his weapon and his dog, the faithful companion of his misfortunes, and fell into a profound sleep. He awoke in an agitated state of mind, and the idea occurred to him of making an eternal sleep follow the temporary one he had so much enjoyed. Pleased with this, he got up, increased the charge of his fowling-piece, and was about to blow out his brains, when he sensibly reflected in this manner—"What! am I about to shorten my days because my unjust and unnatural parents deprive me of their property? This is to give them their utmost desire, and to abandon to them that which they cannot take from me."

Matthew Lovat was born at Casale, a hamlet belonging to the parish of Soldo, in the territory of Belluno. His father's name was Mark, and being in poor circumstances, the son was employed in the coarsest labours of husbandry. His education and habits must have been in accordance with his station; but it appears that, being attracted by the comfortable and easy circumstances of the rector and curate, the only persons in the parish who lived without manual labour, he placed himself under the latter with the desire of entering the priesthood. From him he learned to read and write a little, but he was too poor to gratify this inclination, and betook himself to the trade of a shoemaker. Whether this disappointment had any effect on Lovat we cannot tell, but he never became expert at his trade, and was distinguished for his gloominess and silence. When he grew older, he became subject to attacks of giddiness in the head in the spring, and to eruptions of a leprous character. Except this gloominess and his great attention to religious exercises, nothing remarkable was noticed about Lovat until July, 1802. At this period he performed an operation upon himself, which subjected him so much to the ridicule of his neighbours that he was compelled to remain within doors, and to refrain even from going to mass. He left the village in November, and went to Venice, where he had a younger brother, who recommended him to a widow, with whom he lodged until the 21st of September in the following year, working regularly as a shoemaker, and without exhibiting any signs of insanity. On that day he made his first attempt to crucify himself. Having constructed a cross out of the wood of his bed, he proceeded to nail himself to it in the middle of the street, called the Cross of Biri, and was only prevented by some persons who seized him as he was about to drive the nail through his left foot. He was interrogated as to his motives, but would give no answer, except on one occasion, when he said that the day was the festival of St. Matthew, and that he could not explain further. A few days after this had happened, he left Venice, and went to his native village, but returned soon after, and continued working at his trade for nearly three years without exhibiting further signs of his malady. Having taken a room in a third story in the street Delle Monache, his old delusion again seized him, and he commenced making at his leisure hours the machine on which he intended to accomplish his purpose, and providing the nails, ropes, bands, crown of thorns, &c. He perceived that it would be difficult to nail himself firmly to the cross, and therefore made a net, which he fastened over it, securing it at the bottom of the upright beam a little below the bracket he had placed for his feet, and at the ends of the two arms. The whole apparatus was securely tied by two ropes, one from the net, and the other from the place where the beams intersected each other. These ropes were fastened to the bar above the window, and were just sufficiently long to allow the cross to lie horizontally upon the floor of his apartment. Having finished these preparations, he next put on his crown of thorns, some of which entered his forehead; and then, having stripped himself naked, he girded his loins with a white handkerchief. He then introduced himself into the net, and seating himself on the cross, drove a nail through the palm of his right hand by striking its head against the floor until the point appeared on the other side. He now placed his feet on the bracket he had prepared for them, and with a mallet drove a nail completely through them both, entering a hole he had previously made to receive it, and fastening them to the wood. He next tied himself to the cross by a piece of cord round his waist, and wounded himself in the side with a knife which he used in his trade. The wound was inflicted two inches below the left hypochondre, towards the internal angle of the abdominal cavity, but did not injure any of the parts which the cavity contains. Several scratches were observed on his breast, which appeared to have been done by the knife in probing for a place which should present no obstruction. The knife, according to Lovat, represented *the spear of passion.*

All this he accomplished in the interior of his apartment, but it was now necessary to shew himself in public. To accomplish this, he had placed the foot of the cross upon the window sill, which was very low, and by pressing his fingers against the floor, he gradually drew himself forward, until the foot of the cross overbalancing the head, the whole machine tilted out of the window, and hung by the two ropes which were fastened to the beam. He then, by way of finishing, nailed his right hand to the arm of the cross, but could not succeed in fixing his left, although the nail by which it was to have been fixed was driven through it, and half of it came out of the other side.

This took place at eight o'clock in the morning. Some persons by whom he was perceived ran up stairs, disengaged him from the cross, and put him to bed. A surgeon in the neighbourhood who was called in ordered his feet to be put in water, introduced some tow into the wound in the hypochondre, which he said did not reach the cavity, and prescribed some cordial.

Luckily, Dr. Bergierri, to whom we are indebted for the particulars of this case, was passing near, and came immediately to the house. When he arrived, his feet, from which but a small quantity of blood had flowed, were still in water; his eyes were shut; he gave no answer to the questions of those around him; his pulse was convulsive; his respiration difficult; he was, in fact, in a state which required the most prompt means of assistance. Having obtained permission of the director of police, who had come to the spot to ascertain what had happened, he had him removed by water to the Imperial Clinical School at the Hospital of St. Luke and St. John, of which he then had the superintendence. The only observation Lovat made while being conveyed was to his brother Angelo, who was lamenting his extravagance; he replied, *"Alas! I am very unfortunate."* His wounds were examined afresh on his arrival at the hospital, and it was quite evident that the nails had entered at the palm of the hand, and passing between the bones of the metacarpus without doing them much injury, had gone out of the back. The nail which fastened the feet first entered the right foot between the second and third bones of the metatarsus, and then passed between the first and second of the left foot, laying them open and grazing them. The wound in the hypochondre was found to extend to the point of the cavity.

The patient all this time was quite docile, and did everything that was required of him. The wounds in the extremities were treated with fresh oil of sweet almonds and bread and milk poultices, renewed several times a day. Some ounces of the mixture cardiaca opiata and a little very weak lemonade were taken at intervals during the first six days. On the fifth day the wounds of the extremities suppurated, and on the eighth, that in the hypochondre was perfectly healed.

Dr. Bergierri frequently questioned him as to the motives he had in crucifying himself, and always received the same answer—*"The pride of man must be mortified; it must expire on the cross."* Lovat seldom spoke; he sat with his eyes closed, and a gloomy expression of countenance. The impression on his mind that he must crucify himself was very deep. He seemed fully persuaded that this was an obligation imposed on him by the will of the Deity, and wished to inform the tribunal of justice that this was his destiny, in order that they might not suspect that he had received his death from any other hand than his own. He had expressed these ideas on a paper which he wrote before his attempt, and which afterwards fell into the hands of Dr. B.

He did not complain much of pain during the first seven days, but on the morning of the eighth he suffered severely; this, however, was soon removed by the remedies had recourse to. In the course of a short time Lovat was completely restored to bodily health, but his mind retained until his death the same melancholy caste, although he never had another opportunity of putting his sanguinary project into execution.[86]

---

[86] Vide Frontispiece.

CHAPTER XVI.

CAN SUICIDE BE PREVENTED BY LEGISLATIVE ENACTMENTS?—INFLUENCE OF MORAL IN-STRUCTION.—CONCLUSION.

The legitimate object of punishment—The argument of Beccaria—A legal solecism—A suicide not amenable to human tribunals—Evidence at coroners' courts, *ex-parte*—The old law of no advantage—No penal law will restrain a man from the commission of suicide—Verdict of *felo-de-se* punishes the innocent, and therefore unjust—Are suicides insane, and therefore not responsible agents?—The man who reasons himself into suicide not of sound mind—Rational mode of preventing suicide by promoting religious education.

THE only legitimate object for which punishment can be inflicted is the prevention of crime. "Am I to be hanged for stealing a sheep?" said a criminal at the Old Bailey, addressing the bench. "No," replied the judge; "you are not to be hanged for stealing a sheep, but *that sheep may not be stolen.*" Every punishment, argues Beccaria, which does not arise from absolute necessity is unjust. There should be a fixed proportion between crimes and punishments. Crimes are only to be estimated by the injury done to society; and the end of punishment is, to prevent the criminal from doing further injury, as well as to induce others from committing similar offences.

The act of suicide ought not to be considered as a crime in the legal definition of the term. It is not an offence that can be deemed cognizable by the civil magistrate. It is to be considered a sinful and vicious action. To punish suicide as a crime is to commit a solecism in legislation. The unfortunate individual, by the very act of suicide, places himself beyond the vengeance of the law; he has anticipated its operation; he has rendered himself amenable to the highest tribunal—viz., that of his Creator; no penal enactments, however stringent, can affect him. What is the operation of the law under these circumstances? A verdict of *felo-de-se* is returned, and the innocent relations of the suicide are disgraced and branded with infamy, and that too on evidence of an *ex-parte* nature. It is unjust, inhuman, unnatural, and unchristian, that the law should punish the innocent family of the man who, in a moment of frenzy, terminates his own miserable existence. It was clearly established, that before the alteration in the law respecting suicide, the fear of being buried in a cross-road, and having a stake driven through the body, had no beneficial effect in decreasing the number of suicides; and the verdict of *felo-de-se*, now occasionally returned, is productive of no advantage whatever, and only injures the surviving relatives.

When a man contemplates an outrage of the law, the fear of the punishment awarded for the offence may deter him from its commission; but the unhappy person whose desperate circumstances impel him to sacrifice his own life can be influenced by no such fear. His whole mind is absorbed in the consideration of his own miseries, and he even cuts asunder those ties that ought to bind him closely and tenderly to the world he is about to leave. If an affectionate wife and endearing family have no influence in deterring a man from suicide, is it reasonable to suppose that he will be influenced by penal laws?

If the view which has been taken in this work of the cause of suicide be a correct one, no stronger argument can be urged for the impropriety of bringing the strong arm of the law to bear upon those who court a voluntary death. In the majority of cases, it will be found that some heavy calamity has fastened itself upon the mind, and the spirits have been extremely depressed. The individual loses all pleasure in society; hope vanishes, and despair renders life intolerable, and death an apparent relief. The evidence which is generally submitted to a coroner's jury is of necessity imperfect; and although the suicide may, to all appearance, be in possession of his right reason, and have exhibited at the moment of killing himself the greatest calmness, coolness, and self-possession, this would not justify the coroner or jury in concluding that derangement of mind was not present.

If the mind be overpowered by "grief, sickness, infirmity, or other accident," as Sir Mathew Hale expresses it, the law presumes the existence of lunacy. Any passion that powerfully exercises the mind, and prevents the reasoning faculty from performing its duty, causes temporary derangement. It is not necessary in order to establish the presence of insanity to prove the person to be labouring under a delusion of intellect—a false creation of the mind. A man may allow his imagination to dwell upon an idea until it acquires an unhealthy ascendency over the intellect, and in this way a person may commit suicide from an habitual belief in the justifiableness of the act.[87] If a man, by a distorted process of reasoning, argues himself into a conviction of the propriety of adopting a particular course of conduct, without any reference to the necessary result of that train of thought, it is certainly no evidence of his being in possession of a sound mind. A person may reason himself into a belief that murder, under certain circumstances not authorized by the law, is perfectly just and proper. The circumstance of his allowing his mind to reason on the subject is a *prima facie* case against his sanity; at least it demonstrates a great weakness of the moral constitution. A man's *morale* must be in an imperfect state of development who reasons himself into the conviction that self-murder is under any circumstances justifiable.

We dwell at some length on this subject, because we feel assured that juries do not pay sufficient attention to the influence of passion in overclouding the under-

[87] A singular case of this kind was brought under the notice of the Westminster Medical Society by Dr. Stone, as an argument in favour of the possibility of a person committing suicide when in possession of a sane mind.

standing. If the notion that in every case of suicide the intellectual or moral faculties are perverted, be generally received, it will at once do away with the verdict of *felo-de-se*. Should the jury entertain a doubt as to the presence of derangement, (and such cases may present themselves,) it is their duty, in accordance with the well-known principle of British jurisprudence, to give the person the benefit of that doubt; and thus a verdict of lunacy may be conscientiously returned in every case of this description.

Having, we think, clearly established that no penal law can act beneficially in preventing self-destruction,—first, because it would punish the *innocent* for the crimes of the *guilty*; and, secondly, that, owing to insanity being present in every instance, the person determined on suicide is indifferent as to the consequences of his action,—it becomes our province to consider what are the legitimate means of staying the progress of an offence that undermines the foundation of society and social happiness.

In the prevention of suicide, too much stress cannot be laid on the importance of adopting a well-regulated, enlarged, and philosophic system of education, by which all the *moral* as well as the intellectual faculties will be expanded and disciplined. The education of the intellect without any reference to the moral feelings is a species of instruction calculated to do an immense amount of injury. The tuition that addresses itself exclusively to the perceptive and reflective faculties is not the kind of education that will elevate the moral character of a people. Religion must be made the basis of all secular knowledge. We must be led to believe that the education which fits the possessor for another world is vastly superior to that which has relation only to the concerns of this life. We are no opponents to the diffusion of knowledge; but we are to that description of information which has only reference "to the life that is, and not to that which is to be." Such a system of instruction is of necessity defective, because it is partial in its operation. Teach a man his duty to God, as well as his obligations to his fellow-men; lead him to believe that his life is not his own; that disappointment and misery is the penalty of Adam's transgression, and one from which there is no hope of escaping; and, above all, inculcate a resignation to the decrees of Divine Providence. When life becomes a burden, when the mind is sinking under the weight of accumulated misfortunes, and no gleam of hope penetrates through the vista of futurity to gladden the heart, the intellect says, "Commit suicide, and escape from a world of wretchedness and woe;" the moral principle says, "Live; it is your duty to bear with resignation the afflictions that overwhelm you; let the moral influence of your example be reflected in the characters of those by whom you are surrounded."

If we are justified in maintaining that the majority of the cases of suicide result from a vitiated condition of the moral principle, then it is certainly a legitimate mode of preventing the commission of the offence to elevate the character of man as a moral being. It is no legitimate argument against this position to maintain that insanity in all its phases marches side by side with civilization and refinement; but it must not be forgotten that a people may be refined and civilized, using these terms in their ordinary signification, who have not a just conception of their duties as members of a Christian community. Let the education of the *heart* go side by side with the education of the *head*; inculcate the ennobling thought, that we live not for ourselves, but for others; that it is an evidence of true Christian courage to face bravely the ills of life, to bear with impunity "the whips and scorns of time, the oppressor's wrong, and the proud man's contumely;" and we disseminate principles which will give expansion to those faculties that alone can fortify the mind against the commission of a crime alike repugnant to all human and Divine laws.

THE END